The Alchemy of Laughter

Also by Glen Cavaliero

CHARLES WILLIAMS: Poet of Theology
JOHN COWPER POWYS: Novelist
A READING OF E. M. FORSTER
THE RURAL TRADITION IN THE ENGLISH NOVEL 1900–1939
THE SUPERNATURAL AND ENGLISH FICTION
THE ANCIENT PEOPLE (*poems*)
ELEGY FOR ST ANNE'S (*poems*)
PARADISE STAIRWAY (*poems*)
STEEPLE ON A HILL (*poems*)

The Alchemy of Laughter

Comedy in English Fiction

Glen Cavaliero

First published in Great Britain 2000 by
MACMILLAN PRESS LTD
Houndmills, Basingstoke, Hampshire RG21 6XS and London
Companies and representatives throughout the world

A catalogue record for this book is available from the British Library.
ISBN 0–333–77048–X

 First published in the United States of America 2000 by
ST. MARTIN'S PRESS, INC.,
Scholarly and Reference Division,
175 Fifth Avenue, New York, N.Y. 10010

ISBN 0–312–22551–2

Library of Congress Cataloging-in-Publication Data
Cavaliero, Glen, 1927–
The alchemy of laughter : comedy in English fiction / Glen Cavaliero.
p. cm.
Includes bibliographical references (p.   ) and index.
ISBN 0–312–22551–2
1. English fiction—History and criticism. 2. Comic, The, in literature. 3. Humorous stories, English—History and criticism.
4. Laughter in literature. I. Title.
PR830.C63C38   1999
823.009'17—dc21   99–15265
                                                          CIP

© Glen Cavaliero 2000

All rights reserved. No reproduction, copy or transmission of this publication may be made without written permission.

No paragraph of this publication may be reproduced, copied or transmitted save with written permission or in accordance with the provisions of the Copyright, Designs and Patents Act 1988, or under the terms of any licence permitting limited copying issued by the Copyright Licensing Agency, 90 Tottenham Court Road, London W1P 0LP.

Any person who does any unauthorised act in relation to this publication may be liable to criminal prosecution and civil claims for damages.

The author has asserted his right to be identified as the author of this work in accordance with the Copyright, Designs and Patents Act 1988.

This book is printed on paper suitable for recycling and made from fully managed and sustained forest sources.

10 9 8 7 6 5 4 3 2 1
09 08 07 06 05 04 03 02 01 00

Printed and bound in Great Britain by
Antony Rowe Ltd, Chippenham, Wiltshire

For Roddy and Mary

Contents

Preface	ix
Acknowledgements	xi
1 The Matter of the Work	**1**
The nature of a monolith	3
The perception of diversity	6
The fun of the fair	9
Engaging the monolith	15
2 Aspects of the Comedic Process	**21**
Parody: the verdict of Lady Locke	22
Farce: the lawlessness of Alfred Polly	25
Irony: the benevolence of Lucilla Marjoribanks	28
Satire: the aspirations of George Robinson	30
Burlesque: the appreciation of Emmeline Lucas	33
Wit: the good humour of Auberon Quin	35
Celebration: the self-respect of Charles Pooter	37
3 Parodic Comedy: the Separation of Elements	**42**
First impressions: Jane Austen	43
Gentlemanly relish: Max Beerbohm	48
Saving graces: the Brontës and *Cold Comfort Farm*	54
Matter for laughter: Angus Wilson	57
4 Ludic Comedy: the Dissolution of Elements	**61**
Parlour games: *Tristram Shandy*	62
These foolish things: Ronald Firbank	70
Lucid ridicule: Elizabeth von Arnim	76
Magnificent obsessions: William Gerhardie	80
5 Ironic Comedy: the Conjunction of Opposites	**84**
Basic principles: *Jonathan Wild*	85
Beginner's luck: *Mansfield Park*	88
Old soldiers: *Barry Lyndon*	92
Whispering shades: Henry James	95

viii Contents

6	**Satirical Comedy: the Disjunction of Opposites**	103
	Questions of perspective: *Tom Jones*	104
	The whirligigs of time: *Vanity Fair*	110
	Godliness and good behaviour: *The Way of All Flesh*	113
	Non-conforming consciences: E.M. Forster, D.H. Lawrence	118
7	**Subversive Comedy: the Infernal Marriage**	127
	Egotistical sublimities: *Humphrey Clinker*	128
	Fixed principals: *Martin Chuzzlewit*	132
	Juvenile delinquents: Stalky and Saki	136
	Animal crackers: Gulley Jimson and Mr White	142
8	**Intellectual Comedy: the Distillation of Elements**	149
	Quite the thing: *Emma*	150
	Feasts of reason: Thomas Love Peacock	155
	Striking attitudes: *The Egoist*	163
	Family fortunes: Ivy Compton-Burnett	166
9	**Celebratory Comedy: the Accomplished Work**	172
	The complete consort: *Joseph Andrews*	173
	Innocence abroad: *The Pickwick Papers*	179
	Clerical errors: *Barchester Towers*	187
	A pack of cards: Evelyn Waugh	190
10	**Comedic Stylistics**	197
	In the van: T.F. Powys	200
	Dungeons in Spain: Samuel Beckett	204
	A light pastry hand: Sylvia Townsend Warner	208
	Propitiating magnates: John Cowper Powys	213
	A talent for abuse: Wyndham Lewis	218
	A manner of speaking: Elizabeth Bowen and Henry Green	223
	The ineluctable modality of the oral: James Joyce	229
11	**Epilogue: the Alchemy of Laughter**	238
	Notes	246
	Index	250

Preface

This book is the product of over fifty years of novel-reading, and has been written simply for the pleasure of it. It is a work of celebratory investigation, one which offers a practical approach to the study of comedy in the belief that, in order to discover what comedy is, the surest method is to determine what it does. If we equate it with any of its various elements (satire or farce, for example,) we immediately become entangled in a cat's-cradle of conflicting definitions, for comedy is not a quantifiable object, nor is it merely a literary category: it is a living process, an experience *of* experience, a way of contending with the enigmas, frustrations, contradictions and misfortunes that are the external obstacles to happiness – and also with the vanities, follies and sheer wickedness that human beings breed within themselves. As a consequence, comedy is most readily understood by observing processes rather than by establishing rules.

Although comedy is usually discussed in connection with the stage, I believe that it can be most comprehensively related to its human context through the medium of prose fiction. Novels are a mongrel breed, deriving from allegory, romance, journalism, the drama, travel-writing, biography, the moral essay and the character-sketch: they obey no laws and have no agreed structure or predetermined length, save as commercial practicalities dictate. While making use of the conventions of comedy that have been formulated within the temporal and spatial limitations of the theatre, they do this by so great a variety of means as to embody those conditions of relativity and inconclusiveness in which the comic sense originates. Moreover, the comedic process can be found at work even in novels which would appear to question the validity of comedy's procedures, through their concentration on momentous, harrowing or unavoidably calamitous events. In this study I have accordingly used my chosen novels to illuminate each other by means less of applied than of enacted theory. Through deciphering what they show and say, and through examining the methods by which their authors obtain the effects they do, one stands a good chance of appreciating the nature of comedy itself.

My controlling metaphors are taken from the ancient science of alchemy. I have drawn on the endeavour to transmute base metals into gold as a structural paradigm with which to describe the various comedic processes detectable in prose fiction. Alchemy, an enacted symbol of inward purification, may be less irrelevant to our concerns than the subject's esoteric and arcane associations might lead us to suppose.

I have used the word 'comical' to denote the humorous or 'funny', and have reserved 'comic' for the *conceptual* aspects of comedy – for comedy as a literary genre or category – and have employed 'comedic' to relate to comedy as a *process*. It is the nature and outcome of that process which forms the subject of this book.

The first chapter focuses on comedy's occasion, which I have symbolised in the image of the monolith. It argues that it is personal beliefs and institutional behaviour of an absolutist and authoritarian kind which form the primary material for the imaginative process of comedic transmutation, a process which enlarges human understanding and perspectives, and of which the several categories of comedy (celebration, parody, satire, farce, irony, burlesque and wit) each form a part. The second chapter analyses those seven categories, its successors illustrating each of them in turn; the novels examined in those contexts have been chosen for their representative qualities – no doubt others would have served my purpose equally well. Since comedy is relative to the numberless examples of the monolithic spirit which it encounters and subverts, I am as much concerned with what novels have in common, and with what differentiates them, as I am with questions of influence and evolution: accordingly, the final chapter discusses comedy as a regulative and linguistic procedure, examining it as an element in a novel's form and methodology as well as in its content. For reasons which will become clear, my survey concludes around 1960, when certain far-reaching changes in traditional ways of thinking and feeling became evident in popular behaviour, in moral perspectives and in the economic functioning of social structures. It was a time when new monoliths began drastically to modify the old.

One final point: since human beings (alone apparently within the natural order) are incorrigibly prone to the detection of absurdity, a potential danger lurks in any systematic enquiry into the origins of humour. Comedy is something which not only fictional characters experience, and it tends to resist solemn or over-deliberate investigation, so that even theorists as redoubtable as Freud or Bergson can at times arouse an unintended quiver of amusement. I readily acknowledge that should my own more hesitant conclusions in this matter turn out to be self-defeating, then it follows that the laugh's on me.

Acknowledgements

Among the many people who have contributed to the writing of this book I especially wish to thank Mrs E.E. Duncan-Jones, Dr Paul Hartle and Dr Michael Halls, all of whom have read it in manuscript and made helpful suggestions for its improvement.

1
The Matter of the Work

> It is useless to base any system on a human being.
>
> Henri Bergson, *Laughter*

'Did you ever hear the like of that for impertinence?' Mrs Parsons wound up, brushing the crumbs from her furs.

Why is this so funny? Virginia Woolf obviously intended that it should be: its position in a passage that records the various sounds and movements in a London tea-shop is designed to produce the maximum comic resonance. Consider what leads up to it.

'Pie and greens for one. Large coffee and crumpets. Eggs on toast. Two fruit cakes.'

Thus the sharp voices of the waitresses snapped. The lunchers heard their orders repeated with approval; saw the next table served with anticipation. Their own eggs on toast were at last delivered. Their eyes strayed no more.

Damp cubes of pastry fell into mouths opened like triangular bags.

The observations are dispassionate, no less staccato than the waitresses: the process of ordering and consuming food in public is made to look absurd, since these customers are functional objects related only to what they eat. But then follows a moment of individuation.

Nelly Jenkinson, the typist, crumbled her cake indifferently enough. Every time the door opened she looked up. What did she expect to see?

Here the novelist shows her hand: she considers a character's possibilities. That definite article before 'typist' places Nelly Jenkinson in a social group, while at the same time it differentiates her from the other customers. (Had the indefinite article been used, she would have been appropriated for narratorial ends.) As to that 'enough' – it suggests rôle-playing: Nelly's actual indifference is related to a suppositious one. The rhetorical question that follows forbids any answer; at the same time it marks the writer's momentary assumption of interest in the possibility of one.

Another specific person now appears.

> The coal merchant read the *Telegraph* without stopping, missed the saucer, and feeling abstractedly, put the cup down on the table-cloth.

Bless him, one thinks: the mood has become more intimate; the comical action is both personal and representative, an all too familiar mishap.

And now for Mrs Parsons, third and last and most elaborately presented of these figures. With her we are in the realm of the satirical, recipients of a pictorially encoded message. The flourish of her question, in an idiom that would be recognised by Woolf's original readers as 'not quite quite', is splendidly enhanced by the opulence of those 'furs' – note how different the effect had they been mentioned in the singular. And 'Parsons'? According to this code of discourse 'Perkins' might have been more comical; but 'Parsons', with its clerical echo and broad vowel-sound, conveys precisely the right note of complacent grandeur. The clinching comical device, however, is in the verb 'wound up'; it evokes an auditor and invites the reader's empathy. Finally, as though to underline the musical nature of the passage, there comes a choral aftermath.

> "Hot milk and scone for one. Pot of tea. Roll and butter," cried the waitresses.

This little scene from *Jacob's Room* (1922) is comedic: it takes isolated objects, relates them to each other, and in so doing endows them with vitality. But whereas Mrs Parsons has been rendered as a dramatised personality, the typist and the coal merchant are, by virtue of a definite article, mere signifiers, and in conception monolithic.

The nature of a monolith

A monolith is a single block of stone, its purpose in one form or another monumental. Human ideas and institutions naturally incline to such a petrifaction. So do human personalities: in post-Renaissance stage-comedy we see the obstructive power of monoliths expressed through the comedy of humours. This arose from the belief that human beings were a balance of substances (melancholy, choler, blood and phlegm) which circulated in the body; and that an excess of any one of these 'humours' resulted in distorted personality. The afflicted individual was a natural target for derision, a derision whose apparent cruelty was regarded as justified by the damage which disproportion could be seen to wreak upon the harmonious operations of society as a whole. While it was the function of the comic spirit to draw attention to distortion and excess, it was the work of comedy itself to restore proportion and good order.

The nature of a monolith therefore suggests an analogy with the recalcitrant material on which comedic novelists set to work in order to elicit their world of reciprocally enlivening diversities. To judge from their recurring preoccupations (preoccupations of the emerging commercially-based society in which the naturalistic kind of English novel came to maturity), this monolithic *prima materia* is embodied in four principal human concerns, much as that of the mediæval alchemists was made up of the elements of water, fire, earth and air. It can emerge from an obsession with the *past*, with prescriptive ideas inherited from religion, parentage, environment (both physical and social), sexual rôle-playing, legislation and taboo. When any particular interpretation of these forces becomes immoveable and absolute it turns into an idol – that is to say, a limiting assertion of finality where no real finality exists. Novelists of all kinds rebel against the monolith's restrictive pressures, through one comic procedure or another attacking its usurped authority over the individual's freedom, which is also their own freedom to imagine and invent. Even while acknowledging its potent force, comedy demonstrates the absurdity of that usurpation: from the controlled ironies of Jane Austen to the rumbustious scorn of Kingsley Amis the social monolith is a staple target for English comic fiction.

The monolith likewise establishes itself in the awareness of the *present*, revealed both in a subjection to current fashions, prejudices and attitudes, and in an exaggerated estimate of the claims of personality and self-expression. The two tendencies are in reciprocal relationship: if the claims of society become excessive, then those of its rebellious members will become excessive in their turn – in itself a matter for comedy, as novelists have realised in a whole range of characters, from Dickens's Harold Skimpole to Angus Wilson's Harold Calvert. Comedy is nothing if not self-scrutinising, its turning of the tables being in perpetual revolution.

It is natural to protest at such a constant dance of relativities: if the absolute is not to be located within human nature or human institutions, then let it be known as fate, a philosophical concept which dignifies the apparently inevitable. Once again the monolith emerges: the *future* is to be predictable; regularity, law, logical consequence, right reason are in complete control. But comedy questions even these apparently self-evident monolithic certainties. It draws attention to, and thrives upon, the factor of surprise, that element of sheer chance which upsets all sense of the dependability of a foreseeable predestination. It does not resist, but welcomes, disruptive incursions – as happens in a whole succession of fictions from those of Henry Fielding to those of Evelyn Waugh.

In doing this, comedy appears to point to a supersession of the awareness of past, present and future alike. Such a state of *timelessness*, however, is a postulate which can itself turn monolithic and impose a tyranny of absolutes that extends to prescriptive structural and categorical requirements. But this is a monolith that the more idiosyncratic novelists dismantle in the knowledge that comedy 'has to be recognised as a matrix term that embraces miscellaneous impulses, which can be sensed empirically as effects before they are regarded as intentions'.[1] Accordingly, writers from Sterne to John Cowper Powys have made comedy out of the veridical pretensions of the literary mode they at the same time master and embrace.

Comedy exposes the fallacy inherent in every monolithic interpretation of human experience: it refutes exclusiveness, points out inconsistencies, and harmonises them in a renewed pattern of relationships. It deconstructs the monolith in order to breathe life into it. By its very nature a monolith is both dead and deadening, so that we find monolithic outlooks breeding monolithic institutions, and monolithic institutions nurturing monolithic minds. In personal relationships the monolith may be detected in the self-centredness that refuses to acknowledge the autonomy of others; in social ones it is evident in the inflexible prejudice, the tabloid opinion, the defensive idolisation of the past. It is potential in the monochrome temperament and in every simplistic and compulsive attitude which inhibits personal, political and social harmony.

To perceive that static quality as comical is to challenge the monolith's evaluation of itself: what provokes the comedic action is its apparent immovability. Dickens's novels are full of examples of this process, usually through his use of the narratorial voice, a kind of vocalised Trabb's boy perpetually at his command. And if the young man Pip, encased in snobbery and all his smart new clothes, suffers torments from the derision of Trabb's boy, yet it is that very tormentor who in due course helps to save him from incarceration by the murderous Orlick. *Great Expectations* abounds in such teleological ironies.

This perception of comicality (in whatever shape – character, function, creed or social organism) is developed through a variety of procedures. The monolith can be analysed by presenting it to itself in *parody*, a mirror image which highlights its absurdities: a good deal of eighteenth-century comedy is of this kind, the tradition continuing to the present day, not only in the novel but also in the review sketch and the art of mime in musical and balletic form. Or one can dismiss monolithic pretensions more aggressively, refusing to take them seriously by outraging them in *farce*: slapstick humour is irreversible and fatal to self-arrogated dignity. Alternatively it is possible to take the monolith *ironically* at face value and thus invite its pretensions to betray themselves, the most devastating incidence of this procedure being Swift's *A Modest Proposal for Preventing the Children of poor People in Ireland, from being a Burden to their Parents or Country; and for making them beneficial to the Publick*. Pressing the arguments of commercial logic to the limit, this pamphlet proceeds inexorably to demonstrate that the best use for the children of the Irish poor will be to fatten them and sell them off to the rich as food. The anonymous author protests his own disinterestedness: 'I have no Children, by which I can propose to get a single penny; the youngest being nine Years old, and my Wife past Child-bearing.'

But the literal-mindedness of the majority being what it is, such a methodology is always in danger of backfiring; it is safer and thus more frequent to confront the monolith openly by means of *satire*. Satire presupposes a congenial audience, and is more readily assimilable than irony – hence its proliferation in journalism and shorter forms of fiction. The detachment it involves, however, gives way to a more personally engaged exposure of the monolith's pretensions – *burlesque*. Burlesque grapples with the monolith at close quarters, both through the disrespectful exaggerations of caricature and through the outraging of good taste in 'black' or 'gallows' humour, with its element of collusive relish. (The comical anguish in Samuel Beckett's plays and novels displays this tactic definitively.) It is possible, however, to disallow the monolith's pretensions altogether. This is the attitude of *wit*, for wit is an airy refusal of those claims, one which offers an alternative model of reality, composed of elements which the monolithic point of view keeps separate from each other: whereas farce thumbs a nose at the monolith, wit laughs it out of court. But the true fulfilment of comedy is found in the attitude of *celebration*, one which corrects the monolithic vision by allowing its claims on terms other than their own. While celebration accepts that monolithic attitudes exist, it ignores their self-referential grounds for requiring people to acknowledge that existence.

The perception of diversity

On account of its openness to on-going dissection, a novel tends to evade the solicitations of the monolithic point of view. In English fiction especially, with its diversity and its favouring of pragmatism over academic theory, the categories of tragedy and comedy are seldom exemplified in exclusive form. The number of pure comedies (as distinct from humorous novels) is not large. For if the majority of novels contain elements of the comic, the distillation of pure comedy is usually muddied by the demands of plot, suspense and theme. There are of course innumerable self-styled comic novels, but these are not quite the same thing: they confine themselves to particular aspects of comedy, being farces or satires or burlesques rather than comedies in their totality. *Tristram Shandy, Emma, Barchester Towers, The Egoist, Ulysses* may be placed in the latter category, but not *Great Expectations, Far from the Madding Crowd, Howards End* or *Brideshead Revisited*, rich in various kinds of comic material though they may be. Similarly, among those English novels at one time or another reckoned as canonical, not many are fundamentally tragic: *The Bride of Lammermoor, The Ordeal of Richard Feverel, The Mill on the Floss, The Portrait of a Lady, Tess of the D'Urbervilles* and three or four more of Hardy's novels, the majority of Conrad's, *The Good Soldier, The Death of the Heart* – not many others come immediately to mind, and even of these the majority contain elements which qualify the controlling tragic vision.

The concept of comedy being itself at the service of the comedic process, it can diversify and enrich a novel that would otherwise be monolithically regarded as a tragedy. No better instance of such a modulation can be found than in one of the earliest examples of an intentionally tragic novel, Samuel Richardson's *Clarissa* (1747–49). The argument that the act of reading is an evaluative process in itself is certainly applicable to this monumental work, which, being written in epistolary form, comments upon its own means of progression as it goes along.

It describes an attempt to undermine a potential monolith – the absolute chastity of the nineteen-year-old heroine, the younger daughter of a mercenary and unimaginative landowning family in Hertfordshire. Her resistance to an avowed seducer, Lovelace, is maintained against all odds, not least of them her family's equally unyielding determination that she shall marry against her own interests in order to further theirs. The upshot is tragic in the fullest dramatic sense: Clarissa's rape by Lovelace results in her death of grief at this outrage to her being. But that death is swallowed up in a moral victory. Belford, her violator's comrade, undergoes a change of heart, while the ravisher himself is inconsolable, paying with his death at the hands of Clarissa's avenging champion. Virtue is rewarded, if only by its own probity.

Powerful though its tragic and dramatic aspects are, the book would not retain its hold upon later generations were it not for the comic undertow provided by the letters and attitudes of Lovelace and, to a lesser extent, of Clarissa's confidante, Miss Howe. With her high spirits, indignation at her friend's ill-treatment, and caustic attacks on the oppressors, Anna Howe provides an emotional safety-valve in the enormously protracted progress of Clarissa's story; she allows for readerly participation and for the voicing of a point of view other than the heroine's single-minded adherence to personal integrity and familial duty. But a more potent occasion for the reader's involvement comes through the collision of two monolithic behavioural compulsions – Clarissa's adherence to the dictates of propriety (taken in its most serious sense), and Lovelace's obsession with his own reputation as a rake. For it is one of the grimmer ironies of this novel that the ostensibly 'liberated' worldling should in fact be the slave not only of a need, where women are concerned, to notch up scores, but also of his self-deception in proposing to 'test' the virtue of the one he pretends to love. His personal tragedy is that he does in his own fashion love her, but is incapable of behaving in a manner consonant with what love requires. There is, however, an ambiguity attendant upon Lovelace, whose irresistibly robust and knowledgeably witty letters provide *Clarissa* with its underlying comedic element. 'Underlying', however, does not mean 'repressed': the comedy, the reversal of expectation, issues as a spiritual verdict on the ways of a world which Lovelace and the Harlowe family in their different ways exemplify. Despite the universal eulogies upon her, Clarissa is not monolithically presented. Like Isobel Archer in James's *The Portrait of a Lady*, she has to pay the price for being conscious of her own virtues. She admits to moral complacency and to accepting too readily the general estimate of her character; and on occasion she is subjected to physical indignities which serve comedically to humanise her. During one passionate encounter, Lovelace's violence so alarms her that she struggles and is knocked against a chair. Beholding blood and assuming that she has stabbed herself, he is overwhelmed.

> I was upon the point of drawing my sword to dispatch myself, when I discovered (what an unmanly blockhead does this charming creature make me at her pleasure!) that all I apprehended was but a bloody nose, which, as far as I know (for it could not be stopped in a quarter of an hour) may have saved her head and her intellects. (Letter 267)

The laugh here is on Lovelace; but the faintly comical touch enables one the more readily to empathise with Clarissa. And at other times she is regarded with hostility: as Lovelace's thick-skinned crony remarks,

> Everybody blames him on this lady's account. But I see not why. She was a *vixen* in her virtue. (Letter 436)

It is evidence of how effective Lovelace's own audacious self-exculpation can be that occasionally one feels inclined to endorse that verdict.

An instance of such a seduction of the strictly moral point of view is the 'flyting' of Miss Howe's staid admirer, who is interceding for Clarissa. Lovelace informs him that she has another suitor, 'a misshapen, meagre varlet; more like a skeleton than a man!' But Hickman is sceptical.

> Some East India governor, I suppose, if there be anything in it: the lady once had a thought of going abroad. But I fancy, all this time you are in jest, sir. If not, we must surely have heard of him.
> Heard of him! Ay, sir, we have all heard of him – but none of us care to be intimate with him – except this lady – and that, as I told you, in spite of me. His name, in short, is DEATH! DEATH! sir,

stamping, and speaking loud, and full in his ear; which made him jump half a yard high. (Letter 346)

Such grim farcicality, eloquent of genuine pain, is turned back upon itself with Hickman's dignified rejoinder, one which effectively implicates the reader in Lovelace's bitter jest. The tragic and comic aspects of the drama are in continuous interaction.

On other occasions the comedy is delicately confidential, as in Mrs Norton's account of how the Harlowes belatedly encourage her to visit her former pupil as an ambassadress of their hitherto withheld goodwill.

And sorry I am that I cannot this moment set out, as I might instead of writing, would they favour my eager impatience with their chariot; but as it was not offered, it would have been presumptuous to have asked for it; and tomorrow a hired chaise and pair will be ready; but at what hour I know not. (Letter 483)

This is the kind of inferential observation which Jane Austen was to employ to such good purpose. She owed much to Richardson's use of implied narrative when achieving her own subtle and informative effects.

Comedy requires such tactics: if tragedy is a spectacle, comedy is something shared between those who are in the know. In this respect Richardson's epistolary method serves him well. One can judge the reaction to its fellows of each point of view – the interplay of Clarissa's version of events with that of Lovelace; of Anna Howe's with that of Belford; not to mention the various letters of the supporting characters. Far from detracting from the impressiveness of the tragedy, they frame it within a wider perspective, and raise the possibility of those alternative versions of the truth which it is comedy's function to make apparent. Likewise through the collision between two species of language (the language of sentiment and aspiration and the domestic language of disenchanted worldliness which Lovelace shares with twentieth-century readers) *Clarissa* exhibits complementary versions of reality which are associated with the comic epic and with the contrasting attitudes to life of Don Quixote and Sancho Panza. And it is *Don Quixote* which has as good a title as any prose narrative to be considered the begetter of the European novel.

The fun of the fair

'As we grow older and realise more clearly the limitations of human happiness, we come to see that the only real and abiding pleasure in life is to give pleasure to other people.'[2] P.G. Wodehouse's gently confident assertion reminds us that there are writers whose purpose has been quite simply to keep their readers entertained. Wodehouse is but one of innumerable novelists whose comic sense is not predominantly ironic, satirical or even witty, is not confined to one particular sphere of interest, but whose object has been to build up and to elaborate a world that will be purely pleasurable. Their aim is not to envisage how the human lot can be transformed, but to posit an imaginary existence in which catastrophes are no longer fatal.

Their works are fantasies without the properties of fantasy; indeed, some of them (the socially subversive novels of R.S. Surtees, for example) border upon satire and burlesque. But if Surtees can match Dickens in his capacity to delineate a rogue, to poke fun at social snobbery, husband-hunting and the delinquencies of servants (all of them part of Victorian humorous stock-in-trade), he refuses to disturb his readers with any searching psychological enquiries. His are *sporting* novels: the rural settings and the delight in the chase, in food and drink, and in the niceties of social snobbery, are portrayed with a gusto entirely appropriate to a down-to-earth Arcadia. They create an exuberant world in which a reader can also feel it safe to be.

This carefree sportiveness is sustained by a stable rural society governed by established and generally accepted rules and procedures: the happy land has laws whose infringement can be relied upon only to enhance the sense of universal pleasure. Such stability is likewise an important element in the hunting stories of E.Œ. Somerville and Martin Ross. Theirs is a wilder, more romantically rendered world than that of Surtees, one in which double-dealing is suffused with charm; in which accidents happen at the narrator's expense (and which, because he is a Rural Magistrate, is at authority's expense as well); muddle and mystery are farcically combined. The authorial assumptions as to society and class are more vulnerable to deconstructive analysis than are those of the less sophisticated Surtees; the world of Shreelane and Aussolas, precisely because it is so lovingly (if also caustically) portrayed, is one to be inhabited by means of an act of deliberate imaginative choice. But it does have its shadowy corners and its peepholes into the darker realities from which it draws its being. And, like Surtees, the authors draw on the sheer exhilaration of physical movement, in their case adding the sights and sounds and smells of a lovingly delineated Southern Irish landscape.

Such rural and physical delights are a staple of the earthly paradise that is embodied in so many English humorous novels. They can even be found in such a comparatively prosaic tale as Jerome K. Jerome's *Three Men in a Boat*, a book which, having remained in print since its publication in 1889, may be taken to represent an enduring popular taste. Its predominant mode is satirical slapstick, focusing on the recalcitrance of inanimate objects and the unhandiness of the average male when dealing with them. Here are two men disentangling a tow-rope:

> they feel so angry with one another that they would like to hang each other with the thing. Ten minutes go by, and the first man gives a yell and goes mad, and dances on the rope, and tries to pull it straight by seizing hold of the first piece that comes to his hand and hauling at it. Of course, this only gets it into a tighter tangle than ever. Then the second man climbs out of the boat and comes to help him, and they get in each other's way, and hinder one another. They both get hold of the same bit of line, and pull at it in opposite directions, and wonder where it is caught. In the end, they do get it clear, and then turn round and find that the boat has drifted off, and is making straight for the weir. (Chapter ix)

This is amusing for what it describes rather than for its tone or in the timing of the description. It rests on a base of shared, and thus recognised, experience, and has only friendly designs upon its readers.

Elsewhere one finds a touch of gruesome relish characteristic of popular humour of this kind.

> The pool under Sandford lasher, just behind the lock, is a very good place to drown yourself in. The undercurrent is terribly strong, and if you once get down into it you are all right. (Chapter xviii)

That 'all right' is worthy of Samuel Beckett himself. But more frequently the author, with deliberate ambiguity, adopts the tone of ironic banter beloved of popular comedians to the present day.

Three Men in a Boat seems to have no other purpose than to amuse its readers by arousing their complicity in the enjoyment and acceptance of life's absurdities – an enjoyment and acceptance which it assumes are always there. Its world is classless – one reason, perhaps, for its enduring appeal, since most purely humorous novels require that the reader be prepared to become a part of their particular social worlds, together with those worlds' assumptions and priorities. They play *within* a monolith, as it were, rather than around it or at its expense. But the societies portrayed by Surtees and by Somerville and

Ross are comprehensive enough for their monolithic stability to go unchallenged in the fictions they beget. Matters go very differently when we turn to the literature of 'Society' in the special sense of the word: 'a select class of wealthy and leisured persons, speaking an artificial language of their own and spending all their time and energy in entertaining themselves and one another'.[3] This is the world of Ada Leverson and Saki, and in the latter case one feels it is not altogether a safe one in which to play. But in the farces of P.G. Wodehouse or Ben Travers, even in the more adventurous tales of Dornford Yates, there is an essential jollity, a gallantry even, that flourishes in a way of life as confined by class as that of Saki, and as potentially tyrannical. Theirs is a world in which the possession of money calls the tune; it is also one in which it is always playtime and where it is permissible to make a mockery of the conventions which preserve its being.

Wodehouse is the supreme master of this particular universe, by virtue not only of his linguistic skills and narrative invention, but also of sheer *bonhomie* and good nature – characteristics notably lacking in Saki, and indeed not always evident in Yates, whose comic spokesman, Berry Pleydell, has a line in rhetorical disgust that Saki's Reginald and Clovis might well envy. Here he is, launched on a tirade concerning French bathroom geysers.

> Have you ever seen Vesuvius in eruption? [...] I admit no rocks were discharged – at least, I didn't see any. There may be some in the bath. I didn't wait to look.... Blinded by the steam, deafened by the noise, you make a rush for the door. This seems to have been moved. You feel all over the walls, like a madman. In the frenzy of despair – it's astonishing how one clings to life – you hurl yourself at the bath and turn on both taps.... As if by magic the steam disappears, the roaring subsides, and two broad streams of pure cold water issue, like crystal founts, into the bath. Now you know why I'm so jolly this morning.
>
> (*Jonah and Co.* (1922), Chapter iii)

Yates's world is very much of its time and more firmly rooted in actuality than is that of Wodehouse. His sextet of bright young people have a certain toughness. The men are ex-soldiers, wartime heroes who have paid their dues and are now determined to enjoy themselves to the limit in the company of their spirited, amused and emancipated ladies. But it is precisely because Daphne is so glamorous and charming that Berry's comment, 'I knew our journey would be eventful, because my wife put her teeth in upside-down this morning' is as funny as it is.

It is Wodehouse, however, who piles absurdity upon absurdity to best effect: he contrives to be irresponsible without any taint of parasitical defiance. In their different ways all three of his principal groups of novels exhibit this capacity. In the stories about Psmith, the outrageously nonchalant eponymous protagonist, with his confident flouting of convention and good-humoured bestowal of the sobriquet 'Comrade' on every man he meets, is contrasted with the agreeable, essentially normal Mike Jackson: one can hear an echo of the Don Quixote–Sancho Panza relationship. That Psmith should find his way to Blandings Castle seems inevitable, for that idyllic setting of the second group of tales is proof that the established order can accommodate with infinite flexibility all manner of intruders from outside. Here the sublimely absent-minded Lord Emsworth is attended by a hyper-organisational but by no means omnipotent private secretary – another variant on the Cervantes duo. The latter, however, attain their definitive appearance in Wodehouse's fiction with the partnership between Bertie Wooster and his valet Jeeves, one which reflects the operations of what amounts to a potentially comedic hierarchy.

As a narrator the asinine Bertie has a nicely confidential manner.

I must say Aunt Dahlia's bearing and demeanour did nothing to assist towards a restored composure. Of the amiability which she had exhibited when discussing this unhappy chump's activities with me over the fruit salad, no trace remained, and I was not surprised that speech more or less froze on the Fink-Nottle lips. It isn't often that Aunt Dahlia, normally as genial a bird as ever encouraged a gaggle of hounds to get their noses down to it, lets her angry passions rise, but when she does, strong men climb trees and pull them up after them.

(*Right Ho, Jeeves* (1934), Chapter xx)

It is Bertie's verbal exuberance which enables the author to preserve the balance between him and the omniscient, omni-competent, far-seeing Jeeves. The protective figure who is yet non-parental, Jeeves is a guardian of whom dreams are made. Dilemmas are raised in order that Jeeves may resolve them; perils are encountered in order that Bertie may be delivered from them by Jeeves: the stories almost amount to parables of redemption and salvation. Wodehouse can produce witticisms reminiscent of Saki: 'He was the sort of man who would have tried to cheer Napoleon up by talking of the winter sports at Moscow.' 'I began to understand how a general must feel when he has ordered a regiment to charge and has been told that it isn't in the mood.' But while Saki sets out to disturb, Wodehouse's prevailing tone is not even merely amiable but actively comforting. *Summer Lightning* (1929) opens on a characteristic note: 'It was that gracious hour of a summer afternoon, midway between luncheon and tea, when Nature seems to unbutton its waistcoat and put its feet up.' Even the moments of high drama are exuberant with an athletic sense of timing.

> "Hands up!" said Mr Cootes with the uncouth curtness of one who had not had the advantages of a refined home and a nice upbringing. He advanced warily, preceded by his revolver. It was a dainty, miniature weapon, such as might have been the property of some gentle lady. Mr Cootes had, in fact, borrowed it from Miss Peavey, who at this juncture entered the room in a black and silver dinner-dress surmounted by a Rose du Barri wrap, her spiritual face glowing softly in the subdued light.
> "Attaboy, Ed," observed Miss Peavey crisply.
> (*Leave it to Psmith* (1923), Chapter xiii.4)

For all his absence of pretension, or perhaps because of it, Wodehouse is a genuinely festive novelist.

Comic novels of this kind may represent a species of earthly paradise, an easy gesture towards the reconciliation of opposites that in purely *comedic* fiction is achieved the hard way. The country house world of Wodehouse, the clubland world of Yates, the sporting worlds of Surtees, G.J. Whyte-Melville and Somerville and Ross, no less than the middle-aged middle-class ones of E.F. Benson's Lucia novels, the high-spirited joviality of Compton Mackenzie's Highland farces, or the Dockland yarns of W.W. Jacobs, all have this in common, that although they are wide open to socially orientated, gender-focused critical investigation, they withstand all such assaults by their open appeal to the reader's desire for relaxation and enjoyment. Each of them may be a potential monolith, built up from certain prescriptive attitudes and responses; but to the extent that their authors can arouse our laughter (and how whole-heartedly and cleverly they do) they appeal to that basis of humane response which enables them, without being masterworks of the comedic process, to suggest the nature of the goal at which that process aims.

Engaging the monolith

A comical or purely humorous novel differs from a comedic one by virtue of simplicity. The latter is required to harmonise conflicting monoliths, whereas, taken in isolation from each other, parody, satire and the rest are to a greater or lesser degree dependent on them. Parody needs monoliths in order to provide itself with a model; farce needs them if it is to realise its nature as a feast of fools. Irony assumes their existence while pretending to ignore it; satire requires them as objects to attack. So likewise with burlesque, the very nature of which depends upon them. Only wit and celebration appear to be detached from them; but wit, no less than irony, involves an implicit acknowledgement of their existence; while celebration, by engulfing them, absorbs them into its own carefree realm of disenchantment. But taken as a whole, the comedic process is corrective and remedial, and as such it includes an understanding of the conditions that call out to be anatomised and to be resolved by laughter.

The monolith is exhibited in recurring forms. In the eighteenth and early nineteenth century novel it appears in the shape of character, not only in 'humorous' ones like Hawser Trunnion in Smollett's *Peregrine Pickle* (1751) or Aunt Grizzy in Susan Ferrier's *Marriage* (1818), but also when individuals represent a whole class or an attitude to life – Fielding is adept at such portraits, witness Parson Trulliber and Squire Western in *Tom Jones* (1749). Elsewhere, most notably in Sterne, one finds a character's quirks and oddities portrayed with a sympathetic relish that amounts to celebration: in the case of Uncle Toby and Corporal Trim, those oddities expose the effect upon them of the lives they have led; but it is the people themselves, not the institutions in which they are incorporate, who are the objects of their creator's interest. In the hands of more purely domestic novelists such as Jane Austen, mockery of peculiar characteristics relates to such issues as the marriage market, the disposal of property and the responsibilities of land-ownership and trade. The workings of society itself become the focus of comic scrutiny, with the portrayal of class differentiation being as much a matter of function within the community as of social status.

None the less, monolithic humorous characters remain the norm in a fictive tradition that still followed the patterns of stage drama, with 'serious' hero and heroine, and supporting figures there to provide comic relief. In the novels of Scott, for example, people such as Bartoline Saddletree in *The Heart of Midlothian* (1818) give voice to their overriding obsessions with implacable particularity, despite the fact that even at the time of writing few could share their creator's delight in legal niceties and quibbles of theology. More truly comedic is Nicol Jarvie in *Rob Roy* (1818), whose peculiarities, while conditioned by his caste and occupation, are blended with other, more generally shared characteristics, so that in his diversity he becomes a rebuke to the simplistic notions of a monochrome and thus potentially monolithic portraiture. Indeed, Scott's own humanity is such that it is only when he attends to literary models, rather than to his own experience, that his sense of the comic fails to be persuasive. His inspiration is essentially attuned to comprehensive viewpoints, and while he can accommodate monolithic ones, this is because it would take a monolithic nature to repress them.

Scott's influence on nineteenth-century fiction was enormous, even, one might say, regulative. *St Ronan's Well* (1824) with its satirical picture of the society at a small fashionable watering-place, is focused on personalities and the conjunction of contrasting mannerisms; 40 years later one finds a similar approach in Trollope's account of life at Littlebath in *The Bertrams* (1859) and *Miss Mackenzie* (1865). In his earlier years as a novelist Trollope frequently delineated humorous types, both in his use of tendentious names such as Mr Quiverful and Dr Fillgrave (in which, whether knowingly or not, he was plagiarising Bulwer-Lytton's widely read *Eugene Aram* (1832), which features a manipulative quack doctor called Pertinax Fillgrave) and in the depiction of such consistent personages as the smarmy Mr Slope and the monumentally impassive daughter of Archdeacon Grantley. Even so, his characterisations tend to be more rounded than are those of his contemporary Wilkie Collins: amusing though they are, people such as the valetudinarian Frederick Fairlie in *The Woman in White* (1861) or, in *The Moonstone* (1868), that 'rampant spinster', the Evangelical Drusilla Clack, possess an unvarying tone of voice that keeps them at the monolithic stage. It is Dickens whose sheer creative energy in the realisation of physicality transports the comedy of humours into a surreal world in which psychic energies become material: one has only to cite the names Uriah Heep, Sally Brass or Chadband for their corresponding physiques to come to mind.

But by the mid-nineteenth century a more conscious awareness of social conditioning had infiltrated the imaginations of novelists, evident not only in the expansive canvases of Thackeray and Dickens, but in the more narrowly focused dissections of provincial life by

Elizabeth Gaskell, Margaret Oliphant and George Eliot. Instead of the detailed portrayal of humorous types in isolation from each other, there is a concentration on them as products of their environment and of their inherited social traditions.

Indeed, in the nineteenth century, detection of the monolith shifts from personalities to institutions. Dickens combines both manifestations in *Little Dorrit* (1857), where the Circumlocution Office is derided in much the same manner as are the conversational idiosyncracies of Flora Finching: the element of burlesque opens the way to appreciating both of them as objects for satirical enjoyment, even though the one embodiment is morally objectionable, the other not. And where personality is concerned, Trollope, by reintroducing characters from book to book, modifies our responses to them, most spectacularly in the case of the death of Mrs Proudie, when a majestic figure of fun from *Barchester Towers* (1857) becomes in *The Last Chronicle of Barset* (1867) both pitiable and awe-inspiring. It is Mrs Proudie's opinions which are treated monolithically, not herself.

Later in the nineteenth century, with the advent of George Meredith and Thomas Hardy, fiction takes on a more consciously specialist and intellectual character which issues, in Meredith's case, in novels which specifically propound a philosophy of comedic optimism. Verbal and intellectual energies propel the narratives of *Evan Harrington* (1861) and *Harry Richmond* (1871) to conclusions calculated to induce reflection rather than to minister to pre-emptive expectations. To read a novel by Meredith is not simply a matter of deciphering a demanding text; Meredithian comedy subjects one didactically to the author's own particular world and viewpoint, and is to that extent potentially monolithic.

Hardy's comedy is mainly verbal, arising from the speech of a peasantry conceived in traditional terms of 'character', and is subordinate to the tragi-comic conflicts and obsessions of his better-educated protagonists: none the less, Hardy being Hardy, a troubling note is struck even when he is being most overtly 'quaint'.

"And if Jim had lived, I should have had a clever brother! Tomorrow is poor Jim's birthday. He'd ha' been twenty-six if he'd lived till tomorrow."

"You always seem very sorry for Jim," said old William musingly.

"Ah! I do. Such a stay to mother as he'd always ha' been! She'd never have had to work in her old age if he had continued strong, poor Jim!"

18 *Alchemy of Laughter*

"What was his age when a' died?"
"Four hours and twenty minutes, poor Jim."
(*Under the Greenwood Tree* (1872) II:iii)

Laughter at this point amounts to an entrapment; it is a characteristically bizarre joke on the author's part – for if followed through to its natural consequences, the sentiment, though exaggerated, is not absurd. What is new in Hardy's novels is an ironic rendering of orthodox notions of providential destiny. They refuse the consolations of any prescribed moralistic response. The tragedies, especially the most unrelenting of them, in their very unfolding frustrate the desire for some emotional alleviation of the disasters they portray. In *Tess of the D'Urbervilles* (1891) and *Jude the Obscure* (1895) it is the monolith of received religious opinion which is being challenged.

By the early twentieth century, comedy in fiction had become departmentalised. The nineteenth century had seen plenty of deliberately comic novels, but to the degree that their authors were adjudged to be specialist writers, they were regarded as essentially marginal works. In one case, that of the exuberant Surtees, this was an underestimate: his portrayals of bare-faced social scrounging and ingenious double-dealing in *Mr Sponge's Sporting Tour* (1853) and *Mr Facey Romford's Hounds* (1865) are consonant with both eighteenth and twentieth century tastes for social roguery; but 'serious' novelists used comedy primarily for satirical ends, obvious cases in point being George Eliot and, later, Forster and Lawrence. Where the latter are concerned, the monolith is the materialistic humanism exemplified in such works as John Galsworthy's popular Forsyte saga; and also literally embodied, they assumed, in such readers as did not take up their own satirical novels with approval. The distinction between highbrow, middlebrow and lowbrow was by 1914 firmly established. In the case of the latter, and to some extent in the case of middlebrow writers too, ideas as to what was comical tended to fossilise, and to become monolithic in their turn.

The social upheavals accompanying the two World Wars resulted in a redeployment of monoliths. Irreverence towards established institutions, codes and shibboleths became the norm in fictive comic writing, so that whereas a writer like Wodehouse could exercise his comic gifts within an artificial abstract world which respected and endorsed those standards, his admirer Evelyn Waugh translates social realities into farce, the better to illuminate their imperfections.

In comedy of the period immediately following the Second World War there is a trend towards individual experience and a discarding of any socially prescriptive standard of moral measurement. While naturalistic fiction continued to provide vehicles for satire (witness the novels of Anthony Powell and William Cooper), the element of farce in the writing of, for instance, Kingsley Amis, J.P. Donleavy and, in certain aspects of their work, Angus Wilson and Iris Murdoch, proved equally congenial to popular taste. Both social and psychological self-consciousness had begun to surface in writers and their public alike. Late twentieth century novels are more apt to discuss or to celebrate the comedic process than to enact it.

One prominent factor in this developing self-consciousness was the tendency of post-war journalism to take up a particular literary text and impose it and the age upon each other. An early victim of this procedure was Amis's popular and influential first novel, *Lucky Jim* (1954). Its protagonist came to be labelled an 'angry young man', a term popularly applied to the figure of Jimmy Porter in John Osborne's play *Look Back in Anger* (1956), but originated by Leslie Paul as the title of an autobiography published in 1951. Yet today it is Jim Dixon's vulnerability, lack of assurance, and self-punishing resentment that provide the comic note. His rôle is that of the reluctant anti-hero – for at the end Jim *is* lucky, getting both the girl and the job in fairy-tale fashion. But this Wodehouse quality is offset by anger: Amis is a cogent hater, and few writers equal his power to treat of offence, both given and received. His trading of insults can be a witty and rewarding business, even self-reflexive. 'He disliked this girl and her boy-friend so much that he couldn't understand why they didn't dislike each other.' (Chapter vi)

As a farceur Amis is rather clumsy: the comparison of Jim's disastrous lecture with that of Gussie Fink-Nottle in *Right Ho, Jeeves* is not to his advantage. His principal strength is in his eye for sham and affectation.

> Margaret was laughing in the way Dixon had provisionally named to himself 'the tinkle of tiny silver bells'. He sometimes thought that the whole corpus of her behaviour derived from translating such phrases into action. (Chapter ii)

What Dixon wonders, the novel consistently portrays; and even at the level of simile the author can be deadly in his use of ridicule, as when someone produces 'the curved nickel-banded pipe round which he was trying to train his personality like a creeper up a trellis'. (Chapter iii)

Not one person in the book escapes this kind of mordant, belittling observation. The provincial university which forms its setting is regarded as fair game for mockery: the great monolithic institutions of the past are here experienced in degenerate self-parodic terms. But the comedic work is obstructed by the absolute lack of generosity towards the people and the institutions anatomised, and by the absence of any underlying moral conviction beyond a seedy scorn. Amis's heroes are frequently boozers, womanisers and full of self-pity: they collude with their misfortunes rather than endure them or enjoy them. But such relativity of a purely materialistic kind does offer its own challenge to the comedic sense, and Amis is unflaggingly insistent that conventional comic situations are bound up with structured social expectations. The monolith that *Lucky Jim* attacks so effectively is phoneyness (though an obsessive sensitivity towards the phoney can become a monolith in its turn, just as a reductive outlook does). When one views Amis's work alongside such predecessors as *Tom Jones* or even H.G. Wells's *Kipps* (1905), while one may be aware of a robust and unsparing comic process, one is also conscious of the weakening of a comedic one.

In post-war comic fiction there is found a gradual and, in due course, rapid erosion of social absolutes. Patterns of organisation and behaviour have changed; the very location of taboo has altered. In this respect three factors have been particularly influential. The first of these was the virtual disappearance of domestic servants: one pervasive embodiment of social inequality and of comic contrast was removed. The second factor was the emergence during the 1950s of adolescents as an economically autonomous, self-referential group within society. The consequent upending of traditional aspirations and patterns of behaviour resulted in a distrust of hierarchical structures and of formality of all kinds: the comedy of manners becomes impossible in such a lack of its prerequisite. Thirdly, a radical feminism questions many of the social and ethical presuppositions of earlier societies, so that conventional sexual rôle-playing has been modified and masculine priorities denied. It was a time of the breaking of monoliths; and the popular understanding of what comedy is and what it does was open to redefinition. Traditionally the ingredients of comedy have been in dynamic relation with normative monolithic values, and are thus to that extent dependent on taboo. But while an individualistic liberal society might seem to be a stranger to the experience of *fou rire*, permissiveness can itself congeal into a social monolith, so that new orthodoxies and taboos arise, together with their attendant opportunities for laughter. The comedic process is one of constant adaptation and renewal.

2
Aspects of the Comedic Process

> Nature alone knows no comedy.
>
> Oliver Onions, *A Penny for the Harp*

Alchemists believed that theirs was not just a material science. It was a spiritual one as well: indeed the concept of the purely material was alien to them. Physically their grand experiment was 'to transmute metals by chemical processes, to separate the impure and pure, in order, through continuous transmutations, finally to arrive at the residual precious essence'.[1] But in doing this they hoped to discover the secret of life itself, through a remedial process of transmutation that had its parallels in the teachings of spiritual adepts and the doctrines of Christian mystical theology. Alchemy, in other words, is the transmutation of matter into its teleological fulfilment, a work of redemption and renewal.

Since alchemy presupposed a fusion of physical with spiritual life, its practitioners treated as actual fact what to a later age was metaphor. Bearing this in mind, one can distinguish seven stages in the alchemical process. First the *prima materia*, the matter of the experiment, has to be broken down into its constituent elements and then reduced to formlessness, a state of chaos. Next, the opposing elements of body and spirit are conjoined to secure a balance of higher and lower orders of metal, symbolised in the first marriage of Sol and Luna, gold and silver. That union is then dissolved so that the superiority of the higher element can be asserted – to be reconstituted through a participation of all the original elements in a second marriage (which I have designated an infernal one, since here the inferiority of earthy elements in the previous conjunction is now reversed). This union raises the baser metals to the level of the finer ones; its offspring is the philosopher's stone, the transmuting agent of the final sought-for state of gold. As Morine Krissdóttir defines the process, 'The alchemical opus was a purification of the world of matter so that its golden nature should be revealed.'[2] Esoteric doctrines are not without their exoteric application. Just as alchemy provided a metaphor for spiritual initiation, so one can employ its terminology to interpret the various constituents of comedy. Parody, for example, distinguishes the elements of the primary monolithic literary material through an analysis that forms a requisite prelude to the alchemical comedic process; farce, on the other hand, obliterates those distinctions and reduces its material to absurdity and chaos. And whereas irony conjoins opposing elements – the matter signified and the manner of its signification – in a marriage where intellect is implicitly the dominant partner, satire upends this balance by openly assuming its superiority; burlesque, however, re-unites this purely mental species of awareness with grosser, more instinctual ingredients. The function of wit is to point out the simultaneous operation of such dualities: it resembles the philosopher's stone which transmutes the base monolithic knowledge of human experience into living gold. And if, put in such terms, the comedic process appears to be more cerebral than it really is, in the pages of prose fiction its complexity and tangible procedures become immediately apparent. Comedy is something that happens to people; it is not simply an alteration in awareness. It is *'functional in society*, whether it purports to be or not'.[3]

Parody: the verdict of Lady Locke

When Daisy Ashford's *The Young Visiters* was published in 1919 it ran through thirteen impressions in three months, so that it became fashionable to declare it was a hoax. But it was not. Other writings by the nine-year-old author were issued in the following year, with a confirmatory Preface by Ashford herself, now thirty years older. But *The Young Visiters* is her masterpiece. The tale of Mr Salteena, that 'elderly man of 42' who knew sadly that he was 'not quite a gentleman', is the product not only of sharp-eyed and little-pitcher-eared observation, but also of a keen appetite for society novels. Daisy Ashford unintentionally spells out what their adult readers preferred not to acknowledge; and her very innocence achieves as much as any sophisticated satirist could do. As Mr Salteena and the Earl of Clincham are about to join the royal 'levie',

The earl twiddled his mustache and slapped his leg with his white glove as calmly as could be. Mr Salteena purspired rarther hard and gave a hitch to his garters to make sure. (Chapter vi)

Elsewhere a riverside love scene out of any popular novelette has a decidedly realistic conclusion.

Ethel felt better after a few drops of champagne and began to tidy her hair while Bernard packed the remains of the food. Then arm in arm they tottered to the boat. (Chapter ix)

But the marriage of the Earl is a more prosaic business. Lady Helena Herring 'had very nice feet and plenty of money [...] and she mated well with the earl'. It is exactly what one wants to know. Even had *The Young Visiters* not been genuine, it would have held a worthy place in a well-established literary tradition – that of fiction commenting upon itself. The absurdities of romantic novels, with their emotional clichés and suffocating propriety, their sentimentality and materialistic values, have attracted satirical attention ever since the time of Fielding's *Shamela* (1741).

Reciprocation between the audience for a joke and the maker of it is a vital part of the comedic process. Parody, its basic activity, is essentially intimate and analytic, and only works when its subject matter is familiar: it involves mimicry and even an element of derision. But it also involves a separation of the parodist from the object parodied, and thus asserts that object's independent status, its effectiveness and power. For parody, if an aggressive process, is also a positive one and attacks the monolith of verbal and stylistic stereotypes by affirming their pretensions; at the same time, through imitation (a challenge of power) and by exaggeration (a disowning of serious intent) it exposes those pretensions as absurd. The monolith is shown not to be what it assumes itself to be – the focus of reality – and as a result becomes ridiculous. The distorting mirror of parody ensures that we cannot be certain that others see us as we see ourselves: it represents the initial stage of the comedic process since it takes the monolith apart and exposes its constituents. The parodic viewpoint and its methodology are synonymous.

But parody is not comedic in itself, an instance of this limitation being provided by one of the most celebrated novels of the 1890s. An anonymous self-styled 'skit' on Oscar Wilde, Robert Hichens's *The Green Carnation* (1894) was the literary talk of the town only a short while before its subject's downfall. While the book is a pastiche of Wilde's epigrammatic mode of discourse and his more florid excursions into prose and verse, it also embodies a critique of his effect upon his admirers. A virtuous widow, Lady Locke, declines a half-hearted offer of marriage from Lord Reginald Hastings (Alfred Douglas) on the grounds that he is not a proper man but a mere echo of his friend Esmé Amarinth, a figure who both physically and in all he says and does resembles Wilde.

The book is wafted upon impudence and can still amuse. Not only are Wilde's sayings paraphrased and imitated, but he himself is mentioned several times, as though to provide an authorial alibi; indeed Amarinth disparages Wilde's work, remarking of 'The Decay of Lying', 'That always sends me to sleep. It is like himself, all artfulness and no art.' Ironically, Hichens's imitations of Wilde's colourful periods grow somewhat wearisome (as though he himself were unsure as to how far he disapproved of them); on the other hand, the slick patter of two society ladies is quite as entertaining as that found in the dialogic banter of such contemporary works as Anthony Hope's *The Dolly Dialogues* (1894) or E.F. Benson's *Dodo: a Detail of the Day* (1893), whose success Hichens was later to admit that he was trying to emulate. Elsewhere the book anticipates the world of Ronald Firbank.

"This Bovril is very comforting, Betty; as reviving as – an epigram."
"Yes, my cook understands it. That must be so sweet for the Bovril – to be understood!" (Chapter ii)

The Green Carnation, however, is more than a parody and semi-critique of Wilde and his attendant æsthetes: it also amuses itself with side-swipes at such contemporarily popular and prosaic writers as Walter Besant, Edna Lyall and Mrs Humphrey Ward, and may be read as a historical guide to the literary gossip of the mid-1890s; not even the highbrow Georges, Meredith and Moore, escape the author's mischievous asides. As to the book's principal inspirer, the fact that it had been ascribed to Wilde himself must have proved disconcerting, and he greeted it with public scorn ('middle-class and mediocre') but with private admiration ('Robert Hichens I did not think capable of anything so clever').[4] Indeed Hichens did him justice, and, as Hesketh Pearson observed, he brought out the resemblance between Wilde and that other great nineteenth-century humorist, Sydney Smith.[5] If not a celebration of its subject, neither was the book an attack upon him, and its withdrawal at the time of Wilde's disgrace was at the author's own suggestion.

None the less *The Green Carnation* founders on a discrepancy between what it shows and what it tells. Hichens was a member of the Benson–Douglas circle and himself personally liked and admired Oscar Wilde; elsewhere he portrays the impact of the latter's physical presence, 'the sound of his luscious voice, his ample and suave appearance, his elaborate, condescending manner when before the public, his thick hair parted in the middle, his large shoulders and softly gesturing hands'.[6] But the affirmation of Wilde's influence and philosophy is half-hearted; the presence of Lady Locke voices what appear to be authorial misgivings, most especially when she overhears Lord Reggie promising to give a green carnation to her small son. The endorsement of Wilde's attack on the monolith of social respectability and idolising of the 'natural' is here compromised by an attack on the cult of Wilde for becoming itself another monolith. In this novel there is no comedic transmutation: a discrepancy is registered but not transcended. But if Wilde may have felt himself betrayed, he was to be avenged. The way of the parodist is hard, as the author of *Cold Comfort Farm* was to discover half a century later. Of all the many novels Hichens wrote, *The Green Carnation* is the only one for which he is remembered.

Farce: the lawlessness of Alfred Polly

The mockery that parody induces can turn quite naturally into farce: the perception of the inherent absurdity in one particular monolith here becomes a concentration upon absurdity itself. The monolith is dissolved in an atmosphere that eschews all pretensions to significance: purpose is awash in a sea of fantasy. A resurgence of buried energies releases the inner world of the farceur in a play of incongruities and an unapologetic flouting of conventions. Farce subverts all aspirations towards solemnity, its only purpose being to excite laughter: it turns the solipsistic nature of the monolith inside-out, exhibiting as an object that which the monolith seeks to impose upon others as a subject. And where parody questions literary stereotypes, farce makes hay with social ones: the delighted realisation that there are limits to the ability of human beings to restrict each other's energies is a vitalising element in novelists as different as Charles Dickens, Evelyn Waugh and Iris Murdoch.

Farce also makes use of private fantasy for public ends. This is nicely if ambiguously illustrated in one of the most enduringly popular English comic novels, *The History of Mr Polly* (1910). In this story of an eccentric lower-middle-class shopkeeper's revolt against circumstance, H.G. Wells came close to writing just such a sentimental daydream as the book's numerous imitators were themselves to propagate; yet for all its whimsicality and farcical humour it has an acerbity that keeps it afloat on this sea of potential sentiment. Alfred Polly is the victim of a social system which, having ground him 'in the valley of the shadow of education', has left him at the age of almost 40 with the feeling that

> his life during that time had not been worth living, that it had been in apathetic and feebly hostile and critical company, ugly in detail and mean in scope, and that it had brought him at last to an outlook utterly hopeless and grey. (vii:2)

The horrors of Polly's wedding party are described with a zest that borders on hysteria, a hysteria that springs from an underlying sense of just how deadening a way of life it is which can result in such insensitive vulgarity. Uncle Penstemon, Mr Voules and the rest are portrayed with Dickensian exuberance, as is Mrs Larkin's bonnet, which

> was small and ill-balanced, black adorned with red roses, and first it got over her right eye [...] and then she pushed it over her left eye and looked ferocious for a space, and after that baptismal kissing of Mr Polly the delicate millinery took fright and climbed right up to the back part of her head and hung on there by a pin, and flapped piteously at all the larger waves of emotion that filled the gathering. (vi:4)

(This could itself be a parody of one aspect of Dickens's comic style.) But the true verdict on the Larkins can be read in the perpetually frowning, incompetently anxious drudge that Polly's wife becomes as soon as she sets up house. The vitality of the wedding-party is the vitality of maggots in a corpse.

Mr Polly himself is an unconscious prophet of the disordering which inevitably follows when it is realised that the monolith is not all there is. His breaking up and distortion of traditional language, while it provides a continuous comical linguistic undertow, also voices a temperament that can recognise an epiphany in his father's fury when attempting to move a small sofa up a narrow winding staircase, at a 'moment when self-control was altogether torn aside' he makes 'the shocked discovery of his father's perfect humanity'.

Humanity, as Wells portrays it, is incorrigibly fallible. Often this maddens the perfectionist in him, the novelist who makes Polly realise (fallaciously) that he can change the world (it is only his own world that he can change). But his neighbours' response to the loss of their property (through a fire which Polly has started for his own ends) reveals an acceptance of chance blessings that is at the root of the comedic vision.

> Not one of those excellent men but was already realising that a great door had opened, as it were, in the opaque fabric of destiny, that they were to get their money again that had seemed sunken for ever beyond any hope in the deeps of retail trade. Life was already in their imagination rising like a Phoenix from the flames. (viii:5)

The punning reference to the emblem of the great Insurance Company is a piece of genuine wit.

The History of Mr Polly voices a protest at the apparent unalterability of the life of bread-winning and of social pressures. It provides its hero with a fairy-tale ending, living contentedly with the fat landlady of the Potwell Inn, having in two farcical battles fought with and overcome the ogre 'Uncle Jim'; but he has reached that happy ending by outraging humane standards of behaviour. He has committed arson, deserted his wife, and in a final battle attempted to murder his antagonist. He is no hero, and almost justifies John Batchelor's criticism of him as 'fat, romantic, undersexed ... [with] the mind of a spoilt child, and the violent pleasures also'.[7] If the conclusion of his adventures is idyllic, it is so because without some such possibility of happiness the human game is lost before it is begun. The book ends on a note of resigned and muted nihilism.

> There's something that doesn't mind us [...] it isn't what we try to get that we get, it isn't the good we think we do is good. What makes us happy isn't our trying. [...] There's a sort of character people like, and stand up for, and a sort they won't. You got to work it out, and take the consequences. (x:3)

This bleak outlook provides *The History of Mr Polly* with its credentials as an unsentimental comic masterpiece, but by the same token deprives it of its right to be adjudged in the fullest sense a comedy. Its farcical character is insufficient for the demands the author makes upon it.

Irony: the benevolence of Lucilla Marjoribanks

Ironic discourse is the deliberate voicing of discrepancy between the apparent and the actual; an ironic event occurs when that discrepancy is actualised. Irony therefore attacks the self-perpetuating nature of monolithic feelings, for it is the enemy of every form of sentimental idealism, of easy assurances as to the *status quo* and of the creamy smugness which chooses to pretend that all is well. It is the wit's weapon against stupidity, and the mental attitude which distinguishes intellectuals from their fellows. Irony, indeed, tends to be the preserve of a privileged readership; the light, dry tone adopted, for example, in the extremely class-conscious novels of Anthony Powell assumes a way of life which flatters its readers even when they are not themselves a part of it.

In irony, therefore, respect is (apparently) paid to the status and nature of the monolith, which it takes at face value; the corrective insights of comedy are fused with them in a species of mock-marriage. Irony always appeals over the head of its subject to a like-minded audience: it pretends to say what it does not say, and is a delusive combination of opposites. Its outflanking manœuvering places the monolith in a scheme of values which can afford apparently to tolerate it and to subsume it within a greater intellectual reality. Irony is the experience of celebration in negative terms, its characteristic feature a half-suppressed reluctant smile.

In a predominantly ironic novel like Margaret Oliphant's *Miss Marjoribanks* (1866), for example, the smile, though steady, is composed: the humour is inherent in the design of the book rather than in verbal texture or display. The heroine's youthful self-assurance resembles that of Jane Austen's Emma Woodhouse and the heroine of Oliphant's last Chronicle of Carlingford, *Phoebe Junior* (1876). But the author's interest in religion and theology in this case allows for a profounder resonance than mere social comedy affords.

> "We must leave that to Providence," said Miss Marjoribanks, with a sense of paying a compliment to Providence in entrusting it with such a responsibility. "I have always been guided for the best hitherto," she continued, with an innocent and unintentional profanity [...] "and I don't doubt I shall be so to the end." (Chapter ii)

The story demonstrates with aplomb how right in this she is.
There is no relaxation of the book's controlling irony. Lucilla is resourceful, manipulative, convinced of her own benevolent

motivation and armoured in a clear-sighted view of her prospects and practicable opportunities: she is a born leader and organiser, who has her emotions well under control.

[She] felt no difficulty in discerning the leadings of Providence, and she could not but appreciate the readiness with which her desires were attended to, and the prompt clearing-up of her difficulties. There are people whose inclinations Providence does not seem to superintend with such painstaking watchfulness; but then, no doubt, that must be their own fault. (Chapter li)

That substitution of 'are' for 'were' in the second sentence, by separating the author's voice from that of Lucilla, only serves to press home still further the satire on comfortable religious self-assurance, through widening its application from a purely personal example to the human condition as a whole. Lucilla 'had been brought up in the old-fashioned orthodox way of having a great respect for religion, and as little to do with it as possible, which was a state of mind largely prevalent in Carlingford'. (Chapter xvii)

Miss Marjoribanks is a witty novel in its interplay of irony with satire, and in its unsentimental portrayal of such basically self-centred and morally compromised people as the resentful Barbara Lake and the hapless social climber Harry Cavendish. It also, in the person of the town's mimic, Mrs Woodburn, exposes the limitations of an exclusively satirical perspective, even while the narrative itself is unsparing in its repetition of such self-referential phrases of Lucilla's as those concerning her determination to be a comfort to dear Papa or to wear a plain white dress 'high'. Indeed, Mrs Woodburn's free and welcomed circulation of her various mimicries makes Carlingford society seem even more self-enclosed than it already is: hers is only a temporarily liberating humour. As much as Elizabeth Gaskell's *Cranford*, *Miss Marjoribanks* is a static novel, a portrait rather than a drama; but the world it displays is revealed in a far more chilling light. The very affability both of Lucilla's character and of her creator's presentation of it only serves to make this clarity the bleaker.

Even so, the novel terminates with a final ironic joke at the expense of this exactitude itself – the engulfing of irony and satire as Lucilla discovers that it is only her clumsy cousin Tom whom she has really loved throughout her ten-year reign in Carlingford. This celebratory note is sounded through a use of farce (Tom's familiar awkwardness as he races upstairs to throw himself at her feet) and in a play on intuition and coincidence in the circumstances of his arrival home. Lucilla's stuffy and self-seeking suitors are forgotten in what looks like a fairy-tale conclusion; yet, by a final irony, she never undergoes any moral upheaval or transformation in the process, but remains the self-confident and somewhat humourless Miss Marjoribanks still. But although the impression left by her story is the kind of energising delight we associate with irony when it is spiced with wit, its low-key presentation and disenchanted portrayal of human fallibility ensure that the process of final comedic transmutation is withheld.

Satire: the aspirations of George Robinson

Satire dissolves the ironical mock-marriage of opposites; the monolithic partner is divorced, brought into court and arraigned, and its pretensions analysed in the context of a scheme of values that are once more in the open. Satire may ridicule its object, but it possesses a controlling seriousness of purpose, is essentially moralistic and refuses to judge the monolith by the monolith's own standards. Together with celebration it is the most publicly-orientated and most obviously responsible manifestation of the comic spirit. Accordingly it is the aspect of comedy accessible to the widest spectrum of concerns.

The nature and scope of the subject satirised tends to determine the length of the novel satirising it. Purely intellectual ideas can be parodied and set in play within a small compass, as the satires of Thomas Love Peacock testify; while a specific subject (such as the popular press) can also be treated within a relatively restricted compass, as with Rose Macaulay's *Potterism* or Evelyn Waugh's semi-farcical extravaganza, *Scoop*. But in the expansive fiction of the Victorian age narrowly-focused satire was a rarity, which may be one reason for the unpopularity of Anthony Trollope's single venture in this vein, *The Struggles of Brown, Jones and Robinson*. Serialised in Thackeray's *Cornhill Magazine* in 1861–62, it was decried for its vulgarity and for belabouring an already too-familiar target – advertising. It was not printed in book form until eight years later. Yet it is to some extent a prophetic novel, and its effectiveness, its subject-matter and technique, are likely to be more appreciated by late twentieth-century readers than they were by contemporary ones.

It describes the rise and fall of a draper's shop in the City of London. Brown supplies the initial capital; his son-in-law Jones is the ingratiating shop-walker with his hands in the till; George Robinson, the narrator of the story, is the young aspirant to the hand of Brown's younger daughter Maryanne, and the firm's organising genius. He believes in the supreme importance of advertising, and thus in credit rather than in capital. 'Get credit and capital will follow.' Where social economics are concerned he is an outspoken realist.

There's the same game going on all the world over, and it's the natural game for mankind to play at. They who's up a bit is all for keeping down them who is down; and they who is down is so very soft through being down, that they've not spirit to force themselves up. [...] There is always going on a battle between aristocracy and democracy. Aristocracy likes to keep itself to itself; and democracy is just of the same opinion, only wishes to become aristocracy first. (Chapter i)

The account of the firm's advertising campaign, and its bamboozling of the public, are amusing, and underpinned by a shrewd understanding of the ethos of buying and selling, and of the various tricks of the trade. The satire is straightforward and to the point. But *Brown, Jones and Robinson* is a rather more subtle book than all this might suggest. The story is told by Robinson in the third person, at the suggestion of the editor of 'a first class magazine' – the *Cornhill*. We are reading an account of the book we are reading: Trollope here is anticipating, however remotely, Marcel Proust. But he also anticipates E. Nesbit: while accepting a ghost-writer's help, the exuberant Robinson keeps talking over him, in his own flowery advertiser's style, betraying his presence much as Oswald Bastable betrays his in *The Story of the Treasure Seekers*. Moreover, these switches of style and vocabulary enable the author to bring off some amusing exchanges between Robinson and the indomitably prosaic Poppins.

"My idea of a woman is incompatible with the hard work of the world. I would fain do that myself, so that she should ever be lovely."
"But she won't be lovely a bit the more. She'll grow old all the same, and take to drink very like. When she's got a red nose and a pimply face, and a sharp tongue, you'll be glad enough to see her at the wash-tub then." (Chapter xii)

George Robinson's on/off relationship with the shrewish Maryanne is conducted for the most part in the language of parodic farce; here they are quarrelling over her rival suitor, the butcher Brisket.

"Then go to him!' said Robinson, rising suddenly, and stretching out his arm against her. 'Go to him, and perform your – – sainted mother's wish! Go to the – – butcher! revel in his shambles, and grow fat and sleek in his slaughter-house! From this moment George Robinson will fight the world alone. Brisket indeed! If it be accounted manliness to have killed hecatombs of oxen, let him be called manly! [...] I'll fight him tomorrow – with cleavers, if he will!" (Chapter vii)

But the end for Maryanne is bleak. Having lost both her suitors through over-contrivance, she comes to the conclusion that

As for love, I don't believe in it. It's all very well for them as have nothing to do and nothing to think of, for young ladies who get up at ten in the morning, and ride about with young gentlemen, and spend half their time before their looking glasses [...] You can't afford it, George, nor yet can't I. What a man wants in a wife is someone to see to his cooking and his clothes, and what a woman wants is a man who can put a house over her head. (Chapter xxi)

No wonder that readers of *Framley Parsonage* and *Orley Farm* disliked *Brown, Jones and Robinson*.

For all its high spirits and cogent satire, this is one of Trollope's darker works. It may come from the same genial soil as *The Three Clerks*, but it looks ahead to the spreading panorama of *The Way We Live Now*; what more does Melmotte do than George Robinson plans to do on credit? What else is Lady Carbery but an advertiser? None the less, *Brown, Jones and Robinson* does have one genuinely comedic moment, when the satire is subsumed into celebratory acceptance in old Mr Brown's comment on his creditors' purchase for him of an annuity of £20 a week from the proceeds of the sale of the firm's effects.

"I ain't long for this world, George," he said, when he was told; "and they ought to get it cheap. Put 'em up to that, George; do now." (Chapter xxiii)

It is a moment of triumphant humorous humanity. Dickens himself could not have bettered it. But it remains a rare flash of sunlight in a story that only emphasises the fact that where the comedic process is concerned, satirical observation by itself is not enough.

Burlesque: the appreciation of Emmeline Lucas

The objects of satire are innumerable, and they include all forms of social behaviour, commercial practice, personal pretension, religious hypocrisy – and every manifestation of the power-game. Where satire is concerned, the reader, through his involvement in the matter under scrutiny, is both the judge and the potential victim of the process. As much as irony, satire appeals to a co-operative informed readership, but in this case both author and reader are set over against the subject – rather than the former compromising the latter, as is the case with irony's version of the comedic process.

Such an entrapment, however, does emerge in burlesque, which is irony's complement. For here too we have a marriage of opposites, in which the exaggeration of the monolith as a monolith, and an enjoyment of its pretensions, go beyond parody in exhibiting not only its risible nature but also its threatening aspect. There is an element of the grotesque in this exhibition of what the monolithic essentially is; but burlesque goes beyond mere caricature. Just as derision is more wounding than ridicule, so burlesque contains an element of personal involvement. Through its means, comedy confronts the fundamental suffering involved in being human: what else is so-called gallows humour but the burlesque of that condition, the collusive relishing of what would otherwise be material to send one mad? Dickens at his most outrageous strikes this note, in people such as Daniel Quilp in *The Old Curiosity Shop* or (more intimately painful) the dolls' dressmaker in *Our Mutual Friend*. More frequently burlesque makes use of caricature, and caricature is an exaggeration and distortion of what is plainly visible into an incongruity so great as to effect a reconciliation between the object of burlesque and its participants. The monolithic monstrosity itself becomes a source of pleasure.

This is obviously the case with the fascination exerted by 'the sacred monster', the person one likes to read about but would hate to live with. There are many such in English fiction, from Fielding's Squire Western down to Nancy Mitford's fire-eating Uncle Matthew and to Inge Middleton and others in the work of Angus Wilson. E.F. Benson added to the list when he invented, initially in separation, both the affected, pretentious, domineering Emmeline Lucas ('Lucia') and the devious, manipulative and ineffectively malevolent Miss Mapp; and still more so when he enhanced the particular character of each by bringing them together in *Mapp and Lucia* (1935) and its two successors. By sheer accumulative power of comic reiteration these books, and their three predecessors concerning the pair in separation, not only create a comic world as self-sufficient as that of Surtees, but almost attain the illumination of comedic vision.

Benson's technique is anything but subtle. His characters are monolithically conceived, and are totally predictable in their behaviour. The books rely for their effectiveness on the accumulation of repeated jokes, the reader laughing at his own laughter at such shameless jerking of the strings. Above all, the books' use of burlesque exposes not only the collaborative gusto with which monstrous egotists are appreciated by the communities of which they form the baleful centre, but also the power of any community to turn even its rivalries and divisions to its own advantage: as V.S. Pritchett remarks, albeit a shade unfairly, 'Bitchery is the permanent incentive to Benson's invention and his feline mind.'[8] The repeated efforts of Miss Mapp and Mrs Lucas to score off each other keep the little town of Tilling alive and full of interest. When the two women are presumed lost at sea after being swept away by a flood on an upturned kitchen table, there is avid speculation among their friends as to why the two rivals had been together in the first place.

> A conversational flood [...] was unloosed; a torrent of conjectures, and reconstruction after reconstruction of what could have occurred to produce what they had all seen, was examined and rejected as containing some inherent impossibility. And then what did the gallant Lucia's final words mean, when she said, 'Just wait till we come back?' By now discussion had become absolutely untrammelled, the rivalry between the two, Miss Mapp's tricks and pointless meannesses, Lucia's scornful victories and, no less, her domineering ways were openly alluded to. (Chapter x)

The author is relentless in depicting the jungle-like ferocity that underlies his world of dinner-parties, golf and sketching, bridge and callisthenics. Boredom is the threat against which his human beings struggle even at the cost of their own humanity.

But if the characteristic comedy is static and more akin to burlesque than it is to satire, the action of the Lucia novels as they accumulate takes on something approximating to a comedic tone. For the effect of the struggle for domination in the social world of Tilling is an enhancement of Lucia's character far beyond the mean-spirited ruler of the village of Riseholme, whom one encounters at the beginning of the series in *Queen Lucia* (1920). In its successor, *Lucia in London*

(1923), her snobbery, pretentiousness and blatant social climbing are neutralised and become occasions for an altogether wittier kind of mockery. An appreciative band of Luciaphiles is formed, who see through her and yet appreciate and enjoy her: Benson is fictionalising the readership for the succeeding novels, which provide the invigorating spectacle of people who behave badly without doing anybody any harm; and, as Charles Lamb observes of Restoration comedy, one is 'glad for a season to take an airing beyond the diocese of the strict conscience'.[9] In making fun of the insufferable, Benson's sequence, in its own genteel, addictive way, partakes of that sense of conjoined light and darkness, ugliness and beauty, which issues in the restrained hysteria of gallows humour. But the laughter has something reprehensible about it, a kind of fallen humanity's *fou rire*, only to remain intelligible this side of paradise.

Wit: the good humour of Auberon Quin

The distillation of incongruities is experienced as wit. The connotations of this word have dwindled from its original signification of intelligence and intellectual capacity, and of an ability to know accurately, to its current association with the recognition of similarities and a deft connecting of ideas. Yet in the context of the comedic process those capacities remain related to each other. Wit unifies experience and distils it in mental gymnastics and verbal play, perceiving the absurdities of monolithic pretensions as something to be enjoyed as elements within a game.

For wit no less than irony invites a readerly participation. In this case the monolith is the denial of imagination through the urge to encase reality within the starched prescriptions of pre-emptive theory or inherited behaviour patterns. Wit is the gadfly of the literal-minded. Its willingness both to recognise and to generate absurdity amounts to a record of experience that never hardens into petrifaction. One of the wittiest novels in the language, Jane Austen's *Emma*, celebrates a turning of the tables upon the attempted exploitation of absurdity: the brilliant are innocently out-manoeuvred by the simple. This in itself is a case of comedic irony; but the comedy in this particular story amounts to wit through the ease with which resemblances and discrepancies change places and remain accepted: whereas in parody the literary artefact sees through itself, in wit the comic spirit does the same. And if jokes can get out of hand (as the further reaches of gallows humour testify), they can equally take the form of wit, celebrating their own perceptions in an interchange of humours. Some writers are so consistently, observantly, intelligently humorous as to be witty in their very tone and style; others are naturally epigrammatic, capable of raising a laugh a minute. Few novelists, however, treat of laughter in itself.

One such is G.K. Chesterton – if novelist he can be called. Books like *The Napoleon of Notting Hill* (1904) and *The Man who was Thursday* (1908) are fantasies, yet both are anchored to the material world and to a recognisably contemporary England. The former may be set in the future, but it is the London of businessmen, developers and cabdrivers which provides the setting for a story that questions the nature and place of laughter, and argues the essentially ludic nature of human ceremonial and institutions. The King (elected by now and chosen at random) is Auberon Quin, an incorrigible, not to say a monolithic, joker. To amuse himself he transforms the several London boroughs into virtual city states, with their own heraldry and civic guards. Initially the joke is at the expense of the stuffily conventional powers of big business and bureaucratic management. Forced to wear magnificent uniforms while attending upon His Majesty, the borough officials are ill at ease enough to look ridiculous. The King, however, is resolute in playing the game of government his way. In answer to their protests,

> "The situation is not bad," he said; "the haughty burgher defying the King in his own Palace. The burgher's head should be thrown back and the right arm extended; the left may be lifted towards Heaven, but that I leave to your private religious sentiment. I have sunk back in this chair, stricken with baffled fury. Now again, please." (II:ii)

But the King's frivolity recoils upon him in the person of a literal-minded fanatic with no sense of humour. This idealistic young poet takes the game with total seriousness, and war breaks out between Notting Hill and the neighbouring boroughs. But by the tale's conclusion the two extremes have come to realise that they are

> but the two lobes of the brain of a ploughman. Laughter and love are everywhere. The cathedrals, built in the ages that loved God, are full of blasphemous grotesques. (V:iii)

The underlying message refutes all monolithic feeling and behaviour. 'Every man is dangerous [...] who cares only for one thing.' (I:ii)

Chesterton, no less than his contemporary H.G. Wells, is a didactic writer, but in this book he is didactic at his own expense. Auberon Quin tells a story which he defines as the test of humour.

In a little square garden of yellow roses, beside the sea [...] there was a Nonconformist minister who had never been to Wimbledon. His family did not understand his sorrow or the strange look in his eyes. But one day they repented their neglect, for they heard that a body had been found on the shore, battered, but wearing patent leather boots. As it happened, it turned out not to be the minister at all. But in the dead man's pocket there was a return ticket to Maidstone. (I:iii)

This may or may not amuse; the real joke is that the author himself allows for its being justifiably annoying. What he does endorse, however, is a romanticism based on sound linguistic deductions.

I trust that to very few of you, at least, I need dwell on the sublime origins of these legends. The very names of your boroughs bear witness to them. So long as Hammersmith is called Hammersmith, its people will live in the shadow of that primal hero, the Blacksmith, who led the democracy of the Broadway into battle till he drove the chivalry of Kensington before him and overthrew them at that place which in honour of the best blood of the defeated aristocracy is still called Kensington Gore. (II:i)

Here is a genuine case of verbal play. Wit takes language seriously, acknowledging its capacity to generate meaning and not merely to convey it (as in the monolithic attitude to language, which insists on a one-to-one correspondence and confuses the signified with the sign). Puns, paradoxes, conceits – these extend into a medium of communication that includes parody, farce, satire, even burlesque, in its delighted contemplation of the world. But wit only operates at the contemplative level. Powerless in itself to effect comedic transmutation, it yet remains the seed in which the flowering of comedy germinates. Without the mediation of wit, true celebration is impossible.

Celebration: the self-respect of Charles Pooter

The outcome of the comedic process is the acceptance of diversity, complexity, the incongruous, in a refusal of finality. For when perceived statically, discrepancy is negative; but celebratory comedy is mobile, best figured in terms of a dance. The final term of comedy is festive.

In its light-hearted way *Three Men in a Boat* exemplifies the truth of this: it celebrates frivolity and a world in which the refractoriness of inanimate objects is an integral part of being alive and in which monolithic solemnity is apt to tread on a banana skin. Uncle Podger hanging up a picture, the narrator making himself ill by reading a medical dictionary – human self-confidence and human suggestibility are alike targets of a cheerful mockery that remains essentially affirmative. But celebratory comedy is more comprehensive than this: if Jerome's is a lyrical and sentimental humour, it does not attain to that degree of laughter and pathos that one finds in a no less popular book serialised within a year of *Three Men in a Boat* – *The Diary of a Nobody* (1892) by George and Weedon Grossmith.

On the face of it this is a piece of satire. It appeared initially in *Punch*, in the wake of such popular serials as F.C. Burnand's *Happy Thoughts* (1868), the supposed journal of an ineffective upper-class youth whose book called 'Typical Developments' never gets beyond the opening page. Earlier instances of the genre had been astringent in tone, such as James Beresford's *The Miseries of Human Life or the Groans of Samuel Sensitive and Timothy Testy* (1806) or the better-known *Mrs Caudle's Curtain Lectures* (1846) of Douglas Jerrold, with its perennially popular image of the socially ambitious suburban wife.[10] The Grossmiths' Mr Pooter, however, is contented with his lot and thus differs from his predecessors. He also differs from fictional autobiographers and diarists who came after him, including those who record their lives in the anonymous *Augustus Carp Esq., by Himself* (1924),[11] *The Diary of a Provincial Lady* (1930) by E.M. Delafield, or *The Polderoy Papers* (1943) by C.E. Vulliamy. It is a genre that calls for readerly participation; at the same time it suggests the need for a degree of ironical self-distancing. In Delafield's case the writer of the diary provides that distancing herself; in that of Carp, his conceit is so atrocious that it is too obvious for irony. Closer to the Grossmiths' 'Nobody' is Vulliamy's humourless but by no means unintelligent Henry Polderoy, whose diary covering the years 1868 to 1886 is a delightfully convincing record of what a Victorian country gentleman might have pondered and observed.

The wit shows himself to be superior to other men through his ability to make quick and sharp distinctions. The humorist on the other hand, is just like everybody else, only more so. His art depends less on his power to surprise or impress his reader than on his ability to create an affective bond with him.

Mr Pooter's ancestors are the inhabitants of Thackeray's early fiction, and his diary celebrates the humdrum activities and aspirations of Suburban Man. His villa (The Laurels, Brickfield Terrace, Holloway) typifies the buildings going up in the developing sprawl of north London, and Pooter's pride in his dwelling place reflects, but does not ape, the pride taken in theirs by the upper middle class readers of *Punch* who laughed at him.

> Carrie and I can manage to pass our evenings together without friends. There is always something to be done: a tin-tack here, a Venetian blind to put straight, a fan to nail up, or part of a carpet to nail down – all of which I can do with my pipe in my mouth; while Carrie is not above putting a button on a shirt, mending a pillow-case, or practising the 'Sylvia Gavotte' on our new cottage piano (on the three years' system), manufactured by W. Bilkson (in small letters), from Collard and Collard (in very large letters). (Chapter i)

The fact that Mr Pooter can so dryly note this nice sociological distinction between manufacturer and retailer should alert one against any tendency to patronise him. (The gavotte, a prancing measure full of traps for clumsy fingers, is an especially happy choice.)

Pooter's own sense of humour, issuing in the most obvious of puns, gently parodies the flights of more knowledgeable sophisticates; his sense of his own dignity quietly comments on the more extreme absurdities of gentlemanly self-respect. The summaries that precede each chapter mimic (and to that extent rebuke) those of Pooter's self-styled superiors. Here for instance is the Countess of Cardigan in *My Recollections* (1909).

> Chapter VI. A Royal lover: The Count of Montemolin proposes for me: We become engaged: I visit the Archduchess Beatrix: The late Don Carlos as a Baby: The Count's weakness: I resolve to give up all ideas of a Spanish marriage: I am dogged by Carlist spies: I break off my engagement. The Count's after-career: His death: Fever or Poison?

And now for Mr Pooter.

> Chapter VIII. Daisy Mutlar sole topic of conversation. Lupin's new berth. Fireworks at the Cummings'. The 'Holloway Comedians'.

Sarah quarrels with the charwoman. Lupin's uncalled-for interference. Am introduced to Daisy Mutlar. We decide to give a party in her honour.

(At the end of *My Recollections* the Countess of Cardigan boasted that she had done everything worth doing and known everyone worth knowing: hers could itself be a fictional diary such as Mary Dunn's *Lady Addle Remembers* (1936) with its triumphant claim that 'I have bicycled with Bismarck'.)

The comic methodology of *The Diary of a Nobody* is one of faithfully recording, with the minimum of grotesquerie or heightened juxtapositioning, the petty accidents that punctuate the plod of day to day.

Carrie's mother returned the Lord Mayor's invitation, which was sent to her to look at, with apologies for having upset a glass of port over it. I was too angry to say anything. (Chapter iv)

Anger, indeed, is not one of Pooter's strong points, even when he tries to master it. 'I left the room with silent dignity, but caught my foot in the mat.'

In Pooter's case, Nobody is Everybody. And in the person of Pooter everybody is blessed. All the misadventures which the Diary records end happily; but well before they do, the verdict on Pooter has been pronounced by his employer, following the offer of employment to his wayward son.

Mr Perkupp sent for Lupin, who was with him nearly an hour. He returned, as I thought, crestfallen in appearance. I said: "Well, Lupin, how about Mr Perkupp?" Lupin commenced his song: "What's the matter with Perkupp? He's all right!" I felt instinctively my boy was engaged. I went to Mr Perkupp, but I could not speak. He said: "Well, Mr Pooter, what is it?" I must have looked a fool, for all I could say was: "Mr Perkupp, you are a good man." He looked at me for a moment, and said: "No, Mr Pooter, *you* are the good man, and we'll see if we cannot get your son to follow such an excellent example." I said: "Mr Perkupp, may I go home? I cannot work any more today." (Chapter xvii)

That 'for a moment' says it all: and Pooter's evident self-deception where Lupin is concerned adds as much to the comedy of the situation as it does to its poignance. But Perkupp is right: Pooter *is* a good man, to be laughed with rather than laughed at. *The Diary of a Nobody* is an enduring piece of comic writing because its subject is one we can respect. None the less, affection and respect are all that such material can encompass: there is not enough internal dialectic for the book to attain the transfiguring renewal of comedy. Celebratory it may be, comedic it is not.

Every attempt at the analysis of comedic methodology is essentially self-contradictory and matter for comedy in itself. Certainly these aspects of comedy are aspects of a process; they are not objective literary genres or prescriptive moulds for feeling. Even novels that are overtly comic, and intended exclusively to entertain, exhibit shifting aspects of comedy, so that while being predominantly (say) burlesque, they may contain elements of wit or satire. None the less it remains true that those works of fiction which can be designated 'comedies' have their origins in one or another separate aspect of the comedic process, so that the radical mode of *Mansfield Park*, for instance, is that of irony rather than that of satire or of wit. While it is on this assumption that the succeeding chapters focus on the novels that they do, it remains an assumption that can in every sense be questioned or contested. For the one thing that comedy itself is not is monolithic.

3
Parodic Comedy: the Separation of Elements

> What are the Queens of Sodom to do when their sons come from school?
>
> Logan Pearsall Smith, *Afterthoughts*

> "Shall you go to Cleethorpes this year?" was his next question.
> "I think not. I shall most likely pass the holidays at home."
> "And study electricity?"

It is not surprising that this unremarkable exchange should come from a novel by George Gissing.[1] So faithful a reflection of the humdrum activities of daily life typifies the work of this most pertinacious of late nineteenth-century naturalistic English writers. Indeed, Gissing might here seem to be parodying himself: a blinkered monolithic concentration on method and intention trips him up, as it can with Henry James.

> "It's only as a mother," she added, "that I want my chance."
> But the Duchess, at this, was again in the breach. "Take it, for mercy's sake then, my dear, over Harold, who's an example to Nanda herself in the way that, behind the piano there, he's keeping it up with Lady Fanny."
>
> Henry James, *The Awkward Age* (1899), VIII:xxix.

Dickens likewise is capable of self-parody; but in his case one is conscious more of insufficiently-controlled emotion than of stylistic mannerisms. He invariably gives himself away when his prose turns into blank verse. In the case of James and Gissing it is the excess of a stylistic virtue which can make one smile; but Dickens's more sentimental mannerisms make him sound a humbug. This he certainly was not; but such overwrought appeals to one's emotions suggest a false equation between the nature of his feelings and his readiness to express them, so that he writes like a man distracted – in both senses of that word. But if such passages are fair game for a prodding deconstructive finger, it remains one of the comedic elements in novel-writing that it is not only open to being parodied but can also institute that particular proceeding on its own account.

First impressions: Jane Austen

In the young Jane Austen's case, it was her gift for parody which led her to become a serious writer. Her juvenilia are light-hearted pieces of nonsense with 'a ringing brilliancy like the song of a wren.'[2] They caricature a number of late eighteenth-century fictive models, most often the novel of sensibility; but within three longer pieces, 'Lesley Castle', 'Evelyn' and 'Love and Freindship', there lurks an implied critique of the readers of the kind of books they travesty. One senses a more judgemental authorial presence than in the earlier tales, laced with asperity though the latter are.

If Jane Austen's inspiration came from a perceptive response to literary models, she was keenly aware of how they can impinge upon human behaviour: people not only react to what they read, they also adopt patterns of feeling and behaviour according to its dictates, acccepting the current fashionable scenario and subduing themselves to literary monoliths. Charlotte Lennox had already made entertaining use of this theme in *The Female Quixote* (1752), and early Austenian comedy is likewise devoted to its exploration. Thus in *Northanger Abbey* (1818) the protagonist is set before us in a literary context. Innumerable popular novels provide a standard against which this one is being ironically measured. 'No one who had ever seen Catherine Morland in her infancy, would have supposed her born to be an heroine.' The evenness of tone allows for a dual reading – either that the deduction that she is in fact going to be one is correct; or that the suggestion that she is not is a plain statement of the case. The continuation, however, leads irresistibly towards the first of these conclusions.

Her situation in life, the character of her father and mother, her own person and disposition, were all equally against her. Her father was a clergyman, without being neglected, or poor, and a very respectable man, though his name was Richard – and he had never been handsome. He had a considerable independence, besides two good livings – and he was not in the least addicted to locking up his daughters. (I:i)

And so on: it could be a portrait of the author's own father. The implication is that in the forthcoming narrative a heroine is indeed what Catherine will turn out to be; but the ensuing comedy arises not only from the disparity between model and actuality (which the ironic tone alerts one to expect) but also from the double irony that at Northanger Abbey itself Catherine's attempt to act out the rôle of heroine of a Gothic romance is undermined by the dismantling of her assumptions – though to be subsequently vindicated by the demonstration that at another level of experience she has been right all along. General Tilney may not have murdered his wife, but he remains a monster of paternal arrogance and egotism. *Northanger Abbey* is a satire not on the Gothic novels themselves but on their readers. Isabella's and Catherine's conversation concerning the novels of the day ('Are they all horrid, are you sure they are all horrid?') is a simple piece of ridicule such as the young Fanny Burney, or indeed the author of 'Love and Freindship', might have devised. A more characteristically Austenian touch occurs when Catherine wonders at the number of servants employed at the Abbey.

> How inexpressibly different in these domestic arrangements from such as she had read about – from abbeys and castles, in which, though certainly larger than Northanger, all the dirty work of the house was to be done by two pairs of female hands at the utmost. How they could get through it all, had often amazed Mrs Allen; and when Catherine saw what was necessary here, she began to be amazed herself. (II:viii)

The joke is both at the expense of the impassive Mrs Allen's inability to read romantic novels save in a literal-minded way, and at that of the reader who has smiled at her for doing so. *Northanger Abbey* is concerned not only with other novels and their readership, but also with that connection between imagination and experience which is at the root of the comic novelist's artistry and outlook.

In *Sense and Sensibility* (1811) the critique of romanticism and its literary expression is less smoothly incorporated into the fictive structure. With *Mansfield Park*, this is the most overtly 'moral' of the novels. A number of the characters – the Palmers, Nancy Steele, John and Fanny Dashwood – are eighteenth-century humorous types; they amuse us less in themselves than in their dramatic rôles. But there are others – notably Mrs Jennings – who undergo a modification as the reader's stance is disengaged from that of the two heroines, Elinor and Marianne, in the process of the latter's betrayal by John Willoughby. The Dashwood family circle to which he endears himself is one to which we have been privy from the start, and with which we necessarily collude (rather as one colludes with the Schlegel sisters' view of Leonard Bast in Forster's *Howards End*). It is this shared point of view which ensures the novel's emotional engagement with its readers. Thus we sympathise with the sisters in their subjection to the vulgar insensitivity of Sir John Middleton's domestic circle; but as Mrs Jennings's genuinely warm heart becomes apparent during Marianne's illness, our attitude to her changes. For the most part, however, the comedy in *Sense and Sensibility* is that of situational reversal and mistaken judgements, or of the portrayal of absurdity as treated in characters and types. We are presented with comic spectacle rather than with comedic process.

In *Pride and Prejudice* (1813), spectacle and process, reversal and absurdity combine. Its roots are in the author's juvenilia, the various themes aired in them being here assembled and related to each other – husband-hunting, affectation, snobbery and pomposity, the clash between romantic ideals and common sense and, in the person of Mr Bennet, the temptation of a clever author to indulge and relish a clear-sighted perception of other people's folly. Whereas her father asks, 'For what do we live, but to make sport for our neighbours; and laugh at them in our turn?' (III:xvi), Elizabeth can assure Darcy: 'I hope I never ridicule what is wise or good'. (I:xi) The difference between father and daughter is one of charity.

Pride and Prejudice is the most accessible of Jane Austen's novels, in part through the presence of two characters, Lady Catherine de Bourgh and Mr Collins, who are as funny in what they say as in what they do. They had their birth in the world of her juvenilia, but have matured into real characters who can have an impact upon people whom she would have us take seriously. Mr Collins is absurd to the point of caricature; by marrying Charlotte Lucas, however, he takes on a serious dramatic function. The author's literary strategy in dealing with the tax on one's belief is very deft. On Elizabeth's first visit to the wedded pair, when

Mr Collins said anything of which his wife might reasonably be ashamed, which certainly was not unseldom, she involuntarily turned her eye upon Charlotte. Once or twice she could discern a faint blush; but in general Charlotte wisely did not hear [...] To work in his garden was one of his most respectable pleasures; and Elizabeth admired the command of countenance with which Charlotte talked of the healthfulness of the exercise, and owned she encouraged it as much as possible. (II:v)

That 'owned' is very telling: had 'said' been used we should have remained uncertain as to the friends' continuing intimacy.

For all the dry sparkle of its style, its gaiety and charm, at the root of *Pride and Prejudice* there is a situation of acknowledged pain. Mr Bennet's resignation to his lot, and his self-punishing, self-indulgent amused detachment are implacably anatomised.

Elizabeth [...] had never been blind to the impropriety of her father's behaviour as a husband. She had always seen it with pain; but respecting his abilities, and grateful for his affectionate treatment of herself, she endeavoured to forget what she could not overlook, and to banish from her thoughts that continual breach of conjugal obligation and decorum which, in exposing his wife to the contempt of her own children, was so highly reprehensible. (II:xix)

None the less, the cruelty of his predicament is brought home through the unending imbecility of Mrs Bennet's chatter; its impact is felt uncomfortably in Darcy's apologia to Elizabeth following her rejection of his offer of marriage.

The situation of your mother's family, though objectionable, was nothing in comparison of that total want of propriety so frequently, so almost uniformly betrayed by herself, by your three younger sisters, and occasionally even by your father. – Pardon me. – It pains me to offend you. But amidst your concern for the defects of your nearest relations, and your displeasure at this representation of them, let it give you consolation to consider that, to have conducted yourselves so as to avoid any share of the like censure, is praise no less generally bestowed on you and your eldest sister, than it is honourable to the sense and disposition of both. (II:xii)

The irony that the behaviour of Darcy's own friends and relations is in its way as indelicate as that of Mrs Bennet is left to the reader to

Parodic Comedy: the Separation of Elements 47

observe, who may also detect in Darcy's compliment an echo of Elizabeth's previous suitor.

> And now nothing remains for me but to assure you in the most animated language of the violence of my affection. To fortune I am perfectly indifferent, and shall make no demand of that nature on your father, since I am well aware that it could not be complied with; and that one thousand pounds in the 4 per cents which will not be yours till after your mother's decease, is all that you may ever be entitled to. On that head, therefore, I shall be uniformly silent; and you may assure yourself that no ungenerous reproach shall ever pass my lips when we are married. (I:xix)

But unlike that of Mr Collins, Darcy's proposal is pivotal. It occurs exactly half way through the novel: Elizabeth's ability to convict herself of prejudice marks the turning-point. Her cry of *mea culpa* is the overthrow of the monolith within herself.

> How despicably have I acted! [...] I, who have prided myself on my discernment! I, who have valued myself on my abilities! who have often disdained the generous candour of my sister, and gratified my vanity in useless or blameable distrust [...] vanity, not love, has been my folly [...] Till this moment, I never knew myself. (II:xiii)

The heroine of *Emma* is to come to a similar self-knowledge.

But in *Pride and Prejudice* Elizabeth's conversion is matched by that of Darcy, when he deliberately subdues his pride to secure the marriage of Lydia Bennet to George Wickham, for the sake of love associating himself with a man whom he despises. Whereas the marriage of Jane to Bingley is that between two fundamentally complaisant people who match each other, that between Elizabeth and Darcy is between two who complement each other; it resolves in a positive sense both the disharmony within the Bennet marriage, and the dissociation of aristocracy from trade, with its false equation between good birth and good manners. Jane, Elizabeth and Lydia each gets the husband she deserves – as does Charlotte, who marries Mr Collins 'solely from the pure and disinterested desire of an establishment'.

> I am not romantic you know. I never was. I ask only a comfortable home; and considering Mr Collins's character, connections, and situation in life, I am convinced that my chance of happiness with

him is as fair, as most people can boast on entering the marriage state. (I:xxii)

In marrying a fool she only does knowingly what Mr Bennet has done through want of judgement. Even so, her retort to Elizabeth's instinctive 'Engaged to Mr Collins! my dear Charlotte – impossible!' has a dignity that exhibits the comedic process in its most serious aspect. 'Do you think it incredible that Mr Collins should be able to procure any woman's good opinion, because he was not so happy as to succeed with you?' The rebuke foreshadows Elizabeth's later recognition of the vanity that lurks within her own high spirits.

The literary derivation and literary concerns of Jane Austen's previous novels, in which pre-emptive and conditioned responses are the fruit of fashionable emotional sensibility, nurtured on a diet of novel-reading, and have to be refined in the crucible of challenging and potentially tragic experience, are less immediately obvious in *Pride and Prejudice*. But here too comedy is a chastening process. First impressions have to be corrected by deeper self-knowledge; the question of literary influence inheres in the contrivances of character and plot rather than in the moral evaluation of the text. In subsequent developments of parodic comedy one finds a delight in parody for its own sake, and then a return to Austenian perceptions of it as a means towards moral and sociological evaluation.

Gentlemanly relish: Max Beerbohm

Thirty years after Jane Austen's death popular fiction had proliferated sufficiently for its various types to be parodied with more deliberation. Burgeoning middle-class prosperity had led to a systematic marketing of novels through the circulating libraries, which lent itself to exploitation by writers resourceful enough not only to gauge but also to activate the various currents of popular taste. Novels were becoming increasingly self-referential. Accordingly, when Thackeray contributed a series of parodic sketches to *Punch* in 1847 they were immediately recognisable and popular. Issued in book form nine years later these lively *Novels by Eminent Hands* included among their victims Edward Bulwer-Lytton, Benjamin Disraeli, and the rollicking Irish stories of Charles Lever – all of them easy targets. Their popularity was dwarfed, however, and their range expanded by *Rebecca and Rowena* (1850), in which Scott's Ivanhoe finds himself shackled to a prudish, jealous and managerial Rowena, the epitome of bourgeois respectability. Having had the good fortune to be presumed dead at the wars, he proceeds to lead a pseudonymous existence as the Knight of the Spectacles, finally to be reunited with the Jewess Rebecca, who has conveniently turned Christian. Thackeray is disrespectful towards the solemnities of historical romance while remaining respectful towards Scott himself.

There is plenty of bite in the humorous badinage. The Earl of Huntingdon has become a very different character from Robin Hood the forester.

> There was no more conscientious magistrate in all the county than his lordship: he was never known to miss church or quarter sessions; he was the strictest game-proprietor in all the Riding, and sent scores of poachers to Botany Bay. "A man who has a stake in the country, my good Sir Wilfred," Lord Huntingdon said with rather a patronising air (his lordship had grown immensely fat since the King had taken him into grace, and required a horse as strong as an elephant to mount him), "a man with a stake in the country ought to stay *in* the country. Property has its duties as well as its privileges, and a person of my rank is bound to live on the land from which he gets his living." (Chapter i)

That repetition of 'a stake in the country' is beautifully placed to gain the maximum comic effect: the speech would be less ponderous and complacent without it. Parody has developed into social satire.

By the end of the nineteenth century the parodist had an ever-widening choice of subject. The kind of synchronistic treatment of contemporary issues which marked the Victorian novel in its heyday was being replaced by shorter, more monolithic treatments of particular themes, each presented with its appropriate methodology, and offering an ever-open invitation to the parodist. However, for parody to make its points, a degree of understanding, even of affection, is desirable. In this respect Max Beerbohm, both in his writings and in his drawings, is the supreme master of the genre. None the less, the precise degree of geniality he evinces is open to dispute – and this despite the contemporary verdict that he exercised mockery without any malice – a comment more applicable to his portraits of dead authors than to those of the living. For the assertion may be tested visually as well as through Beerbohm's use of words. Like Dante Gabriel Rossetti and, later, Wyndham Lewis, he belonged to that small band who achieved equal celebrity as writers and as artists; and in each case the pictorial art illuminates the verbal one. But the heavily sensuous periods of Rossetti's verse and the sumptuous colouring of his paintings have nothing in common with the essentially parodic art of 'Max' (as Beerbohm the artist signed himself), whose intuitive grasp of revelatory line enables him with the lightest of touches to transform mere ridicule into pictorial satire.

As a literary satirist Beerbohm is more than Thackeray's equal, for he goes beyond him in using parody as a comedic process which comments on the nature of fiction as such. *A Christmas Garland* (1912) captures with unerring dexterity not only the mannerisms and distinctive style of major literary figures of the time, such as Conrad, James and Kipling, but also such lesser, though currently popular, writers as A.C. Benson, Maurice Hewlett and Edmund Gosse: it constitutes a portrait of an entire literary period. With a few exceptions, notably his piece on Kipling, Beerbohm's treatment of his contemporaries is good-humoured: its pervasive happy scepticism recognises that in the sight of the angels the most solemn creative undertakings are in the nature of a game. And with the good humour – indeed as a product of it – there is a certain sympathy for the victims which provides a scale by which to measure their achievements.

Beerbohm's own fictions are based on pastiche and parody. His earliest writings are exercises in the vein of Wilde's *A House of Pomegranates* (1891), but are more playful, with a vein of worldly cynicism. The conclusion to 'The Story of the Small Boy and the Barley Sugar' (1897, reprinted in *A Variety of Things*, 1928) has, indeed, a sardonic realism worthy of Hilaire Belloc's book of verses, *A Bad Child's Book of Beasts* (1896). But Beerbohm's masterpieces of comedic art, his quintessential literary achievements, are the stories collected under the title *Seven Men* (1919). To say this is to indicate that he was a critical rather than an imaginative artist, for most of these tales are parodic in intent and literary in reference. The two exceptions are 'James Pethel' and 'A.V. Laider', studies of a born gambler and of a compulsive fantasist respectively; it is possible, however, to read the latter as a parody of the artistic urge itself. Of the remainder, 'Hilary Maltby and Stephen Braxton' delicately mocks the chirping Pan-worship of contemporary supernaturalist writers, and also casts an amused glance at the high society world portrayed so meticulously in the tales of Henry James and so disrespectfully in those of Saki; while 'Felix Argallo and Walter Ledgett' recounts a piece of successful literary promotion and financial hedge-betting which remains applicable to the hyper-commercialisation of a later time: this story, written in 1927, was added to the reprint of *Seven Men* in 1950 (the seventh man being Beerbohm himself). The account of Argallo's writing is typical of the author at his most sedately mordant.

> Pity, profound and austerely tender pity, was the keynote of all his writings. He could not, as has often been pointed out, write of anything that did not sadden him. This would have been a serious limitation to his genius, but for the fact that so few things in this world did *not* sadden him.

The description of Argallo's prose style which follows suggests the post-Paterian æsthetic humanism of an A.C. Benson; but the author's comment is also a comment on his own (presumed) assumptions.

> But eloquence, with what it springs from, is out of date. It may come in again? Well, then Argallo will come in again, amid the plaudits of the young.

Such relativity informs the whole of *Seven Men*.

The most obviously comical tale in the collection is that of 'Savonarola' Brown, a definitive parody of costume-drama and of the kind of nonentity who writes it – a portrait of some pathos; but the masterpiece is 'Enoch Soames', which exemplifies Beerbohm's satirical procedures in their purest form. This tale of a Catholic diabolist who sells his soul in order that he may visit the British Museum Reading Room a century hence and discover what posterity will think of him, parodies and sets in interplay a number of contemporary clichés. There is the tale of preternatural terror; there is the tale of the genius whom the world forgot; there is the parody of Soames's inscrutable minor verse; and there is a satire on the question of literary fame and reputation. The latter involves the author himself, whose own attitude towards his subject and to the material of his story is analysed with playful clarity. By introducing himself into each of these stories Beerbohm would seem to assert their historical accuracy; but in 'Enoch Soames' a twist is given to this device when the unhappy poet finds (in 1997) a solitary reference to himself in the only account of his work to survive – the present one, which however is taken as being fictional by a literary historian of a later age. Thus the fictional Soames is doubly confirmed in an ambiguous reality. In his light-hearted way, Beerbohm here anticipates such complex literary contrivances as *A la Recherche du Temps Perdu* (1913–27) and Vladimir Nabokov's *Pale Fire* (1962).

'Enoch Soames' displays one of its author's most happy gifts – a command of tone. Its humour is satirical but never cruel, careless but not complacent. For Soames, so dim, portentous, self-absorbed, is allowed his dignity. His bargain with the sleek, vulgar personage who turns out to be the Devil arises not from wickedness but vanity, and as the author observes, 'No man who hasn't lost his vanity can be held to have altogether failed' – a remark which implicates its maker in the fable, and which lends added pathos to Soames's injunction as he is led away, '*try* to make them know that I did exist!' His plea is at once the occasion of the story and its outcome.

In 'Enoch Soames' parody transcends itself: elsewhere in *Seven Men* it is said that 'one can't really understand what one doesn't love, and one can't make good fun without real understanding'. The speaker here is the lightweight Hilary Maltby; and such humanity is central to genuine comedy, in which human pretensions are both mocked and endorsed in the name of a reality which surpasses them. It is because of this that the monolithic evil of diabolism is derisory; and perhaps the most telling moment in the account of Enoch Soames takes place when the stranger at the next table introduces himself as the Devil and Beerbohm bursts out laughing.

Compared with *Seven Men* the more widely read *Zuleika Dobson* (1911) appears simple and inconsequential. A light fantasy, very much of its time, about the visit to Oxford of a young woman so beautiful that every single undergraduate, bar one, drowns himself for love of her, it seems on a superficial reading to be mere stylish nonsense, a compendium of Edwardian wit and self-congratulation. But like all Beerbohm's work, the novel grows out of parody, in this case of the Victorian romantic novelist 'Ouida' and the sentimental dramas which the author, in his capacity of theatre critic for *The Saturday Review*, so often had to watch. In *Zuleika Dobson* he pays tribute to the enjoyable aspects of literary extravagance and exuberant tosh. It is a pæan of praise not only of the Oxford of his youth but also of the delights of the second-rate: not for nothing is Zuleika herself a conjuror, and an inferior one at that. Her beauty is literally skin-deep, the discrepancy between her appearance and her mind being at the root of the comic absurdity of the tale itself.

For *Zuleika Dobson*, again like the rest of Beerbohm's writings in this vein, contains a sting. The fantasy is ironically anchored to the world of every day. At one level this is evident (and familiar) in Beerbohm's reference to himself as a writer who has influenced Zuleika in her manner of speech, and in the play upon such technical literary terms as ellipsis, aposiopesis and meiosis; he also delves into the question of fictive veracity in a discussion of the present-day function of Clio, the Muse of history – a characteristically comic mythological metaphor. But these literary games are incorporated into the text of the novel itself, as in the confrontation between the Duke of Dorset and his landlady's lovelorn daughter, where their 'literary' dialogue soon degenerates into that of 'servant girl' novelettes as their passions rise: one parody comments on another.

A later generation may find *Zuleika Dobson* less totally delightful than did its contemporary readers. But the book retains its salubrious gaiety and charm, partly through an avoidance of whimsy, partly through its affectionate portrayal of the city that gave it birth. As a piece of essentially comic fine-writing, what could be better than the description of the clocks and bells of Oxford sounding noon?

> Some clock clove with silver the stillness of the morning. Ere came the second stroke, another and nearer clock was striking. And now there were others chiming in. The air was confused with the sweet babel of its many spires, some of them booming deep, measured sequences, some tinkling impatiently and outwitting others which had begun before them. And when this anthem of jealous antiphonies had dwindled quite away and fainted in one last solitary note of silver, there started somewhere another sequence; and this, almost at its last stroke, was interrupted by yet another, which went on to tell the hour of noon in its own way, quite slowly and significantly, as though none knew it. (Chapter iv)

A whole literary tradition is gracefully mocked and in the mockery exalted. As the author's biographer remarks, *Zuleika Dobson* is 'an outstanding example of his characteristic propensity to laugh at what he loved, and to love what he laughs at'.[3] Above all it is a book in which parody, while retaining much of its analytic function, permits itself to relax and enjoy itself in play.

This playfulness is characteristic of Max Beerbohm: all his writings (save for the most incisive and vigorous of them, his dramatic criticism) seem at first sight to amount to a game played with his readers at the author's expense, a delicate game of hide-and-seek with the *persona* he assumes to mask his own identity. The title of his first book of essays, published in 1896 when he was 24 years old, indicates what is to follow. *The Works of Max Beerbohm* – is this a misplaced boast (the essays are only seven in number), or is it a piece of effrontery at the expense of the volumes amassed by well-established authors? Or is it a graceful piece of modesty? Whatever else, it is an act of deliberate evasiveness, a refusal – or, better, a declining – to be monolithic. For who is Max Beerbohm? His characteristics and identity shift from essay to essay, genre to genre. When most confessional, he is most misleading: 'Max's first diversionary tactic was to make himself a funny man in a world that expected its artists to take themselves seriously.'[4] At the same time his tone assumes the existence of a readership that will respond to nuance and a commonly accepted *argot*: he is a writer who whispers over our shoulders as he directs attention to the people and behaviour that he sets before us. 'As others see us' – it is the last thing that most of us come to see for ourselves, and Beerbohm's own literary *persona* is an attempt to create an image which we may accept as being his, while at the same time, through innumerable self-deprecating twists and confidences, he dissolves the monolithic quality of the image itself, so that we are unable to laugh *at* him. But his strategy is as much polemical as self-defensive.

For what his literary parodies and pictorial caricatures have in common is an underlying belief in the reciprocal requirements of civility. Beerbohm's appeal to the 'us' element in his readers is a reminder of sociable relativity, of the mutual derivation of all members of any cultural group. To the extent that any one member gets exaggerated notions as to his or her monolithic singularity and importance, that member creates a self-caricature. In Beerbohm's art, good manners are the natural defence against such distortion: if we parody each other we are no less liable to parody ourselves. The cult of 'Max' is itself a witness to that liability; but at their best, his writings provide a 'comic mode for rescuing civility from the disruptive demands of the imperialistic personality'.[5] That is a verdict which both Max Beerbohm and Jane Austen would have been pleased to hear pronounced upon their work. For both of them, morality and civility were intimately connected.

Saving graces: the Brontës and *Cold Comfort Farm*

In keeping with its wayward nature, English fiction boasts a procession of eccentric and misleading titles. If there is a 'no-nonsense' quality about eighteenth century ones (names, places, subjects are the norm), the Victorians were altogether more inventive. They could be rhetorically uncertain (*What Will He Do With It?*; *Can You Forgive Her?*;

Did He Deserve It?), or enigmatically tendentious (*Put Yourself In His Place*; *The Woman Who Did*). Often a title was a hook baited for a certain kind of reader: *Wee Wifie, Red As A Rose Is She, Unkist, Unkind!*, or *Snares*. Later titles were often enigmatic – *Some Do Not, Go She Must!, As Far As Jane's Grandmother's, Novel On Yellow Paper* and *My Wife's The Least Of It*; while apparently not to be outdone, the later twentieth century can offer *Ever Singing Die Oh! Die, The Sacred and Profane Love Machine, Sexing the Cherry* and *Paddy Clarke Ha Ha Ha*.[6]

With this record of allusiveness, the title of Rachel Ferguson's *The Brontës Went to Woolworths* (1931) sounds parodic; and the author was indeed a parodist, contributing to *Punch* and in this novel emphasising both the delights and dangers of the parodic art. A widowed mother and her three daughters invent an on-going parodic saga built up of private jokes and knowing social references about people whom they have seen but never met; it is a not uncommon sport in close-knit domestic circles. The book steers an uneasy path across a morass of self-indulgent whimsy into which it never quite subsides, its peculiar interest lying in an awareness and avoidance of just such a possibility. *The Brontës Went to Woolworths* is an uncommon case of self-indulgence exercising a critical self-scrutiny.

For the family actually come to know the principal subject of their fantasies – a High Court Judge and his wife. Two realities are brought up disconcertingly against each other, albeit to reconciliatory effect. The dangers attendant on such a potentially contradictory collision are reflected in the experience of the youngest daughter, still virtually a child, to whom either aspect of reality is liable to be discredited by the other, to stultifying effect. Moreover, the family are psychic. By means of a table-tapping session in the presence of a resentful governess, Charlotte and Emily Brontë materialise: the effect is as eerie as it is comical. The resolution fuses psychic and physical reality in the family's decision to control the fantasy in the name of love and healing. The comedy may be at the expense of the monolithic single vision that only perceives the surface of things; but it is not so unqualified as to be sentimental. The cruel pain endured by the unlucky unimaginative governess in this teasing household of in-jokes and self-conscious charm is punishingly evident. Ferguson is a true comedic artist because she never allows a joke to determine its context, nor does she permit the whimsy to get out of hand. In a singular refinement of analysis she directs parody towards the parodic process itself, and, in doing so, reveals an understanding of its essentially preparatory function. As much as Jane Austen and Max

Beerbohm she sees parody as an aspect of morality, and its overindulgence as restricting its remedial possibilities.

A similar perception informs that most popular and influential of twentieth-century parodic novels, Stella Gibbons's *Cold Comfort Farm* (1932). In this lively fable the author by laughing at a genre created a mythology. Following Hardy's creation of a literary 'Wessex', a fashion of novels about rural life persisted through the first three decades of the twentieth century; but now it was so tellingly ridiculed that, in popular esteem at any rate, it could no longer command imaginative assent. Gibbons's portrayal of the Starkadder family – sulky, backward, sexually smouldering and presided over by Great Aunt Ada Doom who notoriously once saw 'something nasty in the wooodshed' – came to be considered as itself the norm of rural fiction and to have blasted forever the reputations of the tradition's more popular practitioners.

In fact, however, the parodic element in *Cold Comfort Farm* is by no means all there is to it. The descriptive passages, with their Baedeker star ratings to indicate fine writing, occur mainly in the first half of the book, which sets up a model for the rationalistic young protagonist Flora Poste to dismantle and constitute anew. If the model is what most people remember, what gives the book its force is the corrective consequence of the parody. *Cold Comfort Farm* attacks the self-conscious, essentially adolescent attitudinising which any adherence to a pre-emptive literary model indicates. Stella Gibbons is following in the footsteps of the young Jane Austen: by taking such stereotypes at their own valuation and then introducing them into the world of the rationalistic novel, she exposes their absurdity. Her heroine, however, is not without absurdity herself: so bustling, crisp, methodical a dedication is as extreme in its way as is the brooding introversion of the Starkadders. But if Flora is a do-gooder, she yet succeeds in doing good. Hers is a rational wish for happiness, her Bible *The Higher Common Sense*, a fictional book of apophthegms by 'the Abbé Fausse-Maigre' – itself a piece of fictive parody. The upshot of her endeavours is the humanising of the Starkadders, their conversion from creatures of fantasy and stereotype to products of a humane naturalism. *Cold Comfort Farm* moves from parody by way of farce and ironic satire to celebration. It ends with a succession of unlikely marriages, and on a note of light-hearted foolishness, having begun with the exposure of self-centred posturing and the merely silly. And what Stella Gibbons achieves in terms of self-referential parody, later writers were to put to use in the context of a more comprehensive consideration of culturally conditioned standards of behaviour.

Matter for laughter: Angus Wilson

As a literary concern, parody seems trivial in the face of the despairing recognition of a universal absurdity, a recognition which the two World Wars rendered well nigh universal. If in such a climate parody itself can be regarded as the only appropriate mode of literary expression (and is thus rendered self-defeating since it becomes in its turn a criterion for normality), it can also become an indulgence exposing the self-defensiveness of its practitioners. This particular tension activates most, if not all, of the novels of Angus Wilson, probably the sharpest-eyed and most ambitious of mid-twentieth century English novelists. In his work parody becomes both a tool of responsible enquiry and a means of expressing the problems and difficulties of an over-developed personal social self-awareness.

Few writers have so exact and critically informed an ear. His novels and stories are remarkable for the precision with which they pounce on tell-tale turns of phrase and expose nuances of competitiveness and cruelty both in speech and in behaviour. The topicality of many of their references and the exactitude of their details should provide a field day for future annotators. Much of Wilson's work may be classed as satire bordering on burlesque. For all his gifts of mimicry, for staging a literary music-hall turn, his novels indicate that life itself is no laughing matter. Indeed, the most ambitious and impressive of them carries that phrase as its title. Ironically it is also the one of them to make the fullest use of parody.

This is not simply a matter of employing literary models or of directing our attention to the formative power of language. Wilson's concern is with language as the expression of pre-conditioned attitudes, and with literary form. Spanning the first 60 years of the twentieth century, *No Laughing Matter* (1967) describes the fortunes of six brothers and sisters whose parents are a couple of irresponsible, self-referential attitudinisers; but it does not employ the straightforward chronology or omniscient narrator found in most domestic family sequences since Galsworthy's *The Forsyte Saga*. Rather, Wilson eliminates the narrator altogether and mediates his story through the consciousness of his eight main characters, rather as Virginia Woolf handles her six principals in *The Waves*, though without cloaking them, as she does, in an overriding authorial tone of voice.

For *No Laughing Matter* is an essentially dramatic novel. Deploying as his narratorial method points-of-view rather than interior monologue of the stream-of-consciousness variety, Wilson avoids any danger of creating separate instances of solipsism. He punctuates his narrative with formal dramatisations, above all by 'the game' whereby the Matthews sons and daughters ape their parents and declare themselves to be interconnected performers in a drama that transcends them. They thus intensify, and to that extent become responsible for, the continuation of the very forces in their parents' world which have made them what they are. Wilson hereby achieves an impression of continuity between past and present: parody is used both to highlight its subject-matter and to dismantle it.

> Was the man or the woman able to be another [...] the most suited to defend that other's interest? Yes, for simulation, whatever its motive, demands identification. But was he or she sufficiently detached to be able to offer a defence intelligible to others as defending counsel should, without the confusions and blurs of subjective statement? Yes, for simulation and mimicry also demand observation: in them compassion is tinged by mockery or mockery by compassion, and identification is distanced by the demands of technique.

Here apparently is parody's moral justification; but this is a novel which questions the validity of its own literary strategies, and so

> could this simple mixture of opposites which mimicry requires, of affection with distaste, of respect with contempt, of love with hatred – be justly defined as a sort of reasoned apology?
>
> (Book I, 'The Game')

At the very start, the family's visit to the Wild West exhibition in West Kensington in 1912, and their several mental identifications with what they see, creates a communal consciousness by parodic means, enabling one both to empathise with their various self-projections and to perceive their limitations. The clichés of a fictional world illuminate and endorse the corresponding behaviour of the so-called real one. Personal and popular consciousness are fused in a manner reminiscent of James Joyce's *Ulysses*.

To the children as they grow up, parody becomes a method of distancing their parents and of coping with the domestic oppressions they endure. But each child's parody is also a parody of what he or she is to become: Sukey, the domesticated daughter, may mimic her conventional old grandmother, but a conventional old grandmother is what at the novel's close she is herself – although not without modifications as the result of time and a degree of learning from experience. And so likewise with the other five – the political journalist, the businesswoman, the actor, the novelist, the artistic connoisseur: the Matthews are a microcosm of society itself, and in parodying what has formed them, they expose the forces that govern the civilisation of their time. Funny though Wilson's comic scenes can be, their ultimate purport is indeed no laughing matter. When Quentin Matthews, the disenchanted soldier back from the front, apologises to his youngest brother for upsetting him, he is told:

> You showed that you too have a sense of humour like the rest of us. It's obligatory, you know, in this house. Only yours is of a fiercer brew than we're used to.
>
> (Book II, '1919')

That dialogue might have been between Angus Wilson and his early readers. His mastery of social satire is accompanied by a gift for creating frequently appalling comic characters and a power to register the finer shades of morally-compromised embarrassment. Here is the æsthete Marcus Matthews with his working-class temporary lover.

> "Oh, well," Ted said, "What's 'e matter to us? You're all right, you know. I mean larks apart. I don't know as I've met another bloke I've liked as much as you [...] I was lucky meeting you. *And you can cook.*"
>
> He offered the joke to Marcus perfunctorily, but then, perhaps remembering the number of pickups to whom he had said it when it had no meaning, he added, "No, I mean that. That fish you done for tea was as good as Lyons. Better." He belched to show his appreciation.
>
> (Book III, '1937')

Ted is displayed on the wings of his creator's gift for mimicry, and one laughs to hear him; but the laughter is uncomfortable, for we have also been given Marcus's terror of being sucked down 'into the vast, empty emotional gulf of Ted's shapeless life, a fluid mess of random thoughts, chance feelings and appetites, half formed words, glottal stops that took mould only as now from a desperate attempt to suit the mood of the person he was with'. That Wilson's comic characters are not mere caricatures is due to his ability to use parody for purposes of ethical discrimination and analysis. Because his people are the products of a particular society, he isolates and sifts them, highlighting those qualities which demonstrate most forcibly their capacities for good or evil – evil in particular, since it is precisely in such isolation that distortion becomes evident.

Few, if any late twentieth-century English novels have been so ambitious in their scope as *No Laughing Matter*, for the temper of the post-war world does not encourage broad generalisations or magniloquence of outlook. But Wilson's use of parody is an ironic way of forestalling the pre-emptive forces of traditional chronological exposition and its accompanying moral commentary. Moreover, both in Margaret Matthews's preoccupation with how, as a novelist, to combine sympathy with detachment, and in her brother Rupert's attempts to resolve the ambiguities of Malvolio's character in performance, one sees a quest for sincerity in a world which the corresponding extremes of social competitiveness and sentimentality have rendered both supercilious and wary. In the late twentieth century, parody has come to perform the function less of critical dissection than of reconciliation, its mood approximating to burlesque in its affirmative ferocity.

As both Fielding and Jane Austen had already demonstrated, parody strips away the disguises of literary, behavioural and even religious models: it subverts the epistemology of monolithic attitudes by reflecting them in terms of caricature and disrespectful imitation. It also becomes increasingly critical, not only of its original material but also of the effects of the parodic act upon the parodists themselves. Even when parody is largely celebratory (as it is with Beerbohm) it is also purposeful, its target the tyranny of the monolith, its aim to be liberating and remedial. Both the strength and the weakness of any literary artefact can be illuminated by a parody, for here the primary elements of the comedic experiment are set out in what is the preliminary stage in the alchemical comedic process.

4
Ludic Comedy: the Dissolution of Elements

> Somehow there were very extraordinary noises over-head, which disturbed the dignity and repose of the tea party.
> Beatrix Potter, *The Tale of Tom Kitten*

English novels can be as eccentric as their titles, but Stevie Smith's *Novel on Yellow Paper* (1936) is the only one quite literally to describe itself, for on yellow paper it was written, typing paper from the office in which the author worked. Composed at top speed and sounding like it, the book forms an extended breathless interior monologue, free-associating, breaking off chattily to address the reader, and regularly commenting on its own progression. At times the voice sounds like a cross between James Joyce's Molly Bloom and Anita Loos's Lorelei Lee, that blonde whom gentlemen preferred; but Smith's persona, Pompey Casmilus, is undoubtedly her own woman.

> Because I can write only as I can write only, and Does the road wind uphill all the way? Yes, to the very end. But brace up chaps, there's a 60,000 word limit.

Novel on Yellow Paper farcically dismantles the traditional naturalistic novel; even the fiction of Virginia Woolf looks conventional beside it. But Stevie Smith is not so much an experimental woman of letters deliberately writing a new kind of fiction as yet another instance of an individual expressing an artful artlessness within the freedom of a literary tradition that goes back two hundred years and more to when Laurence Sterne began to publish *Tristram Shandy*, a tradition in which the authorial presence makes us feel uncertain as to whether what we are reading is fictional or not. In works as unpredictable as these, the monolith of structured imitative naturalism is not so much undermined as disregarded.

Parlour games: *Tristram Shandy*

'... irresponsible (and nasty) trifling'[1] – F.R. Leavis's sneer at *The Life and Opinions of Tristram Shandy* (1759–67) echoes an earlier verdict from a more celebrated moralist and critic. 'Nothing odd will do long: *Tristram Shandy* did not last.' Johnson's remark was made in 1776, nine years after Sterne's death. It was delivered parenthetically and perhaps should not carry the critical deliberation that has been ascribed to it. In any case time has rendered the pronouncement null and void. Sterne's novel (as one may as well call it) continues to challenge notions of literary decorum, affronting both the platitudes of socially-prescriptive sensibility and the norms of what is logically persuasive and dispassionately ordered. Its combination of buffoonery with tearful sentiment puts established procedures out of countenance; and to this day the book remains the most distinguished exemplar in English fiction of the property of farce.

Sterne's clowning lies, as clowning usually does, not far from tears: he once wrote to a friend that 'if God [...] had not poured forth the spirit of Shandeism into me, which will not suffer me to think two moments upon any grave subject, I would, else, just now lie down and die'.[2] Shandeism, although deriving from the Pantagruelism of Sterne's master, Rabelais, is a mode of feeling which the complexities of *Tristram Shandy* both exemplify and measure. In Sterne's writings farce is not merely self-indulgence; it is set to work, in the name of a transcendent sanity.

The book is in continual dialogue with itself, the narrator incorporating not only his own reservations, apologies and explanations, but also his readers' comments and enquiries.

> How could you, Madam, be so inattentive in reading the last chapter? I told you in it, *That my mother was not a papist.* —Papist! You told me no such thing, Sir. —Madam, I beg leave to repeat it over again, That I told you as plain, at least, as words, by direct inference, could tell you such a thing. —Then, Sir, I must have missed a page. —No, Madam, —you have not missed a word. (I:xx)

And so on; finally the lady is dismissed the room and the remaining readers are addressed by the narrator while she is deciphering the disputed passage for a second time. Our involvement is so close as almost to obliterate the notion that this is a printed book at all. On the other hand, Sterne repeatedly insists that that is what it is; he presents us with blank pages, displaced chapters, blacked-out paragraphs, diagrams of his own narratorial progress with all its accompanying digressions, not to mention an unabashed and unacknowledged lifting of passages from other authors. He even compares the actions recorded in the story with the time it has taken us to read about them. *Tristram Shandy* both insists upon its own complexity as artefact and assumes that its world is a verifiable one which its readers know and share. By qualifying the distinction between author and reader, it subverts the monolithic status of the artefact as object.

This particular methodology is appropriate to a narrative which is itself a jest at the expense of traditional notions as to time and space. The constant digressions and back-trackings, the reflexive commentaries and the procedure by way of mental association are reminiscent of *The Tale of a Tub*; yet in deploying Swift's literary tactics Sterne resorts to the tone of Robert Burton and Sir Thomas Browne, and crosses them with the urbanity of Addison and Steele, to end up with a voice distinctively his own, an essentially confiding voice, one that eschews all confrontation. He speaks throughout to an individual rather than to a collective (and thus impersonal) readership: even when addressing reverend Sirs and disapproving Madams, he does so, as it were, over the head of a sympathetic and co-operative companion. At the opening of the sixth volume this reader is invited to sit down upon a pile of the preceding five; and at another point Tristram's calculations bid fair to bring the entire process of writing and reading to an end.

> I am this month one whole year older than I was this time twelve-month; and having got, as you perceive, almost into the middle of my fourth volume – and no farther than to my first day's life – 'tis demonstrative that I have three hundred and sixty-four days more life to write just now, than when I first set out; so that instead of advancing, as a common writer, in my work with what I have been doing at it – on the contrary, I am just thrown so many volumes back – was every day of my life to be as busy a day as this – And why not? – and the transactions and opinions of it to take up as much description – And for what reason should they be cut short? as at this rate I should just live 364 times faster than I should write – It must follow, an' please your worships, that the more I write, the

more I shall have to write – and consequently, the more your worships will have to read. (IV:xiii)

Had this been Swift at work, the succeeding paragraph might have proceeded to develop some fantastical metaphysic; but this is Sterne, and what we find instead is the isolated line, 'Will this be good for your worships' eyes?' The query is typical Shandean sentiment; but it also undermines the potential grandiosity of the preceding passage. It is farce, but farce motivated by compassion.

The medium of *Tristram Shandy* is the narrator's consciousness: time is internalised, events are described not as they chronologically occur but as they surface in Tristram's mind. The narrative focuses on his father and his Uncle Toby in their armchairs before the fire in Shandy Hall. Around them Mrs Shandy, Corporal Trim, the Widow Wadman, Doctor Slop, Parson Yorick, Obadiah and other servants come and go; but the heart of the book is the comedic collocation of two contrasted mentalities, one of them a contorted wrestling of prejudice with speculation, the other simple, benign and entirely literal-minded, in Hazlitt's words, 'one of the finest compliments ever paid to human nature'.[3] It is the conjunction of these two attitudes which forms the comic heart of the novel's apparently random and farcical contrivances. Everything goes wrong with Walter Shandy's monolithic notions for his son's welfare, the most carefully-laid plans and intentions being foiled both by accident and by the total unawareness of them exhibited by other people. But in terms of Uncle Toby's ability to transform life into a game (which is what his fortifications in the garden amount to) this matters not at all. A master of contrivance himself, Toby accepts human life as it comes.

Sterne's refusal to be limited to clock time (signalled in the famous opening account of Mrs Shandy's unfortunate enquiry at the moment of her son's conception) is accompanied by a similar refusal to be restricted to conventional concepts and usages of space. He accomplishes this through a number of methodologies. One of these is to concentrate on the nature of space as such, as in the account of Walter Shandy's left-handed attempt to extract a handkerchief from his right-hand pocket. As with Toby's fortifications (indeed, as with the whole question of hobby-horses, which infuses the book, wherein monolithic mental concepts existing in time are arrested and reified in space), physical movement is converted into structure. Indeed, all the characters are enclosed in their own obsessions, and, since they exist in the past of Tristram's recollections or reportage, they become spatial rather than temporal beings.

Sterne's extended use of *double entendre*, however laboured it may seem to present-day ears, is a demonstration of the spatial quality of language and its simultaneity of signification. The puns which trick the reader into self-confounding misinterpretations are as much a part of the book's comedic structure as are the physical collisions and coincidences that qualify and contradict the over-simplifications of monolithic consciousness. All the same, the narrative allows for an opposite point of view. When, for example, Dr Slop so angers Mr Shandy senior with his immoderate laughter over 'curtins and hornworks', Toby patiently explains that he has made a mistake, for these objects refer not to bedsteads but to fortifications – thus expelling one hobby-horse by means of another; and it is hard to determine among the three men at whose expense the jest is being made. The book abounds in such outflanking comedic manœuvres. Indeed, its entire structure and narratorial procedure demonstrate the limitation inherent in any simplistically authoritarian point of view.

If its governing mode is farce or play, *Tristram Shandy* does contain, as all major comic fiction will, its share of other elements as well. Sterne's use of parody, and his treatment of the pre-Enlightenment model of the humours, and of the possibility of an absolute knowledge of scientific processes, has received ample critical attention, and is the aspect of the novel which most appeals to scholarly readers: indeed the examination of the author's use of plagiarism has been agreeably pursued ever since Ferriar's *Illustrations of Sterne* appeared in 1798. But Sterne is too individual a stylist to be effective as a mimic: Slawkenbergius's tale and that of the two nuns and the mules are hardly Rabelaisian, whatever the author's intention may have been. But in moments of pure farce, such as that of Obadiah's disastrous collision with Dr Slop, his particular bent of humour produces a characteristic effect of slow motion, so that movement itself becomes phenomenalised.

> What could Dr Slop do? —he crossed himself + —Pugh! —but the doctor, Sir, was a Papist. —No matter; he had better have kept hold of the pummel. —He had so; —nay, as it happened, he had better have done nothing at all: —for in crossing himself he let go his whip,—and in attempting to save his whip betwixt his knee and his saddle's skirt, as it slipped, he lost his stirrup, —in losing which he lost his seat; —and in the multitude of all these losses (which, by the bye, shews what little advantage there is in crossing) the unfortunate doctor lost his presence of mind. So that, without waiting

for Obadiah's onset, he left his pony to its destiny, tumbling off it diagonally, something in the style and manner of a pack of wool, and without any other consequence from the fall, save that of being left (as it would have been) with the broadest part of him sunk about twelve inches deep in the mire. (II:ix)

The humour of this is as much in the telling as in the matter told: the interruption from the supposititious reader, the word-play, the pedantic qualifications, the misplaced scrupulosity of that 'as it would have been', all issue in what may be termed a stylistically induced hilarity.

Such verbal complexities substantiate and exemplify the irony which pervades the whole book. All Walter Shandy's plans for his son are defeated by accidents that he has in one way or another brought upon himself – just as the processes of mental association frustrate Tristram's intention of producing an ordered narrative. Moreover, irony even presides over the deployment of satire that is frequently directed at human reasoning based on the mental logistics of scholasticism. A good instance of Sterne's undermining of his own processes even in this connection occurs at the conclusion of the debate as to whether a mother is of kin to her own child, which in a parody of logic concludes that

> there is no prohibition *in nature*, though there is in the levitical law—but that a man may beget a child upon his grandmother—in which case, supposing the issue a daughter, she would stand in relation both of— But who ever thought, cried Kysarcius, of laying with his grandmother?— The young gentleman, replied Yorick, whom Selden speaks of—who not only thought of it, but justified his intention to his father by the argument drawn from the law of retaliation.— "You layed, Sir, with my mother," said the lad— "Why may not I lie with yours?" (IV:xxix)

Once again literal-mindedness and simplistic argument are blown sky-high.

If we are invited to mock at the absurdities of the various characters, we are also compelled to recognise the absurdity of such mockery in itself: the simplicity of Uncle Toby is not something to be laughed at but something to be laughed with. The third chapter of Volume Four provides an instance of this distinction. Tristram's father, lying upon the bed, is lamenting the accident to his newborn son's nose.

Did ever man, brother Toby, cried my father, raising himself upon his elbow, and turning himself round to the opposite side of the bed, where my uncle Toby was sitting in his old fringed chair, with his chin resting upon his crutch—did ever a poor unfortunate man, brother Toby, cried my father, receive so many lashes? —The most I ever saw given, quoth my uncle Toby, (ringing the bell at the bed's head for Trim) was to a grenadier, I think in Mackay's regiment.

—Had my uncle Toby shot a bullet through my father's heart, he could not have fallen down with his nose upon the quilt more suddenly.

Bless me! said my uncle Toby. (IV:iii)

That is all there is to the chapter; the next one commences with Toby questioning Corporal Trim as to the truth of his recollection. The incident is thus self-contained, comically exhibiting the excesses of self-pitying rhetoric and the simplicity of Toby's literalness of mind. But its peculiarly Shandean quality springs from its attention to domestic detail and corresponding evocation of familiarity; its juxtaposition of satirical comedy with the harshness and cruelty of life outside Shandy Hall, and the force of the penultimate sentence, which seems to enact what it describes (Sterne is a master of this sort of thing); and the reiteration of the word 'Toby', a chime which has the effect of immobilising the events into a tableau. The final comment is ironic in its dual exhibition of Toby's imaginative limitations and his innocent goodness of heart. By making him delightfully funny, Sterne renders him morally significant – as is evident in the succeeding conversation with Trim as to the grenadier's innocence: the result is the chastisement of Walter Shandy's histrionics.

Toby's embodiment of the benevolent norm is also evident in a verbal coincidence which relates to one of the book's more celebrated moments. This occurs during the scene in the servants' hall when Obadiah breaks the news of Bobby's death, and Mrs Shandy's maid Susannah realises that her mistress will have to go into mourning and that she herself is thus likely to inherit her 'green sattin night-gown'. Sterne uses the occasion to poke sly fun at Locke's theories of an associative language (since for Susannah the word 'mourning' signifies 'night-gown'); but he also lowers the tone with an observation far more rich in implication.

We had a fat, foolish scullion—my father, I think, kept her for her simplicity; —she had been all autumn struggling with a dropsy. —

He is dead, said Obadiah, —he is certainly dead! —So am not I, said the foolish scullion. (V:7)

Such directness might seem to be a Swiftian indictment of the lumpen insensibility of the general run of uneducated humankind; but earlier one finds Toby using identical words as a response to Dr Slop's enthusiastic reading of Ernulphus's curse.

> I declare, quoth my uncle Toby, my heart would not let me curse the devil himself with so much bitterness. —He is the father of curses, replied Dr Slop. —So am not I, replied my uncle. (III:xi)

The effect, as so often with Sterne, is to transpose from one mode of humorousness to another, from ridicule to a celebratory acceptance. In that light, the scullion's reaction can be seen as that of simple, if stupid, being. The nature of Sterne's satire is never blistering, always kind.

Hence it is that in *Tristram Shandy* burlesque is found not so much in the bawdy anecdotes as in the shocked reactions to them which the elaborate play with verbal ambiguity would appear to assume and to pre-empt. Once again the reader finds himself implicated in verbal nets and tripwires: the jokes recoil upon him, just as satire is outflanked by irony. Indeed the whole comic interplay of *Tristram Shandy* amounts to a species of wit, the recognition of the relativity of each response with regard to its fellows: all alike are dissolved into a mood in which laughter is pervasive but within which it does not exist as a distinct ingredient.

At the same time, the book is designed to be remedial. 'If 'tis wrote against anything, – 'tis wrote, an' please your worships, against the spleen' – and then the author goes on to parody the medical interpretation of spirit that still formed part of the common consciousness,

> in order, by a more frequent and a more convulsive elevation and depression of the diaphragm, and the sucussations of the intercostal and abdominal muscles in laughter, to drive the *gall* and other *bitter juices* from the gall bladder, liver and sweet-bread of his majesty's subjects, with all the inimicitious passions which belong to them, down into their duodenums. (IV:xxii)

The lip-smacking relish of this arcane vocabulary erupts into a wilder absurdity of collocation with the introduction of 'his majesty's subjects' in such a context. Indeed, much of Sterne's writing might be characterised as the comedy of contexts misapplied. A good example of this occurs when Mrs Shandy informs her husband of his brother Toby's supposed impending nuptials. 'Then he will never, quoth my father, be able to lie *diagonally* in his bed again as long as he lives.' The sheer surprise of this is funny enough; and the humour is compounded by the fact that we have just been informed that Walter Shandy was at that time 'musing within himself about the hardships of matrimony' (VI:xxxix). Indeed, the relations between husband and wife are vital to the book's humorous perspective. Mrs Shandy, as much a foil to her husband as is Uncle Toby, possesses a simplicity of character which is even more prevalent than is his. She is the embodiment of that acquiescent, unenquiring placidity of outlook which is the intellectual's and the artist's perpetual stumbling-block. We are informed that

> she had a way [...] that was never to refuse her assent and consent to any proposition my father laid before her, merely because she did not understand it, or had no ideas of the principal word or term of art, upon which the tenet or proposition rolled. She contented herself with doing all that her godfathers and godmothers promised for her – but no more; and so would go on using a hard word twenty years together – and replying to it too, if it was a verb, in all its moods and tenses, without giving herself any trouble to enquire about it. (IX:xi)

Such a temperament might equally become the object of indignant or indulgent satire; but Sterne's recognition that it is fundamental to ordinary human nature renders it truly humorous in all senses of that word. And the full measure of his sensitivity can be gauged in the masterly scene in which Mrs Shandy discovers her husband lamenting the death of their eldest son, with characteristic theatricality both invoking and quoting the speech of Socrates before his judges, with its appeal 'I have three desolate children.' This is too much for his wife, who exclaims that in that case 'you have one more, Mr Shandy, than I know of'. He leaves the room in anguish, and it is left to Toby to explain that her husband was referring to the children of Socrates, to which she objects that he has been dead for a hundred years.

> My uncle Toby was no chronologer—so not caring to advance a step but upon safe ground, he laid down his pipe deliberately upon

the table, and rising up, and taking my mother most kindly by the hand, without saying another word, either good or bad, to her, he led her out after my father, so that he might finish the éclaircissement himself. (V:xiv)

The modulation is very sure, the idiosyncracies of each character only serving to further the pathos, while at the same time preventing it from becoming mawkish. It is a perfect instance of the kind of compassionate sanity engendered by this author's comic vision, of the serious attitude to life that underlies his verbal play. But it was not an attitude which later ages were to find it easy to adopt.

These foolish things: Ronald Firbank

It was not *Tristram Shandy* but *A Sentimental Journey* which was to influence the Victorian age: the intellectual curiosity and witty manipulation of the concepts of time and space which mark its seemingly introverted predecessor were alien to nineteenth-century Protestant concepts of work and duty. Bulwer-Lytton's *The Caxtons* (1849), for example, is an essay in Shandeism, but its domestic whimsicalities owe more to the Yorick persona of the *Journey* than they do to that of *Tristram*. If we are to look for a re-surfacing of Sterne's outlook and methodology, then we must do so not among the Victorian novelists but in such modernist writers as Ronald Firbank, William Gerhardie and James Joyce.

But there is a third aspect of Sterne's comedic art which does erupt towards the end of the nineteenth century, to reach full expression in the Edwardian period, and that is the element of farce. The delighted pin-pointing of human absurdities which helped to popularise Walter Shandy and My Uncle Toby is found subsequently in Dickens, from Mrs Leo Hunter in *The Pickwick Papers* to the monumental Mr Thomas Sapsea in *The Mystery of Edwin Drood*; and it is a distillation of such perceptions which glistens in the work of Oscar Wilde, reaching its apogee in *The Importance of Being Earnest*, a play whose particular style of nonsensical hyperbole was to perpetuate a whole world of comic sensibility, one which transforms the weighty power-structures of social differentiation into what is essentially a game. Wilde wrote no comic novel, but lesser luminaries took fire from him, and in the 'Society' fiction of Anthony Hope, Ada Leverson and Saki a delight in triviality is expressed in dialogue form, to expand with increasing exuberance in the farcical narratives of

Dornford Yates and P.G. Wodehouse. In all of them the solemnity of human social and moral pretensions is dissipated not in moralistic satire but in a cloud of willed unknowing.

Vainglory (1915) by Ronald Firbank belongs very much in the Wildean tradition. Firbank's novels ('a tiresome fribble to most of us', Q.D. Leavis called him)[4] are with Samuel Beckett's among the most purely abstract in the English language: their world is one of total self-enclosure, resisting all attempts to relate it to any normative scale of reference. The author, in E.M. Forster's words, is 'completely absorbed in his own nonsense'.[5] *Vainglory* is a murmuration of half-abstracted voices: overlong for any attempt at concentrated attention, it is alive with that luminous sense of the absurd which is Firbank's hallmark.

> "A Last Supper at *two tables*," Mrs Pontypool said confidentially, "struck one as—scarcely— —" (vi)

Or, to switch mythologies, from *Inclinations* (1916):

> "They showed me the smartest set of tea-things [...] that I ever saw. It belonged to Iphigeneia—in Tauris." (I:xii)

Firbank's work has parodic roots. His particular method is to apply to the worlds and characters of contemporary novelists 'his own private brand of fantasy, pickling them, as it were, in his own special brine'.[6] Thus his earliest mature work, *The Artificial Princess* (posthumously published in 1934) plays with the decadent world of the eighteen-nineties – the Princess laments that the Devil 'neglects our Court ever since Fräulein Anna Schweidler giggled so disrespectfully at a Black Mass'. (Chapter i) Where *Vainglory* reflects and adapts the epigrammatic dialogues of 'Society' novels, *Caprice* (1917) enters the world of the then currently popular theatrical fiction of Compton Mackenzie (who was to adopt the Firbankian world of *Inclinations*, with its eccentric ladies on their Mediterranean travels, for *Vestal Fire* (1927), a highly entertaining novel about expatriates on Capri in the 1920s). In *Valmouth* (1919) Firbank offers his own version of the bucolic world made familiar at the time by writers such as Mary Webb and John Trevena; while *The Flower Beneath the Foot* (1923) adapts the still-flourishing literature deriving from Anthony Hope's invention of Ruritania. In its turn *Prancing Nigger* (1924) mischievously transfers the satire of social aspirations to the West Indies, while Firbank's last completed novel, *Concerning the Eccentricities of Cardinal Pirelli* (1926) returns to the familiar nineties world of ecclesiastical extravagance already plundered in *Valmouth* and which had been definitively realised in the *Stories Toto Told Me* (1898) of Frederick Rolfe, the self-styled 'Baron Corvo'. As to the unfinished *The New Rythum* (posthumously published in 1962) it moves in Firbank's re-creation of the New York of Scott Fitzgerald. His fictive world is not so solipsistic as it appears to be.

In technique it is he, if anyone, who is the heir of Sterne – the Sterne of *A Sentimental Journey*. That interplay between the record itself, the recording voice and the recipient of the recorded message, which makes Sterne's second work of fiction the uniquely intimate thing it is, is achieved by Firbank through means that are less obtrusive but just as deft. Compare Yorick's seduction of the lady at the theatre with Charlie Mouth's encounter with his mother in *Prancing Nigger*. In the first case there is a description of two people trying to get out of each other's way while passing through a door, a description both naturalistic and erotic, following which

> I ran and begg'd pardon for the embarrassment I had given her, saying it was my intention to have made her way. She answered, she was guided by the same intention towards me; so we reciprocally thank'd each other. She was at the top of the stairs; and seeing no *chichesbee* near her, I begg'd to hand her to her coach; so we went down the stairs, stopping at every third step to talk of the concert and the adventure. Upon my word, Madame, said I, when I had handed her in, I made six different efforts to let you go out. And I made six efforts, replied she, to let you enter. I wish to heaven you would make a seventh, said I. With all my heart, said she, making room. Life is too short to be long about the forms of it, so I instantly stepp'd in, and she carried me home with her. And what became of the concert, St Cecilia, who, I suppose, was at it, knows more than I.
>
> ('The Translation. Paris')

The prose enacts the event, involving the reader by means of a process of grammatical modulation in the penultimate sentence which, through the delaying ambiguity of 'life is too short to be long about the forms of it' (Yorick's reply to the lady? a general proposition to the reader?) ensures that by the time it is resolved Yorick is in the coach and away, on the wings of a *double entendre*. Never was a pick-up so elegantly, so breathlessly achieved: the monolithic disposal of subject and object is tossed in a bouquet to St Cecilia.

Firbank's effects are achieved more sensuously, as Charlie 'resigned himself to sit down upon his heels, in the shade of a potter's stall, and consider the passing crowd'.

> Missionaries with freckled hands and hairy, care-worn faces, followed by pale girls wielding tambourines of the Army of the Soul, foppish nigger bucks in panamas and palm-beach suits so cocky, Chinamen with osier baskets, their nostalgic eyes aswoon, heavily straw-hatted nuns trailing their dust-coloured rags, and suddenly, oh, could it be? – but there was no mistaking that golden waddle. "Mamma!" [...]
> And, oh, honies! Close behind, behold Miami, and Edna too: the Miss Lips, the fair Lips, the smiling Lips. How spry each looked. The elder (grown a trifle thinner), sweet *à ravir* in tomato-red, while her sister, plump as a corn-fattened partridge, and very perceptibly powdered, seemed like the flower of the prairie sugar-cane when it breaks into bloom. (Chapter viii)

Here narrator and character combine in the language of a common consciousness, the one interpreting the other, as in the potentially ribald 'waddle' and 'tomato'. A total subjectivity is achieved.

Firbank's most striking humorous effects are inextricably confused. In *Valmouth*, the devout Mrs Hurstpierpoint, alarmed by an approaching storm, requests her maid to bring her a saint's relic out of her collection.

> "Any one in particular, 'm?" the maid enquired, slipping, with obedient alacrity, across the floor.
> "No; but not a leg-bone, mind! a leg-bone relic somehow—" she broke off, searching with her great dead eye dreaming the sad camphor-hued hills for the crucifix and wayside oratory that surmounted the topmost peak.
> "You used to say the toe, 'm, of the married sister of the Madonna, the one that was a restaurant proprietress (Look alive there with those devilled kidneys, and what is keeping Fritz with that sweet omelette?), in any fracas was particularly potent. (Chapter vi)

The narrative slides back and forth between direct speech with authorial comment and the mind of Mrs Hurstpierpoint, doing so by means of that 'dreaming' rather than (say) 'searching'; and away from maid and narrator alike in the bracketed phrase which so ludicrously and robustly contrasts the language of piety with that of everyday – indeed, the juxtaposition is so immediate that there is hardly room for contrast. Firbank's is a uniquely sophisticated and self-destructive mode of narratorial discourse.

The novels are full of jokes. The names of the characters are one abundant source of these: only Dickens, Thackeray and Trollope had been as inventive as Firbank in this respect. In their case the names are both expressive of character and, one is inclined to feel, determinative of it. Firbank, however, appears to invent names out of sheer exuberance – Olga Blumenghast, Mrs Barleymoon, Lady Lucy Lacy, Lady Charlotte-Cadence-Stewart, Mrs Guy Fox, Father Nostradamus, Lily Quickstep, Winsome Brookes, Dismalia, Duchess of Meath and Man, to name a happy few; at other times, though less frequently, he invents a name to pinpoint a type or indicate a social rôle (as does Trollope with his Miss Thoroughbung or Dickens with his Wackford Squeers) – 'Mrs Julia Portland Stone, the distinguished classic actress' being one felicitous example.

Firbankian comedy operates not so much within the action of his novels (which is usually tragic, wry, pathetic, wistful and in terms of plot anything but funny) as in relation to the reader's expectations: it is a comedy of incongruity and displacement that outrages normative associations – as when, in *Cardinal Pirelli*, Pope Tertius II, having lamented, 'Why can't they all behave?', cheers himself up by reflecting on the increasing number of English people in his audiences, bearing out 'the sybilline predictions of their late great and sagacious ruler – Queen Victoria'.

> "The dear *santissima* woman," the Pontiff sighed, for he entertained a sincere, if brackish, enthusiasm for the lady who for so many years had corresponded with the Holy See under the signature of *the Countess of Lostwaters*.[7] (Chapter iv)

A more systematic affront to normal expectations occurs in the Valmouth ladies' sporting recollections.

> "One could count more alluring faces out with the Valmouth, my husband used to say, than with any other pack. The Baroness Elsassar – I can see her now on her great mauve mount with her profile of royalty in misfortune – never missed. Neither, bustless, hipless, chinless, did 'Miss Bligh'! It was she who so sweetly hoisted

me to my saddle, when I'd slid a-heap after the run of a 'fairy' fox. We'd whiffed it – the baying of the dogs is something I shall never forget; dogs always know! – in a swede-field below your house from where it took us by break-neck, rapid stages – (oh! oh!) – to the sands. There, it hurried off along the sea's edge, with the harriers in full cry; all at once, near Pizon Point, it vanished. Mr Rogers, who was a little ahead, drew in his horse with the queerest gape – like a lost huntsman (precisely) in the *Bibliothèque bleue*."
"It's a wonder he didn't vomit." (Chapter iv)

The mastery of mimetic rhythm ensures the effect of the contrasts when they come: Firbank's world is ordinarily so hyper-refined that the occasional blunt word obtrudes with maximum force.

But to what purpose? This appears to be a comedy of bafflement, even of 'nasty (and irresponsible) trifling'. Certainly it discards all pretensions towards endorsing either conventional moral or conventional literary standards, even where fantasy or whimsy are concerned. To call such books 'novels' is as much (and as little) a joke as it would be to apply the term to the very different (but not entirely different) tales of Beatrix Potter; yet they are composed with total dedication, no fewer than 58 notebooks attesting the deliberation of their composition. And what offends certain people about them is in fact the secret of their enduring appeal and actual strength – the quality of sheer silliness, a resourceful silliness which is a comic antidote to pain. That Firbank was a practical man of affairs and an artist of peculiar dedication accounts for that resourcefulness: but he was also a homosexual and an æsthete at a period when it was more than usually dangerous to be either. If his fiction constitutes a disguised attack on the kind of society it so delightfully portrays, the particular plangency of his comic vision none the less arises from a collusive pleasure in the frivolities and impertinencies of that society's activities and conversation.

As in the case of Sterne, a sense of melancholy underlies the absurdities, so audacious in their affront to monolithic dignity. But the novels' underlying sadness arises more from plaintiveness than grief; nor are they strictly farcical, for they are too static to engender the tearaway ribaldry, so potentially destructive, of that comedic mode. But they do preserve in their peculiar kind of amber the possibilities of farce, and portray a world whose constituent ingredients are separated and dissolved in a luminous haze. And those ingredients are the structures and hierarchies and materialistic concerns of the monolithic point of view.

The novels may not aspire to serious moral or metaphysical statement, but they are certainly serious by implication.[8] *The Flower Beneath the Foot*, itself the most robust of them, ends on a physical image of despair and agony, as a nun's hands are lacerated by the broken glass that defends her convent wall.

Firbank's world is one of single people: at the conclusion of *The Princess Zoubaroff* (1920), effectively a novel in the form of a play, the men and women go their separate ways. Singleness suggests singularity: in that world the entire social fabric of law and custom and conventional rôle-playing becomes a game. Firbank's art invigorates by its innocent obliquity; it converts a nihilistic attitude towards monolithic pretensions into an order of gaiety and outrageous disregard that, for all its outward sophistication, is entirely free from spite. It is a commendable achievement; but the continued enforcement of social, not to say societal, monoliths, was to ensure that it remained a rare one.

Lucid ridicule: Elizabeth von Arnim

Firbank's ludic world is irrigated by a stream of feminine frivolity in which women – or more strictly the socially prescribed version of them known as 'ladies' – are an unending source of amusement and delight. For the monolithic mother-figure itself has at times to be dismantled, no less than that of the father, and it is comedically appropriate that some of the most reductive comic portrayals of inadequate or domineering mothers should have come from women novelists. But the tyranny of masculine presumption and complacency was a no less frequent target, a target which was pierced repeatedly by the writer who for more than 40 years published her novels under the anonymity of 'The Author of *Elizabeth and her German Garden*'. Mary Annette Beauchamp was invariably known by this penname, 'Elizabeth'. She married Count Henning von Arnim in 1891, and following his death in 1910, she married Francis, Earl Russell, elder brother of Bertrand Russell. (Her work is now reprinted as by Elizabeth von Arnim – with regard to her last ten novels, a doubly inaccurate designation.) Writing to Hugh Walpole in 1927, Beerbohm remarks of the author that 'she writes as a lark sings [...] or rather as a lark *would* sing if it had a powerful little brain'.[9] Elizabeth was indeed that rare being, a feminine farceur who, in undermining the monoliths of social propriety and cant, made telling use of flippancy and ridicule, her methods being the more effective in that her talent

Ludic Comedy: the Dissolution of Elements 77

for making mischief was so self-assured. Here, for example, is the opening of her penultimate novel, *The Jasmine Farm* (1934).

> At Shillerton that week-end, the week-end before Whitsuntide, they had gooseberry tart – or is it pie? Daisy Midhurst, in whose house it was eaten, never quite knew, but anyhow it was the thing with pastry on its top instead of its bottom, – for luncheon on Sunday; and it was a hot gooseberry tart, because pastry is better hot, though gooseberries are worse; and the guests, having eaten it, were hot too, and not only hot but uncomfortable; for the gooseberries, on whose sourness no amount of sugar flung and cream emptied had the least effect, almost immediately, on getting inside them, began to ferment.

The offhand frivolity of this is characteristic. But Elizabeth was seldom concerned simply to make fun. The best of her novels contain a serious undercurrent and are peppered with an occasionally blistering wit.

In the first two, centred on the German garden, mockery of an authoritarian husband – 'The Man of Wrath' – is only occasional; but the domineering male in all his dullness and brutal egoism was to become the focus of many of the later books, most memorably in *The Caravaners* (1909), *The Pastor's Wife* (1914) and *Vera* (1921). In the first of these the self-righteous narrator gives himself away with every word, and at the end seems stupefied by the animosity he has aroused: through his very unawareness the author exposes the egotistical mentality, so monolithic in its concentration on itself. But while the satire is amusing, the target it attacks is obvious.

The Pastor's Wife and *Vera* are more complex, exposing as they do the reciprocal attraction between masculine arrogance and female self-distrust. In the former novel, the dutiful daughter of an English bishop is wooed by a middle-aged German pastor, whom she marries out of gratitude for having been desired at all. Her subsequent engulfment in the deadly monotony of life in an East Prussian rural parish is funny but alarming (humour and danger are frequent neighbours in Elizabeth's fictive world). But the story takes a farcical turn when Ingeborg, that incorrigible innocent, on 'holiday' with a cultivated young Englishman, thwarts his attempts at seduction through her all-absorbing appreciation of the delights of foreign travel, and then by a sense of outrage that is less a matter of morality than of disappointment: in her companion's pretended 'liberation' she divines yet another form of tyranny. In penitence she returns to a husband who scarcely notices that she has been away. This farcically ironical conclusion barely masks the pain of a story that is ultimately without hope.

In *Vera* a devouringly egotistic widower, who has driven his first wife to suicide, persuades a sentimental young woman to replace her – the authorial inference being that she will do so in that ultimate respect as well. No more in Lucy's case than in Ingeborg's is there any prospect of escape. Their stories are chilling; but the indictment of conventionalised sexual rôle-playing is accompanied by a keen sense of the ludicrous. Elizabeth has a piercing eye for incongruities, and a trick of deflating solemnity by the use of reductive metaphors coined by her characters themselves. Here, encased in self-importance and respectability, is the Bishop of Redchester lamenting Ingeborg's protracted absence from home and duties.

> What had really been cruel was the muddle his papers and letters had got into owing to her prolonged absence. Grave dislocations had taken place in the joints of his engagements, several with far-reaching results; and all because, he could not help feeling, Ingeborg, in spite of precept and example, did not in her earlier years use her toothbrush with regularity and conscientiousness. Manifestly she did not, or how could she have needed nine enormous days to be set in repair? He himself, who regarded his body as a holy temple, which was the one solution of the body question that at all approached satisfactoriness, and had accordingly brushed his teeth from the point of view of their being pillars of a sacred edifice after every meal for forty years, had never had a toothache in his life. (Chapter vii)

The accumulation of parentheses is matched by the inexorable flow of fallacious logic.

Elsewhere Elizabeth employs a more direct method of attack. In *Vera* the grossness of Everard Wemyss is portrayed in action.

> Wemyss held forth. He stood on the hearthrug filling his pipe – he was used to smoking in that room when he came to tea with Lucy, and forgot to ask Miss Entwhistle if it mattered – and told everybody what he thought [...] and what he thought was what *The Times* had thought that morning. Wemyss spoke with the practised fluency of a leading article. He liked politics and constantly talked them at his club, and it created vacancies in the chairs near him.

Ludic Comedy: the Dissolution of Elements 79

But Lucy, who hadn't heard him on politics before and found she could understand every word, listened to him with parted lips.
(Chapter xi)

Vera comes under the category of black humour or burlesque: the relentless way in which the author piles one instance of tyrannical behaviour upon another induces readerly hysteria as indignation struggles with collusive merriment.

An instance of this author's particular brand of the absurd occurs in *Father* (1931). The heroine, awaiting the return of the country clergyman from whom she wishes to rent a cottage, grows chilly in his unheated study, and is provided by an obliging servant with a coat,

> but it happened to be the Vicar's winter-coat, and he, when he arrived home ten minutes later and found a strange woman in it, didn't like it at all [...] But he was upset silently, as became a clergyman. His resentments padded about inside him with muffled footsteps, and not once in recent years had got out and made a real noise, his wife having been dead some time.

That last phrase is slipped in with disarming casualness; but a more specific satirical observation is involved.

> He [...] was increasingly provoked by his inability to say the only thing he really wanted to say, which was "why have you got my coat on?" He knew the Duke would have said it at once; and it added to his annoyance to have it brought so disagreeably to his notice that he belonged to the in-between class which couldn't be simple, and was called – he had always disliked the word – middle.
> (Chapter xi)

The situation is prolonged (Elizabeth is adept at slow-motion narrative) and mutual incomprehension grows. But it all comes to nothing, merely illustrating that continual eruption of the farcical which is liable to unseat monolithic postures and responses at any opportunity.

But in combining sentiment with farcicality and sardonic rage, Elizabeth plays a dangerous game; few of her books avoid an occasional declension into humbug or facetiousness, and she lacks the dedicated artistry of the single-minded satirist. Yet in her final and most accomplished novel, *Mr Skeffington* (1940), she does achieve a resolution that is genuinely comedic. An ageing society woman, following a series of disastrous visits to her former admirers, during which she is compelled to recognise the ravages of time and the futility of her existence, is re-united with her ex-husband on discovering that he is blind and thus unaffected by her loss of beauty. Were this all, the resolution would be cheap and slick; but Fanny's compassion for Mr Skeffington is genuine, and she accepts their reconciliation without exploiting it. In a gallant gesture at the end, when her maid enquires as to which dress she shall lay out for the first dinner of the master's return, the reply comes, 'but *of course*, the new white lace'. Bitter irony is leavened with a touch of wit: at her best Elizabeth combines absurdity with tenderness in situations that might seem to warrant neither treatment. In this respect she is an enlightening instance of the comedic potential of frivolity and farce. But to be realised, that potential called for a wider social and formal context than she was in a position to provide.

Magnificent obsessions: William Gerhardie

Whereas the novels of both Firbank and Elizabeth indicate that the farcical dissolution of conventional restraints is not necessarily a cause for laughter, a book like William Gerhardie's suavely absurd *The Polyglots* (1925) shows that neither is it necessarily one for tears. The author's own complicated parental background (he was of mixed German, French and Flemish ancestry) is woven into the tragi-comic portrait of uprooted people – English, Belgian, Russian, Japanese, American – all of them stranded in the Far East during the chaotic aftermath of the First World War. The novel is infused with a kind of astringent whimsy; but beneath its illogicalities and haphazard unfolding of events there sounds a note of anger, pathos and, on occasion, absolute tragedy. It is a rare mixture of lyrical beauty and frivolous detachment.

The narrator, George Hamlet Alexander Diabologue, regards his fellow-characters as no more crazy than are the manipulators of the world that they inhabit.

> They were good, well-behaved lunatics, trim and neat in their diminutive, harmless lunacy, compared with our war lords in their raving, disorderly madness. They were floating in a sea of bewilderment and confusion, but we who were waging this colossal war with seriousness and with method were more destructively futile in our pretensions, more grievously self-deluded. (Chapter xxxv)

Lunacy is at the heart of *The Polyglots*: most of its people are governed by obsessions, some of them comical, others self-destructive, some both.

> Now and then Captain Negodyaev suffered from an acute attack of persecution mania, when, often in the middle of the night, he would bid his wife and child get up and dress in readiness for flight at a moment's notice. And they would sit there, all dressed up, in their furs and overcoats and hats and muffs and warm goloshes, in the heated drawing room, Mme Negodyaev looking as if somebody had hit her suddenly between the ears with an umbrella, and she could not quite reconcile the fact with what had taken place immediately before. But Natasha seemed to take it all for granted. With her parasol in her gloved hands, she would sit there, grave and quiet, one hour, two – until at last he would declare the danger over, and send them back to bed. (Chapter xxviii)

But Natasha, so touchingly and tenderly observed, is to die at sea, her father's obsessions simultaneously refuted and fulfilled.

A different act of lunacy confirms the tragi-comic bias of the novel – the suicide of George's Uncle Lucy, who hangs himself while dressed up in his sister's underclothes. It is an act of grotesquerie, permitting neither untrammelled grief nor careless laughter. Even Aunt Teresa, the sister in question, finds it difficult to respond becomingly, for

> she did not mourn him as she felt she should have done, because she secretly resented the highly unconventional manner of his end. It did not follow the canons of good taste. It was not pre-eminently a respectable death [...] It was awkward to tell people how he died. What made it worse was that the crêpe-de-Chine camisole and knickers – green, embroidered with flowers – were the General's souvenir brought back from Japan. (Chapter xlii)

George goes on to comment that 'She did not know that one could laugh and be serious at the same time.' But the reader too is involved with her in her outbreaks of *fou rire*.

Such ambiguities are reminiscent of Sterne, a novelist whom Gerhardie resembles at several points. Both writers employ an assumed persona, and both talk freely about the reading process that accompanies what they are writing; Gerhardie even involves us in his characters' eventual fate. George tells his story in order to make money with which to finance his various relations and their dependents, and therefore

I invite the reader to co-operate with me in a spirit of good will to make the end a happy one for all concerned: buy this book. If you have already bought it, buy it again, and get your brother and mother to buy it. And the end, for Aunt Teresa and Aunt Molly and the Negedyaev family, will be different – very different – from what it might otherwise become. So tell your friends, tell all your friends – my aunt wants you to. (Chapter l)

The gallery of characters – Aunt Teresa, *grande dame* of *les crises de nerfs*; the incurably susceptible Uncle Emmanuel; Sylvia, that sweetly vacuous scatterbrain; Major Beastly with his 'stinks'; the irrepressible small boy Harry; the harassed parvenu General Pshemovich-Pshevitski – engaging as they all are, are bundled out of the book with the same ruthlessness that Thackeray displays at the conclusion to *Vanity Fair*. But in *The Polyglots* the difference between fact and fiction would appear to be non-existent. For the author suggests that even a novel as exquisitely humorous and touching as this one is, is but one way of passing time. For 'there is no way out, as there is no way in: for all is life, and there is nothing to get out into'. It is this belief which underlies George's definition of comedy.

The inestimable advantage of comedy over any other literary mode of depicting life is that here you rise superior, unobtrusively, to every notion, attitude, and situation so depicted. We laugh – we laugh because we cannot be destroyed, because we do not recognize our destiny in any one achievement, because we are immortal, because there is not this or that world; but endless worlds; eternally we pass from one into another. In this lies the hilarity, futility, the insurmountable greatness of all life. (Chapter l)

The Polyglots is its own universe: it both relates to the post-war world and yet floats free of it. Just as at the height of the conflict the valetudinarian Aunt Teresa can remove her soldier husband from Flanders to Manchuria in order to escape it – and then contrive to convey her family and retainers back again – so the arbitrary nature of fictive events is commandeered by the author to present a view of life in which human absolutes are dissolvable in each other. *The Polyglots* is not so much a novel concerned with farcical happenings as an embodiment of that melting-down of artificial protections and barriers which constitutes the particular function of farce in the comedic process.

As early as 1815 Mary Russell Mitford, the future author of the influential pastoral prose idyll *Our Village*, was expressing a wish to see a novel 'undertaken without any plot at all'.[10] She may be reacting against the Gothic fiction of the day, but implicitly she voices a desire for the kind of reliance on the free movement of imaginative association which Sterne alone among English novelists had hitherto exhibited. But his deliberate dismantling of the formalised structure of dramatic fiction did not, probably could not, become an established tradition in its turn; for all its deliberate intellectual and moral seriousness his work remains *sui generis*, his genius outstripping that of all subsequent farceurs by virtue of its sheer intelligence.

In later writers such as Firbank and Gerhardie one finds an irruption of the interior life actualised dramatically in terms of fantastic farce. In their fictions, as in those of Elizabeth, there is an assertion of frivolity which avoids the trivial through its absence of a sense of moral purpose – though in her case it could be argued that her work demonstrates that spiritual freedom is the result (to borrow a phrase contentiously used by David Cecil about Jane Austen) of 'sunshine and unselfishness'.[11] But through their disregard of dramatic norms all these writers express a dissatisfaction with the restrictive nature of monolithic understandings of social structures and behaviour. They are all in one way or another Lords of Misrule, declining to confront the monolith on terms that would permit it to reassert its sovereignty, declining, indeed, to confront anything. Farce may mock at humanity's efforts to maintain control over its affairs; but the way out of farcical disintegration is always forward, never back. In *The Flower Beneath the Foot* the city streets were known in the Convent of the Flaming-Hood as 'Sinward ho'.

5
Ironic Comedy: the Conjunction of Opposites

> We can only be ignorant of that which we can know.
>
> Arthur Machen, *Far Off Things*

The history of English fiction is full of ironies. *Novel on Yellow Paper*, written at the suggestion of a publisher who had turned down the author's poems, was in its turn to be rejected. In view of the book's freakish nature, this is hardly surprising; but a more unusual irony attends the well-known case of Barbara Pym. This deceptively quiet-voiced satirist of English church life and middle-class manners was to discover in the mid 1960s that her hitherto successful novels were suddenly deemed unmarketable; and her reputation went into eclipse for 15 years until a fortuitous championing by Philip Larkin and Lord David Cecil (a surprising collocation) made her work imediately fashionable. It was now applauded, even excessively so, and the 'guilty' publishers were excoriated; yet when, following her death, the novel they rejected was put in print it was considered to be inferior to her previous work. They had not been so undiscerning after all.

Pym's novels are themselves predominantly ironic; but the real irony in this connection is that her popular reputation should still be that of a benign domestic novelist in the tradition of pre-war women writers such as Dorothy Whipple and O. Douglas. On a superficial reading the ascription may seem reasonable, in view of their sheltered settings and concentration upon trivial details of behaviour: Pym excels at capturing moments of intimate private amusement.

> I could not imagine Everard Bone breaking a casserole! It was a silly, trivial thing, but every time I thought of it I smiled, sometimes when I was by myself in a street or in a bus.
>
> (*Excellent Women* (1952), Chapter xx)

Such feelings are pleasantly familiar; but the expectation that the unmarried narrator has of life suggests the pessimistic outlook that makes the appreciation of such small delights so great:

> what had I really hoped for? Dull, solid friendship without charm? No, there was enough of that between women and women and even between men and women [...] This thought led me to worry again about Everard and his meat and how I had refused to cook it for him, and it was a relief when the church clock struck and I realised that it was time to go to the meeting in the parish hall.
> (Ibid., Chapter xxiv)

The very flatness of the prose reflects the determination of the understatement. Barbara Pym's fictive world is unusual in that, despite its amused reflection of the absurdities of daily life and its quiet response to virtue, truth and beauty, it is also informed by a resignation so great as almost to obliterate its origin in a sense of irony. Indeed Pym's novels reveal an outlook on life almost as chilling as those of Samuel Beckett, and it might be argued that a naturalistic technique such as hers brings home the horrors of loneliness, old age and the sheer littleness of life's opportunities more uncomfortably than do deliberately stylised symbolic figures encased in existential dustbins or buried in the sand at a safe distance on the stage.

Basic principles: *Jonathan Wild*

Irony is born of indignation; but while voicing dissatisfaction with things as they are, it simultaneously recognises that they *are* as they are, and thus combines acceptance of them with an unvoiced protest. Such a conjunction, however much, as in the case of Pym's heroines, it may appear to do so, does not constitute passivity. By its very nature, irony assumes standards that transcend the present moment, and a shared knowledge of them which illuminates provisional assessments. Even at its most savage it aims at signification and containment, at a marriage of apparent incompatibilities. In consorting with the monolith on the monolith's own terms, it includes an element of hope.

On occasion that element can be so suppressed as to be invisible. This happens in an early and sustained piece of irony by Henry Fielding, *The Life of Mr Jonathan Wild the Great* (1743), a work of fiction inspired by the recent execution of a well-known thief. By taking at face value the world's reckoning of what constitutes a great man, and by applying those moral measurements to the life of his infamous 'hero', the author demonstrates the essential inhumanity, not to say the criminality, of the standards imposed upon themselves by the ambitious.

Initially the narrative proceeds upon the assumption that 'far the greatest Number are of the mixt Kind; neither totally good nor bad.'

> If we view one Side of [Wild's] Character only, he must be acknowledged equal, if not superior to most of the Heroes of Antiquity: But if we turn the Reverse, it must be confessed our Admiration will be a little abated, and his Character will savour rather of the Weakness of modern than the uniform Greatness of ancient heroes. (I:i)

This questions the contemporary reverence for classical tales of heroism and conquest. The weakness referred to is, of course, that occasional amelioration of Wild's character which is evidence of the novelist's, as distinct from the romancer's, sense of moral relativities. The inversion, however, is camouflaged by the ironic statement of what appears to be an impregnable moral position.

> We would not therefore be understood to affect giving the Reader a perfect or consummate Pattern of human Virtue; but rather by faithfully recording the little Imperfections which somewhat darkened the Lustre of his great Qualities, to teach the Lesson we have above mentioned, and induce our Reader with us to lament the Frailty of human Nature, and to convince him that no Mortal, after a thorough Scrutiny, can be a proper Object of our Adoration. (I:i)

Had Fielding been prepared to trust this close-knit ironic method, the book would have been the more effective. As it is, his overriding moral concerns lead him at times to cloud the issue by intruding comments which, while pointing towards an irony, are not themselves ironical.

> There is one Misfortune which attends all great Men and their Schemes, *viz.*, That in order to carry them into Execution, they are obliged in proposing their Purpose to their Tools, to discover themselves to be of that Disposition, in which certain little Writers have advised Mankind to place no Confidence.... (III:v)

The point is neatly made, but too explicitly for the full ironic impact that emerges elsewhere as a turn of phrase.

> She accompanied these Words with so tender an Accent, and so wanton a Leer, that *Fireblood*, who was no backward Youth, began to take her by the Hand, and proceeded so warmly, that, to imitate his Actions with the Rapidity of our Narration, he in a few Minutes ravished this fair Creature, or at least would have ravished her, if she had not, by a timely Compliance, prevented him. (III:vii)

One can understand how Jane Austen would have acquired a sense of verbal economy from Fielding.

Elsewhere we find him prepared to be satirical at his readers' expense by attacking popular notions with regard to what is funny – as when the prison officer demands a bribe before allowing Heartfree to say farewell to his wife.

> On this hint, *Friendly*, who was himself half dead, pulled five Guineas out of his Pocket; which the GREAT MAN took, and said, he would be so generous as to give him ten Minutes; on which one observed, that many a Gentleman had bought ten Minutes with a Woman dearer, and many other facetious Remarks were made, unnecessary to be here related. (IV:v)

A different writer would have ended the passage on the word 'dearer'; Fielding, however, will not play for laughs or afford the remark such a measure of importance, but handles it instead with an offhand dismissive scorn. Such moments reject the merely humorous in the name of comedy itself; and it is to this purpose that the author appears to return at the conclusion of his narrative. Having observed that 'a Man may go to Heaven with half the Pains which it costs him to purchase Hell' he proceeds to point out a continuing discrepancy.

> For while the Majority of Mankind, while Courts and Cities resound the Praises of the said GREAT MEN, there are still some in Cells and Cottages, who view their GREATNESS with a malignant Eye; and dare affirm, that these GREAT MEN, who are always the most pernicious, are generally the most wretched and truly contemptible of all the Works of the Creation. (IV:xvi)

The irony appears to be dissolved; but the retention of that word 'malignant' with its witty combination of political with normal meanings is there to give *Jonathan Wild* its final, triumphantly ironic twist. If the narrative declines any comedic dissolution of its own negative vision, Fielding could ensure that his readership would understand him.

Beginner's luck: *Mansfield Park*

Jane Austen is, of course, the supreme instance of a novelist who uses irony to communicate with a readership not so much spectatorial as complicit. Her strategy is both intimately personal (in the sense of an assumed intimacy of narrative confidentiality) and also confidently public: she voices an accepted code of conduct and manners, while being at the same time aware of the relativities imposed by human fallibility. Nowhere is this dual relationship with her readers more apparent than it is in what is not usually reckoned to be a comedy at all – *Mansfield Park* (1814). This is the most sombre of her novels; but although her notorious disclaimer 'let other pens dwell on guilt and misery' may seem to betray a heartless irresponsibility and a monolithic moral code, the words take on a different shading when read in conformity with the ironic spirit which pervades and controls the story as a whole. For the adoption of the nine-year-old Fanny Price by her uncle, the affluent and complacent Sir Thomas Bertram, provides a classic case of two-edged reward and retribution. An ambivalence runs through the family's treatment of her – practical generosity is offset by heartless condescension, neglect by increasing indulgence. Through Fanny's refusal to marry the unprincipled Henry Crawford, the Bertrams are both punished and rewarded by her being the unconscious instrument of their disgrace; at the same time she is left to be their consolation. To the extent that he learns to value her at her true worth, Sir Thomas atones for the shortcomings and contradictions involved in the upbringing of his own children.

There is irony in every aspect of the plot. At the very start, when Fanny's adoption is being canvassed, her aunt Norris (invariably wrong in her prognostications)[1] dismisses any romantic attachment between her and her male cousins as 'morally impossible'; later on this is precisely the definition applicable to Maria and Edmund Bertram's feelings for the sophisticated worldlings, Henry and Mary Crawford. And the underlying irony throughout the story is that Fanny herself does, until the very end, endorse the family's view of her. As she protests to Edmund, 'I can never be important to anyone.' Yet it is her behaviour which in fact determines the fates of all the principal people in the book.

Hidden from everyone save Fanny herself (and the reader) is the factor which governs the action – her love for her cousin Edmund. Henry Crawford 'knew not that he had a pre-engaged heart to attack'. It is this which enables Fanny to resist the blandishments of both Crawfords. That an attachment should be invisible is beyond their reckoning; it is the unseen rock on which all their projects founder. Even so, there is a further irony, one at the expense of any absolute moral closure, when the author remarks, in an unwonted aside to her readers,

> Would [Henry] have persevered, and uprightly, Fanny must have been his reward – and a reward very voluntarily bestowed – within a reasonable period from Edmund's marrying Mary. (III:xvii)

The subtlety with which the Crawfords are portrayed is the most remarkable feature of *Mansfield Park*. Both brother and sister, shallow and trivial at heart though they be, are almost transformed by genuine love; but frustration and delay bring out their essential venality. Mary in particular is an embodiment of the author's sense of irony. She is given much of the charm and delicate audacity of an Elizabeth Bennet, yet displays the moral vulgarity, though not the spitefulness, of a Lucy Steele: her confidences to Fanny concerning Edmund have much of the painfulness of those inflicted by Lucy upon Elinor Dashwood in *Sense and Sensibility*; but in Mary's case these are made in ignorance. Nor does she guess Fanny's secret, even when the latter almost gives herself away on being urged to consider the likelihood of Edmund's marrying someone else.

> "No," said Fanny stoutly, "I do not expect it at all."
> "Not at all!" – cried Miss Crawford with alacrity. "I wonder at that. But I dare say you know exactly – I always imagine you are – perhaps you do not think him likely to marry at all – or not at present."
> "No, I do not," said Fanny softly – hoping she did not err either in the belief or in the acknowledgement of it. (II:xii)

The use of those stage directions – 'stoutly', 'with alacrity', 'softly' – is exact and telling. Austen's mastery of dialogue is such that she can convey not only what is said but what is in mind while it is being said.

Mary's bantering mode of speech is itself laced with ironies, though delivered with a charm that smacks of self-consciousness, leading to a falsity of tone and resultant falsity of step that has its own comic reverberations.

"Certainly, my home at my uncle's brought me acquainted with a circle of admirals. Of *Rears*, and *Vices*, I saw enough. Now, do not be suspecting me of a pun, I entreat."

Edmund again felt grave, and only replied, "It is a noble profession." (I:vi)

The same recklessness, in both senses of the word, betrays her when writing to Fanny from London concerning Tom Bertram's illness, an illness that could leave Edmund the heir to Mansfield.

I confess I cannot help trembling. To have such a fine young man cut off in the flower of his days, is most melancholy. Poor Sir Thomas will feel it dreadfully. I really am quite agitated on the subject. Fanny, Fanny, I see you smile, and look cunning, but upon my honour, I never bribed a physician in my life. (III:xiv)

The sheer bad taste and impercipience of this is genuinely shocking. Austen's ironic stance encourages her characters to give themselves away.

If Mary Crawford oscillates between unconscious vulgarity and genuine goodness of heart (as when she champions Fanny against Mrs Norris's nagging), the author's own tone can vary between cruel and tender irony. An instance of the former may be found at the close of chapter xiii of Volume Three.

Three or four Prices might have been swept away, any or all, except Fanny and William, and Lady Bertram would have thought little about it; or perhaps might have caught from Mrs Norris's lips the cant of its being a very happy thing, and a great blessing to their poor dear sister Price to have them so well provided for.

The anger that informs this passage is only just held in check: it is an aspect of Austen's writing that permits the ascription to her, in D.W. Harding's well-known phrase, of 'regulated hatred'.[2]

Where Fanny is concerned, there may be a degree of authorial irony at the expense of the reader. Her nervousness, fragility, self-effacement and sense of personal obligation are not qualities that immediately endear themselves; while later novelists and psychologists have taught twentieth-century readers not to take them at face value. But the reader should not fall in with the assessments made by a Maria Bertram or a Mrs Norris. There is enough textual evidence to reveal a stubbornness, a determination, and a capacity for indignation in Fanny which rebuke the too-easy patronage bestowed on seemingly weak and ill-conditioned people. Her furious reaction to Edmund's letter concerning Mary Crawford is heartfelt, and comes as a relief to any reader impatient of her long-suffering behaviour – and as an irony this time, arguably, at the author's own expense.

The various ironies of plot and characterisation are, moreover, enclosed in an embracing sense of what to Jane Austen herself were the ironic workings of Divine Providence. *Mansfield Park* is a novel firmly based on the Christian ethic of its time and on an interpretation of the respective rôles of social conditioning and free will. One thread running through the novel is the concept of good luck. It is mentioned in the very first sentence and in the process renders the novel's ironies comedic.

> About thirty years ago, Miss Maria Ward of Huntingdon, with only seven thousand pounds, had the good luck to captivate Sir Thomas Bertram, of Mansfield Park, in the county of Northampton, and to be thereby raised to the rank of a baronet's lady, with all the comforts and consequences of an handsome house and large income.

The statement is bald, precise and apparently dispassionate. Yet that word 'luck' is subtly deflationary: 'good fortune' would have been a more formal, even a more proper, term to use in such a connection. There is a deliberate refusal of solemnity, a refusal that takes on a keener edge in the succeeding sentence.

> All Huntingdon exclaimed on the greatness of the match, and her uncle, the lawyer, himself, allowed her to be at least three thousand pounds short of any equitable claim to it.

The straight-faced presentation of what is thereby rendered an essentially commercial transaction, the amused participation implicit in 'all Huntingdon' and 'her uncle, the lawyer' (as opposed to 'a' lawyer) alike preserve that sedate balance, allowing for implied comment and readerly participation, which is a quintessential element in Jane Austen's style.

This faintly denigratory use of the word 'luck' is developed further when Henry Crawford appropriates it in his account of his happening upon Edmund's parish of Thornton Lacey, 'with my usual luck – for I never do wrong without gaining by it – I found myself in due time in the very place which I had a curiosity to see' (II:vii). The irony here has a dramatic resonance, since the comment is so drastically to be disproved. And 'luck' is used in a genuinely bitter manner in connection with Lady Bertram's finding in her eldest son's illness interesting subject-matter for a letter: it is her 'hour of good luck'. A further turn of the screw comes a few pages later when Fanny

> was more inclined to hope than fear for her cousin – except when she thought of Miss Crawford – but Miss Crawford gave her the idea of being the child of good luck, and to her selfishness and vanity it would be good luck to have Edmund the only son. (III:xiv)

And the final placing of the idea of luck occurs in connection with the Rushworths' divorce, which 'ended a marriage contracted under such circumstances as to make any better end, the effect of good luck, not to be reckoned on'. (III:xvii).

Luck, the product of chance, has nothing to do with fortune, which is the work of Providence and the domain of duty, loyalty and a care for others. The ironies of *Mansfield Park*, with their exposure of human self-deception, are all directed towards what is essentially a religious vision, one of a truth that can be apprehended behind the appearances and which reconciles the opposites which irony connects and displays in its efforts to control them. If not formally a comedy, this novel's story is none the less comedic in its import; but it presses the extremes of happiness and sorrow so close together that such a conjunction was one which a later age, lacking the hard-headed theological perspective of Jane Austen's own, would find it hard to visualise.

Old soldiers: *Barry Lyndon*

It is itself an irony that tales of guilt and misery should in due course become popular as vehicles for romantic stylistics that were by no means always mock-heroic. The cult of the so-called 'Newgate' novel, concerning the lives of highwaymen, murderers and forgers, reaches its apogee in the *Jack Sheppard* (1839) of Harrison Ainsworth and the sentimental falsifications of the ever-timely Bulwer-Lytton's *Eugene Aram* (1832). It was with a view to destabilising the repute of this potentially corrupt tradition that Thackeray wrote his own versions of the genre – *Catherine* (1840) and *The Luck of Barry Lyndon* (1844). The former is a straightforward case of systematic debunking, a 'telling it as it is'; but *Barry Lyndon* is a sustained piece of irony that is of especial interest as a characteristically ambiguous nineteenth-century version of what Fielding essays more confidently in *Jonathan Wild*. Not only is it one of Thackeray's darker novels, it is also one of his most technically ambitious in its attempt to be ironic through the medium of first-person narrative. In such a case the novelist cannot signal to the reader over his protagonist's head, since both of them are, as it were, the same height as the narrator himself.

Barry Lyndon is an adventurer. A brute, a braggart, and a self-deceiver, he is not an obvious hypocrite: his youthful circumstances arouse a certain sympathy, while his period of service in the Seven Years War accustoms him to cynicism and corruption. But as soon as worldly success is within his grasp his behaviour becomes the more alienating from his frank admission of its callous nature: this book is a study in specious honesty.

Thackeray's touch is typically varied. Initially the irony is straightforward, as in Barry's description of his mother: 'often has she talked to me and the neighbours regarding her own humility and piety, pointing them out in such a way that I would defy the most obstinate to disbelieve her' (Chapter i). The irony here is even more at Barry's expense than at his mother's, since he plainly cannot recognise the absurdity of his own statement. This sets the tone for much of what follows. A more subtle and generally applicable form of irony occurs when he comes to tell how

> My uncle, like a noble gentleman as he was, knew the pedigree of every considerable family in Europe. He said it was the only knowledge befitting a gentleman; and when we were not at cards, we would pass hours over Gwillim or D'Hozier, reading the genealogies, learning the blazons, and making ourselves acquainted with the relationships of our class. Alas! the noble science is going into disrepute now; so are cards, without which studies and pastimes I can hardly conceive how a man of honour can exist. (Chapter ix)

We are accordingly prepared for such pointed comments as these on members of the Irish Parliament.

> In the House of Commons there were some dozen of right pleasant fellows. I never heard in the English Parliament better speeches than from Flood, and Daly, of Galway. Dick Sheridan, though not a well-bred person, was as amusing and ingenious a table-

companion as ever I met; and though during Mr Edmund Burke's interminable speeches in the English House I used always to go to sleep, I yet have heard from well-informed parties that Mr Burke was a person of considerable abilities, and even reputed to be eloquent in his more favourable moments. (Chapter xiv)

This is marvellously deft: its very casualness of tone makes the reminiscence the more damning. And in the final third of the book the irony reaches its full flowering as Barry, confiding with complete self-assurance in his readers, exposes himself with every word he utters. How felicitous Thackeray's handling can be is evident in the following fallacious argument concerning the spoliation of Barry's wife's estates.

Let this be flung in the teeth of my detractors, who say I never could have so injured the Lyndon property had I not been making a private purse for myself; and who believe that, even in my present painful situation, I have hoards of gold laid by somewhere, and could come out as a Crœsus when I choose. I never raised a shilling upon Lady Lyndon's property but I spent it like a man of honour; besides incurring numberless personal obligations for money, which all went to the common stock. Independent of the Lyndon mortgages and incumbrances, I owe myself at least one hundred and twenty pounds, which I spent while in occupancy of my wife's estates so that I may justly say the property is indebted to me in the above-mentioned sum. (Chapter xviii)

Such reasoning is characteristic of the egoistic personality, which usually feels itself aggrieved; and it is consonant with Barry's later report on his relations with his step-son.

After a scene or a quarrel between us, it was generally to the rectory-house that the young rebel would fly for refuge and counsel; and I must own that the parson was a pretty just umpire between us in our disputes. Once he led the boy back to Hackton by the hand, and actually brought him into my presence, although he had vowed never to enter the doors again, and said, "He had brought his lordship to acknowledge his error, and to submit to any punishment I might think proper to inflict." (Chapter xviii)

All well and good: Barry Lyndon can respect an honest man. But at once

I caned him in the presence of two or three friends of mine, with whom I was sitting drinking at the time; and to do him justice, he bore a pretty severe punishment without wincing or crying in the least. This will show that I was not too severe in my treatment of the lad, as I had the authority of the clergyman himself for inflicting the correction which I thought proper.

By now the irony is in complete control; and yet Barry is allowed one genuine sentiment, his grief for the death of his own nine-year-old son.

I have got a lock of his soft brown hair hanging round my breast now: it will accompany me to the dishonoured pauper's grave; where soon, no doubt, Barry Lyndon's worn-out old bones will be laid. (Chapter xix)

Here is a cadence to which the author was to resort with ever greater frequency: the end of Barry Lyndon begins to sound like that of the Colonel in *The Newcomes* (1855). But nowhere does the soliloquy acknowledge that the child's death was the outcome of his father's carelessness; while the touch about the pauper's grave, and still more Barry's naming of himself, exhibit the self-pitying sanctimoniousness attendant on the softening of rascality. *Barry Lyndon* is a text which invites its readers to re-interpret it for nearly every page of its length. One of the few places where it does not comes in the account of the ageing Barry's visit to his former home in Ireland. This passage anticipates the plangency of the late Thackeray to a degree that is insidiously persuasive. There is a near-fatal softening of tone.

It is precisely this softness, occurring more than once in the course of the narrative, which dissolves the irony into open satire. The attempt to hold together two points of view (Barry's and the author's) breaks down, so that a distance opens up between the reader and the fictional characters. *Barry Lyndon* lacks the unrelenting bite of *Jonathan Wild*. The compensation, however, is a greater humanity and responsiveness to pain. But comedy? One senses the desire for its capacity to transform the bitterness the tale instils, but no belief that it exists. With the nineteenth century's exaltation of emotion, ironic comedy would need to turn to the intellect to find expression.

Whispering shades: *Henry James*

In ironic comedy collaboration between author and reader is the pervasive mode of discourse; and in Henry James's baffling late novel,

The Sacred Fount (1901) one even finds that procedure itself becoming the subject of the comedy. The whole thrust of the narrative in this most undervalued of his fictions is at the expense of the novelistic mind, the *hubris* of the imagination which results from excess of ingenuity, and from 'the joy of the intellectual mastery of things unamenable, that joy of determining, almost of creating results'. (Chapter xi) The anonymous narrator is accordingly arraigned at his story's close by the formidable Mrs Brissingham in a critique that might be applied to James himself by many of his would-be readers:

> people have such a notion of what you embroider on things that they're rather afraid to commit themselves or to lead you on: they're sometimes in [...] for more than they bargain for, than they quite know what to do with, or than they care to have on their hands. (Chapter xiv)

The excess of speculation in this instance arises from the neat irony that it is this very Mrs Brissingham who has set the ball of speculation rolling, since she appears to have regained her youth through marriage, at the cost of ageing her very much younger husband. The narrator develops this suggestion of vampirism to account for the apparent improvement in intelligence of a hitherto rather stupid fellow-guest: he starts to look for a woman lover/victim whose wits have been correspondingly destroyed. The idea is preposterous enough to alert any reader to the dangers of crediting the narrator with a monopoly of insight. The search for the supposititious lady takes place at one of those Great House weekend-gatherings which James evokes so well; and in this case the setting provides a further warning not to take the story at its progenitor's face value.

> This especial hour, at Newmarch, had always a splendour that asked little of interpretation, that even carried itself with an amiable arrogance, as indifferent to what the imagination could do for it. I think the imagination, in those halls of art and fortune, was almost inevitably accounted a poor matter; the whole place and its participants abounded so in pleasantness and pictures, in all the felicities, for every sense, taken for granted there by the very basis of life, that even the sense most finely poetic, aspiring to extract the moral, could scarce have helped feeling itself treated to something of the snub that affects – when it does affect – the uninvited reporter in whose face a door is closed. (Chapter ix)

One's implication in the obsessive deductions of the narrator provides the comic texture of the novel. The latter's final disabusing of his case – all his basic premises seemingly turn out to be incorrect or to be misinterpreted – amounts to a joke at the reader's expense as well. But not altogether so: the evidence even of the collapse of this human house of cards is there to be assessed and judged. The whole story amounts to a witty gloss on the allurements and pleasures of practising and deciphering the art of fiction; and what is true of the narrator and Mrs Brissingham at the end of the novel has been true of the author and his reader all along.

> It could *not* but be exciting to talk, as we talked, on the basis of those suppressed processes and unavowed references which made the meaning of the meeting so different from its form. We knew ourselves – what moved me, that is, was that she knew me – to mean, at every point, immensely more than I said or than she answered; just as she saw me, at the same points, measure the space by which her answers fell short. (Chapter xii)

This is at once a prescription for interpreting the novel and an exhibition of the attendant perils. The reader is thus free to endorse or not Mrs Brissingham's verdict on the would-be monolithic narrator at the novel's close: 'I think you're crazy'.

But *The Sacred Fount* is a middle-aged writer's *jeu d'esprit*. To see Jamesian comedy both at its wittiest and most deeply-felt one must turn to the early *The Europeans* (1878) and to the late and still more masterly *The Ambassadors* (1903), both of them novels which illustrate abundantly that whereas irony may be a function, even an outcome, of the comedic process, it is not to be equated with that process in itself.

The Europeans, for all its discreet charm, is a somewhat chilly piece of writing. The novelist is fully in command of his characters and of their several functions in this essentially static encounter between a puritanical New England family and their worldly-wise and faintly raffish continental relatives. This is a novel in which the monolith is not to be monolithically located: if the Wentworths' sobriety and caution, their obsession with duty and distrust of pleasure, are the objects of James's not unfriendly satire, it cannot be said that the Baroness Munster and her hedonistic brother serve as liberated foils to such a state. These Europeans are encumbered by their very sophistication; but whereas Felix's self-confidence and easy-going readiness to charm enable him to succeed in his quest for love-plus-a-modest-fortune, the more calculating Eugenia overplays her hand and, through excessive contriving and anxiety to please, arouses, fatally, the mistrust of a potential husband. Indeed, the novel's crowning irony consists in one's uncertainty as to whether it is calculation or self-restrictive conservative morality which the more effectively assists the monolithic self to attain its ends.

The Wentworths' moral seriousness is certainly one form of defensive armour against external claims.

> The sudden irruption into the well-ordered consciousness of the Wentworths of an element not allowed for in its scheme of usual obligations required a readjustment of that sense of responsibility which constituted its principal furniture. To consider any event, crudely and baldly, in the light of the pleasure it might bring them was an intellectual exercise with which [they] were almost wholly unacquainted, and which they scarcely supposed to be largely pursued in any section of human society. (Chapter iv)

To the Europeans this very simplicity is perplexing: as the Baroness complains, 'in this country [...] the relations of young people are so extraordinary that one is quite at sea'. (Chapter ix) Each civilised tradition is shocked by the license of the other. But to get the full point of this a collaborative readership is called for, and it is to just such a readership that James's fictive artistry makes its appeal. His urbanity of style, by assuming its existence, both creates it and depends on it.

James was to explore the differing nature of social conventions on the two sides of the Atlantic in a more heartfelt and decisive way in *The Ambassadors*. In this novel the journey is reversed: New England visits the Continent and with a purpose as ostensibly disinterested as the Baroness and her brother were implicitly self-seeking. The middle-aged Lambert Strether arrives in Paris as the emissary to the supposedly erring son of the formidable wealthy widow whom he is on his probation to marry. She is characterised with a good deal more direct comic vigour than are the Wentworth family. As Strether tells his expatriate friend Maria Gostrey, her nature is monolithic:

> she doesn't admit surprises [...] she's all, as I've called it, fine cold thought. She had, to her own mind, worked the whole thing out in advance, and worked it out for me as well as for herself. Whenever she has done that, you see, there's no room left; no

margin, as it were, for any alteration. She's filled as full, packed as tight, as she'll hold.... (XI:i)

By the time that Strether has come to this conclusion he has been exposed to the romance of Paris and to the sophisticated toleration of the European mind. As Maria Gostrey remarks, Mrs Newsome, in her attitude to her son's sojourn in Paris, 'imagined stupidly' (XI:i), and what she imagined was his seduction by the Parisienne of vulgar cliché. As James himself remarks in his Preface to the New York Edition of the novel,

> There was the dreadful little old tradition, one of the platitudes of the human comedy, that people's moral scheme *does* break down in Paris; that nothing is more frequently observed; that hundreds of thousands of more or less hypocritical or more or less cynical persons annually visit the place for the sake of the probable catastrophe, and that I came late in the day to work myself up about it.

But Chad Newsome's mistress is an elegant, enlightened older woman who deeply loves him; and Strether, converted by her own character and by the improvement he sees in the hitherto ungainly Chad, is compelled to renounce the monolithic morality of Mrs Newsome and her daughter Sarah, herself the target of some of James's most masterly comic writing – as when he portrays her 'dressed in a splendour of crimson which affected Strether as the sound of a fall through a skylight'. (XI:i) Sarah's relation to Strether and to her mother is characterised with what, for her creator, is an unwonted idiomatic vigour.

> She was in no position not to appear to expect that Chad should treat her handsomely; yet she struck [Strether] as privately stiffening a little each time she missed the chance of making the great *nuance*. The great *nuance* was in brief that of course her brother must treat her handsomely – she should like to see him not; but that his treating her handsomely, none the less, wasn't all in all – treating her handsomely buttered no parsnips; and that in fine there were moments when she felt the fixed eyes of their admirable absent mother fairly screw into the flat of her back. (X:i)

The Ambassadors, however, would not be the profoundly satisfying novel it is were it simply a witty refutation of the limited imagination of the materialistic mind. At its heart is Strether's lamentation for the life he never lived and the glow of his appreciative revelling in a discriminatory nostalgia. His innocence and discretion delight the worldly-wise Parisians, and the no less detached expatriates; but the novel touches tragedy when at the end, in seeking to realise the rural paradise he has glimpsed in art, he stumbles upon the true nature of the 'virtuous attachment' between Chad and his mistress. It is an episode recounted with supreme Jamesian subtlety and grace; and it is not the least of the book's triumphs that this final disillusionment remains incorporate in Strether's newly-found determination to live henceforth from his own imaginative resources. The comedic process, however, even in this resolution, retains a touch of ironic bitterness. The real victim of this invasion of the old world by the new is Maria Gostrey, who has to lose Strether in his determination to go back to America and to live his new life on the old ground. With the insight of friendship she perceives that his exalted self-realisation is itself potentially a monolith. To her own question 'But why should you be so dreadfully right?' she adds the gloss, 'It isn't so much your *being* "right" – it's your horribly sharp eye for what makes you so'. (XII:v) The author here, one feels, is acknowledging the potential dangers of even his own powers of exquisite discrimination.

The Ambassadors fairly gleams with the polish of an attuned, attentive sensitivity of response to the graciousness, as James sees it, of the European style. But if the comedy is barely sustained in the resolution of Strether's story, it lapses altogether in the prospective one of the relations between Chad and Marie de Vionnet. Her love for him is clearly doomed, as one sees in his closing protestation of his loyalty.

> "Of course I really never forget, night or day, what I owe her. I owe her everything. I give you my word of honour," he frankly rang out, "that I'm not a bit tired of her." Strether at this only gave him a stare: the way youth could express itself was again and again a wonder. He meant no harm, though he might after all be capable of much; yet he spoke of being 'tired' of her almost as he might have spoken of being tired of roast mutton for dinner. (XII:iv)

Nowhere in James's work is the contradictory nature of materialistic emotionalism more drastically exposed. The irony of that final insight contains the seeds of a well-nigh unbearable lucidity.

James's explorations into personal behaviour and his ironic sense of the human inability to communicate in an objective manner is summed up in his assessment of Strether's dilemma in corresponding with his alarming wife-to-be.

> No one could explain better when needful, nor put more conscience into an account or a report; which burden of conscience is perhaps exactly the reason why his heart always sank when the clouds of explanation gathered. His highest ingenuity was in keeping the sky of life clear of them. Whether or no he had a grand idea of the lucid, he held that nothing ever was in fact – for any one else – explained. One went through the vain motions, but it was mostly a waste of life. A personal relation was a relation only so long as people either perfectly understood or, better still, didn't care if they didn't. (III:ii)

Comedy is one way of acknowledging that particular truth, and one which provides a methodology for its constructive implementation. And irony, the marriage of acceptance with rejection, is at its root.

Irony depends for its force on a readership informed and warily intelligent enough to respond to its ambiguities. For confirmation of this one need go no further than the notorious fourth book of *Gulliver's Travels* (1726), a signal instance of fictionality being the clue to a fiction's true signification. If taken simply as a piece of satire, the disillusionment with human nature voiced in the voyage to the kingdom of the supremely rational horses, the Houyhnhnms, is misleading. The voyage needs to be read in the context of Swift's composition as a whole, which addresses itself to a readership for whom the Augustan ideals of rationality were in tension with the insistence upon human fallibility to which Swift, as an Anglican divine, subscribed.

In the preceding voyage to Laputa we find Gulliver recording how 'The natural Love of Life gave me some inward Motions of Joy', and it is precisely this feeling which the Houyhnhnms' view of life does not include, and therefore imperils. Gulliver, on his return to England, is virtually dehumanised; he is unable to bear the company of his wife and children, preferring that of his horses, and is thus de-Christianised as well. But the final joke is one at his expense. The penultimate paragraph commences with a declaration that he desires to accept his fellow men; but there is one obstacle.

> My Reconcilement to the *Yahoo*-kind in general might not be so difficult, if they would be content with those Vices and Follies only which Nature hath entitled them to. [...] But when I behold a Lump of Deformity, and Diseases both in Body and Mind, smitten with *Pride*, it immediately breaks all the Measures of my Patience; neither shall I be ever able to comprehend how such an Animal and such a Vice could tally together.

Satire and irony coruscate together along the surface of the prose; but it is an extreme of irony that controls the closing sentence.

> I dwell the longer upon this Subject from the Desire I have to make the Society of an *English Yahoo* by any means not insupportable; and therefore I here entreat those who have any Tincture of this absurd Vice, that they will not presume to appear in my Sight.

The double negative is delicious: this pharisaical smugness may be read as Swift's last grim joke at the expense of his own misanthropy. It brings us back full circle to the letter from the narrator to his publisher with which *Gulliver's Travels* opens, and in which he complains that it has not resulted in any such reformations as 'I firmly counted upon by your Encouragement; as indeed they were plainly deducible from the Precepts delivered in my Book.' The pretence of synchronicity between appearance and reality is as plain at the beginning of *Gulliver's Travels* as it is at its conclusion.

It takes an informed readership to appreciate the inflexibility with which Swift's ironic standpoint is maintained. Not many writers have achieved a similar poise – Jane Austen, certainly, and Henry James. But even Fielding wobbles now and again, and Thackeray more often still: amelioration will keep breaking in. And there is even less poise to be found in the more philosophically and morally uncertain twentieth-century novelists – Lawrence has it on occasion, as do Elizabeth Bowen and Barbara Pym, all three the products of greater certainties than later writers could maintain; while Beckett acquires his poise through a savage re-working of ironic conjunctions in burlesque. But this sustained irony contains the seeds of tragedy. There is anger implicit in it, an element of repressed protest, as much in the suavities of James and Austen as in the self-punishing unease of Thackeray and the contempt for the plausibility of evil displayed by Fielding. One smiles at the tricks these authors play upon us, but one does not laugh.

6
Satirical Comedy: the Disjunction of Opposites

> If there is a paradise there are many natures who will always worry whether they ought not to be somewhere else.
>
> Henry Green, *Pack My Bag*

> Mrs Linnet had become a reader of religious books since Mr Tryan's advent, and as she was in the habit of confining her perusal to the purely secular portions, which bore a very small proportion to the whole, she could make rapid progress through a large number of volumes. On taking up the biography of a celebrated preacher, she immediately turned to the end to see what disease he died of; and if his legs swelled, as her own occasionally did, she felt a stronger interest in ascertaining any earlier facts in the history of the dropsical divine [...]

Probably everyone follows this method with regard to some branch of reading or another. But this is George Eliot writing, a mastersatirist, and imperceptibly our attention is drawn from Mrs Linnet to the religious verbosity which she so deftly side-stepped.

> She then glanced over the letters and diary, and wherever there was a predominance of Zion, the River of Life, and notes of exclamation, she turned over to the next page; but any passage in which she saw such promising nouns as 'small-pox', 'pony', or 'boots and shoes', at once arrested her.[1]

In *Scenes of Clerical Life* (1858) Eliot set out to frustrate admirers of 'society' fiction and all the snobbery that accompanied it by providing instead a faithful portrait of provincial life as she herself had known it. She describes simple people, not in order to laugh at them but to present them as they are, even when they are 'men of complexions more or less muddy, whose conversation is more or less bald and disjointed' and who would normally be despised and rejected by readers who prefer 'the ideal in fiction; to whom tragedy means ermine tippets, adultery, and murder; and comedy, the adventures of some personage who is quite a "character".'[2] Eliot is returning to an earlier eighteenth-century tradition in seeking to pursue these aims. She was concerned to off-set a literary fashion that was catering for limited imaginations, such as a supposititious 'Mrs Farthingale', who in her own way is as restricted in her outlook as is Mrs Linnet.

But Mrs Linnet is in the right of it. Her own choice of reading may be an implicit satire on people of her kind; yet the laugh is partly on their side. In her small way she is drawn, as was her creator, to the same kind of practical reality that Fielding was seeking to portray in *Tom Jones*. In the introductory chapter to Book XV he makes short work of the kind of book that Mrs Linnet's circle liked to read.

> There are a set of religious, or rather moral writers, who teach that virtue is the certain road to happiness, and vice to misery, in this world. A very wholesome and comfortable doctrine, and to which we have but one objection, namely, that it is not true.

For Fielding, as for George Eliot, a novel was worth nothing unless it gave an accurate account of how human life was actually experienced.

Questions of perspective: *Tom Jones*

Although a later age may see in the concept of a comic epic something ponderous (the noun discrediting its qualifying epithet), *The History of Tom Jones: a Foundling* (1749) is self-assured without being self-inflationary, its text articulate enough to acknowledge its own artifice while insisting on its protagonist's normality. It refutes the monolithic claims of prescriptive rationality to be the principle that governs human behaviour, and satirises the compulsion to be in the right.

Tom Jones may thus be read as a playful yet precise interpretation of the phrase, 'Just So'. Through comic exposure it questions any notion that human character and circumstances can be precisely known, or governed, by the discerning mind alone. It also questions the notion that the *status quo* must of necessity be just. The very ascription of the hero's name makes this apparent: 'a Foundling'. The infant Tom, discovered so embarrassingly in Allworthy's bachelor sheets, is a challenge to the order established on the latter's potentially idyllic Somerset estate. But whereas the housekeeper, innately resistant to change, finds the bastard smelly, Allworthy accepts the changeling and shelters him with love. It is Tom, not the legally born Blifil junior, who is the true heir of his heart and home; and so at the tale's conclusion he turns out to be. Yet Tom remains a bastard: the fact that he is Allworthy's nephew is not in itself a legitimising of his status. In *Tom Jones* the monolithic nature of the social hierarchy is compromised and challenged in a manner that would not have been the case had its hero turned out not to be a bastard after all.

The novel also works against the stereotyping of individual human beings: 'we do not pretend to introduce any infallible characters into this history; where we hope nothing will be found which hath never yet been seen in human nature'. (III:v) Even Allworthy's own monolithic all-worthiness leaves him open to delusion where the Blifils are concerned; Thwackum, sadistic and self-righteous, is allowed to be a conscientious scholar; Lady Bellaston, reluctant to grow old, is pathetically the prey of her emotions; Sophia, the all-beautiful, virtuous, tender-hearted object of Tom's romantic quest, is subjected to a couple of ignominious tumbles from her horse. Even the solemn intrusion of the Man of the Hill is compromised by the local people regarding him as a curiosity; Molly Seagrim's battle with the village women is at once elevated and belittled by the mock-heroic language with which it is described; Tom's honourable purposes are regularly undone by the ham-fisted indiscretions of his Sancho Panza, Partridge. There is scarcely a person in the book who is not at one time or another presented in a qualifying light, ranging from the blatant exposure of Square in Molly's attic bedroom to the insidious corruption of Honour Blackmore once she has entered Lady Bellaston's employ. (Significantly it is Honour, hitherto one of the most engaging people in the story, who alone goes unnoticed at the end.)

The dexterity of the characterisation depends in part on what is left unsaid: Fielding exhibits his people in action rather than through extended analysis or exposition. The worthy Mrs Miller's excessive garrulity suggests an insensitiveness that reveals itself at the novel's end in opposing Allworthy's concern for Blifil; Mrs Fitzpatrick's shady morals are exhibited not only in her wary account of her misfortunes but in her ready acceptance of the help of the notorious Irish peer, who was

> as bitter an enemy to the savage authority too often exercised by husbands and fathers, over the young and lovely of the other sex, as ever knight-errant was to the barbarous power of enchanters; nay, to say truth, I have often suspected that those very encounters with which romance everywhere abounds, were in reality no other than the husbands of those days; and matrimony itself was perhaps the enchanted castle in which the nymphs were said to be confined. (XI:viii)

The reader is invited to participate in the author's exposition, since a shared moral standard is assumed, reference to which makes satire possible. It can work at the personal level; indeed,

> I hope my friends will pardon me, when I declare, I know none of them without a fault; and I should be sorry if I could imagine, I had any friend who could not see mine. Forgiveness, of this kind, we give and demand in turn. It is an exercise of friendship, and perhaps none of the least pleasant. (II:vii)

But this moral standard is not to be equated with any particular class or social group: the various innkeepers, landladies, hostlers and post-boys who cross Tom's path are all allowed their individuality and are never laughed at condescendingly. No doubt Fielding, the magistrate, had seen too many people of all types and conditions in the dock for that. And all the adventures on the road which form the middle third of the action take place against the potential destabilisation of society through the advance of the Jacobite rebels of the 'forty-five on London.

This is no accidental part of the design. The comic epic is also a satire on notions of historical momentousness. Indeed, it does not even take itself all that seriously: the essays which introduce each book serve to distance the reader from the action, to invite participation by response and dialogue, rather than through imaginative absorption. Perfectly shaped and rendered though it is, *Tom Jones* refuses to regard itself as monolithic. Its appeal is to the common good sense and compassionate humanity of its readers.

But it remains in its pervading character a satire, the main force of which is directed against the corrosiveness of cant, cant being the prevailing vice of a society given over to an idolisation of rationality and order. The villainous younger Blifil, who would be aptly described in our own contemporary parlance as a creep, is an instance of excessive prudence and self-management; while quite early on in the story his father's precept that charity is a theoretical rather than a practical matter shows us from whom his way of life derives.

> Those [...] came nearer to the Scripture meaning, who understood by it candour, or the forming of a benevolent opinion of our brethren, and passing a favourable judgement on their actions; a virtue much higher, and more extensive in its nature, than a pitiful distribution of alms, which, though we would never so much prejudice, or even ruin our families, could never reach many; whereas charity, in the other and truer sense, might be extended to all mankind. (II:v)

As against such a view, Tom's character is one of *ad hominem* kindliness exerted through an *ad hoc* methodology. He never takes himself too seriously, so that when he discovers Square behind Molly's curtain he bursts out laughing and offers him his hand – a perfect instance of what may be designated comic alchemy. And in his debate with the misanthropic Man of the Hill he voices a moral relativity that is genuinely affirmative.

> Indeed you here fall into an error, which, in my little experience, I have observed to be a very common one, by taking the character of mankind from the worst and basest among them; whereas indeed, as an excellent writer observes, nothing should be esteemed as characteristical of a species, but what is found among the best and most perfect individuals of that species.

If sounding a little pompous here, he proceeds to turn the tables neatly.

> This error, I believe, is generally committed by those who, from want of proper caution in the choice of their friends and acquaintance, have suffered injuries from bad and worthless men; two or three instances of which are very unjustly charged on all human nature. (VIII:xv)

Tom himself, of course, is guilty of gross indiscretion and irresponsibility, to offset his warmth of heart: indeed, the action of the novel derives from an interplay between the imprudence of Jones and the remedial activity of a benevolent overriding Providence. Irony is thus sustained throughout the book, recurring in a different key when Tom is temporarily saved from the blandishments of Mrs Waters through his still greater appreciation of his dinner. This comic reductiveness satirises many of the clichés of romance literature. A nice instance occurs when Squire Western and Parson Supple are pursuing the runaway Sophia, and the former is lamenting his misfortune. The parson's reassurances are couched in lofty clericalese.

> "Sorrow not, sir," says he, "like those without hope. Howbeit we have not yet been able to overtake young madam, we may account it some good fortune, that we have hitherto traced her course aright. Peradventure she will soon be fatigued with her journey, and will tarry in some inn, in order to renovate her corporeal functions; and in that case, in all moral certainty, you will very briefly be *compos voti.*"
>
> "Pogh! d–n the slut!" answered the squire, "I am lamenting the loss of so fine a morning for hunting. It is confounded hard to lose one of the best scenting days, in all appearance, which hath been this season, and especially after so long a frost." (XII:ii)

Again and again Fielding mocks the pretensions of affectedly conformist diction and the self-indulgent attitudes of sentimentalists. Rather than contrasting the rich with the poor, he contrasts the natural with the artificial. Squire Western, for all his outrageously extravagant behaviour, is very much a natural man; his creator's real disdain is reserved for those who do not possess enough vitality to be worth satirising.

> But to let my reader into a secret, this knowledge of upper life, though very necessary for the preventing mistakes, is no very great resource to a writer whose province is comedy, or that kind of novels, which, like this I am writing, is of the comic class. (XIV:1)

For Fielding, this is a serious indictment; the vitalising effect of the comedic process springs from its ability not merely to laugh at life but to laugh with it. One sees this happening with superb audacity when Tom for a brief while is under the impression that he has committed the sin of Oedipus and had carnal knowledge of his mother. But Mrs Waters makes a charmingly inadequate Jocasta. Her letter to Jones in prison, following the apparent discovery, is a profound instance of

Satirical Comedy: the Disjunction of Opposites 109

comedy in action, since both Tom and Partridge are under the impression that she means by it the same enormity as they do.

> Since I left you, I have seen a gentleman, from whom I have learnt something concerning you which greatly surprizes and affects me: but as I have not at present leisure to communicate a matter of such high importance, you must suspend your curiosity 'till our next meeting, which shall be the first moment I am able to see you. O Jones, little did I think, when I past that happy day at Upton, the reflection upon which is like to embitter all my future life, who it was to whom I owed such perfect happiness. Believe me to be ever sincerely your unfortunate
> J. Waters
> P.S. — I would have you comfort yourself as much as possible, for Mr Fitzpatrick is in no manner of danger; so that whatever other grievous crimes you may have to repent of, the guilt of blood is not among the number. (XVIII:ii)

The impertinence of this (in the proper sense of the word) is breathtaking. And the joke is as much at the reader's expense as it is at that of Jones and Partridge, for he is as much in the dark as they are concerning what she is about to disclose.

Hazlitt quotes Fielding's comparison of his work with that of official historians and his declaration that 'in their productions nothing is true but the names and dates, whereas in his every thing is true but the names and dates'.[3] But though naturalistically conceived, Fielding's work is presented with open artifice, its truth inhering not in itself but pointing beyond itself, so that it is 'true to life' in the sense of being 'true to experience'. And its moral truth is brought home through the use of satire and the exploding of fallacies and literalistic equations. Tom Jones's humanity is an average humanity, not an heroic ideal. Unlike Richardson's monolithic model of all the virtues, the hero of *Sir Charles Grandison* (1754), he exemplifies the necessary relativity of all standards of human behaviour.

None the less, in creating him, Fielding does posit an absolute, though an absolute which is, as absolutes must necessarily be, transcendent and inaccessible. Tom's goodness of heart may point towards it, but does not embody it: Fielding was no sentimentalist. The noble figure of Grandison, on the other hand, is an idol, product of the supposition that the absolute is to be apprehended in a given particular form. The same might be said of the virtuous heroine of

Fielding's *Amelia* (1752); but in the person of her husband, the shiftless Captain Booth, the author is true to his own belief in the relativity of all human standards and achievements. Every comic writer delights in the fact that the world is an untidy place.

The whirligigs of time: *Vanity Fair*

The comic epic of *Tom Jones* suggests that all absolute human evaluations, being human, are necessarily relative and partial. Such moral clarity would not come so readily in the Victorian age: the inroads of sentimental cant are detectable even in so essentially an eighteenth-century inspiration as that of Thackeray. Personal factors, it is true, may account for the injection of mawkishness which taints all but his finest work; but as a satirist he was having to contend also with the effects of individualistic Evangelical piety, of the post-Romantic cult of personal feeling, and of the idolisation of domestic virtues, all of which were to muffle outspokenness and sincerity in the writings of contemporary novelists.(The three unmarried Brontë sisters, however, are notable exceptions to this rule.) Such a confusion of personal sentiment with moral values was inimical to the comedic process, and nowhere is this more apparent than in Thackeray's acknowledged masterpiece, *Vanity Fair* (1848).

This extraordinary novel combines an unrelenting sense of passing time with a close attention to domestic and naturalistic detail: it is both general and specific in its methodology and application. The elegantly-contrived account of the complementary fortunes of its two protagonists gives it a shapeliness and a sense of narrative control; yet its sub-title, 'a Novel without a Hero', rebuts any intention of traditional dramatic resolution, and indeed suggests (as by the end is so obviously the case) that this is a novel without a heroine also. Instead it presents a disenchanted portrayal not merely of human society, and of the corrupting effects of commerce and social mobility upon its members, but also of the human condition itself. To this extent *Vanity Fair* is an epical satire comparable with *Tom Jones*; but it cannot, as *Tom Jones* can, be considered an exemplar of the remedial comedic process. The tone of the novel lacks Fielding's good-humoured detachment. *Vanity Fair* may be a satire: it is not a comedy.

There is, of course, much excellent comic business in the course of its progress towards its sober, all-too-equalising conclusion – the portrait of that shamelessly irresponsible old rake, Pitt Crawley; that of the portly, self-deluding East Indian administrator, Jos Sedley; the disastrous visit of

Sir Pitt's undergraduate grandson to his crusty spinster aunt. But the comedy is riddled with pain. Sir Pitt's effect upon his family and his property is totally destructive; Jos's self-absorption almost brings disaster on the Sedleys; Miss Crawley's wealth gives her nothing but dissatisfaction and makes her the prey of all who come in contact with her. Nor are the novel's situational ironies cause for merriment or intellectual delight: Becky Sharp's manœuvrings and exploitation of other people's foibles bring her merely a feeling of futility. And if Amelia Sedley, the paragon of simplicity of heart and unworldly innocence, eventually attains domestic peace, it is as a parasite upon a faithful lover who has become disillusioned with his image of her. Becky's lot as a respectable do-gooder in Cheltenham is scarcely less enviable than hers.

Vanity Fair is, indeed, potentially a bitter, disagreeable book. But the author's controlling commentaries, which ring the changes on incisive satire, genial irony, and blunt reportage (as in the celebrated account of George Osborne's death at Waterloo), are all absorbed into the cadences of as relaxed and relaxing a prose style as any English novelist provides. The geniality, though tart, is also whimsical, a whimsy which, where Amelia is concerned, all but compromises the dissection of sincerity and sentiment that is Thackeray's concern. For although William Dobbin's disenchantment with his hard-won prize underlines the warning against all premature absolute assessments, none the less the repeated appeals to the charm of Amelia's simplicity and weakness, with the constant resort to that demeaning ascription 'little', appear to endorse rather than to scrutinise the confused moral evaluation that blurs the edges of the author's vision. That he exhibits a liking for Becky Sharp enhances the book's satirical status; that he wavers in his portrayal of Amelia does not.

Thackeray refers to *Vanity Fair* as 'this Comic History'. (Chapter l) Comic it certainly is, through the standard satirical method of contrasting pretensions with actuality. Its focus is on money, on the fluctuations of the market, on the competitiveness of society, on snobbery and knowingness. It might be specifically describing the late twentieth-century world, were it not describing commercialised society as it always has been. But there is an ambiguity about Thackeray's indictment. Early on he remarks of Becky that she

> was not [...] in the least kind or placable. All the world used her ill, said this young misanthropist, and we may be pretty certain that persons whom all the world treats ill deserve entirely the treatment they get. (Chapter ii)

Such an apparent endorsement of worldly standards is confusing; but the gullible unworldly people in the story – Amelia, Lady Jane, the hapless old-maid companion, Briggs – are not ridiculed. They are victims of what the deplorable George Osborne calls 'a ready money society'. (Chapter xx) one in which his unmarried sister can be hailed as a possible 'fifty thousand pounder' when her brother alienates their purse-proud father by his marriage to the penniless Amelia. In *Vanity Fair* people are marketable commodities, and the author can be ruthless as to the result of subscribing to the standards of such a self-seeking world. Concerning Sir Pitt's senescent end he comments,

> this was all that was left after more than seventy years of cunning and struggling and drinking and scheming, and sin and selfishness – a whimpering old idiot put in and out of bed and cleaned and fed like a baby. (Chapter xl)

Such clear-sightedness is reinforced by the author's insistence on 'the awful kitchen inquisition which sits in judgement in every house, and knows everything'. (Chapter xliv) It is the servants and the attorneys' clerks who really understand what is going on. The powerful are supported by an army which can see through them and which is not easily to be disabused. Comic discrepancy lies at the heart of capitalist society itself.

But the emotional tone of *Vanity Fair* consorts uneasily with such clarity of outlook. The author may, early on, take care to dissociate himself from his characters:

> Otherwise you might fancy it was I who was sneering at the practice of devotion, which Miss Sharp finds so ridiculous; that it was I who laughed good-humouredly at the reeling old Silenus of a baronet – whereas the laughter comes from one who has no reverence except for prosperity, and no eye for anything beyond success. Such people there are living and flourishing in the world – Faithless, Hopeless, Charityless; let us have at them, dear friends, with might and main. Some there are, and very successful too, mere quacks and fools: and it was to combat and expose such as these, no doubt, that Laughter was made. (Chapter viii)

He may also recognise that this society is not so much moral as squeamish. But he is too involved in it, too soft-hearted maybe, for his satire to be bracing. It is too confiding, too gentle (not to say genteel) in tone to offer a vision of renewal or of any ultimate belief in a sovereign power of virtue by which the ways of the world are judged.

> O brother wearers of motley! are there not moments when one grows sick of grinning and tumbling, and the jingling of cap and bells? This, dear friends and companions, is my amiable object – to walk with you through the Fair, to examine the shops and the shows there; and that we should all come home after the flare, and the noise, and the gaiety, and be perfectly miserable in private. (Chapter xix)

Such a statement is a good instance of comic method, rounding on itself and declining even a whimsical portentousness; but at the same time it constitutes a flat denial of that confident upending of conventional priorities which marks the comedic process. *Vanity Fair* is arguably the last of the great eighteenth-century social panoramas, one that is already overtaken by the mid-Victorian forces of social propriety, sentimentalist introversion, and their resultant cant and humbug.

Godliness and good behaviour: *The Way of All Flesh*

The expansion and opening-up of social groupings which took place in the Victorian age was matched by a corresponding enlargement of expectation as to what a novel might encompass. A survey, such as *Vanity Fair* presents, is more socially analytic than is that found in *Tom Jones*, and is developed in personal and economic terms in Dickens's *Bleak House* (1851), Eliot's *Daniel Deronda* (1874) and Trollope's *The Way We Live Now* (1875). The procedure called for a different kind of observation and narratorial structuring than was appropriate to the relatively confined circumstances of Jane Austen's fictive world. Perhaps because of this, portraits of small-town provincial life like Elizabeth Gaskell's *Cranford* (1853) and Margaret Oliphant's *Chronicles of Carlingford* (1863–76), while superficially resembling Austen's art, the first in its celebration of community life, the second in their asperity, exhibit a less subtle conflation of disparate comic modes.

In *Cranford* the humour, delicate and charitable, is suffused with an obvious affection that indulges its object rather than analysing or enhancing it. The Cranford ladies seem to be enshrined in amber (admittedly an amber that glows with abundant warmth) and are held in the light of an appreciative smile rather than transfigured in any vitalising comedic process. The humour, engaging as it is, is largely contemplative and static, its subject a bygone way of life – this is a sensibility that goes back to Addison's essays in *The Spectator*. But Charlotte Brontë's reaction to the author was perceptive. Writing on May 22nd 1852 she commented, 'Satirical you are – however; I believe a little more so than you think.'

For the characters in *Cranford* do react, however mildly, against the monoliths of prescriptive propriety and inherited familial tradition; and the author's satire is directed as much towards what conditions them as towards their willingness to conform. A good instance is her treatment of the social superiority of the inert and stupid Honourable Mrs Jamieson, with her pug-dog and tremendous butler, of whom the ladies are far more in awe than they are of his employer.

> I saw Mrs Jamieson eating seed cake, slowly and considerately, as she did everything; and I was rather surprised, for I knew she had told us, on the occasion of her last party, that she never had it in her house, it reminded her so much of scented soap. She always gave us Savoy biscuits. However, Mrs Jamieson was kindly indulgent to Miss Barker's want of knowledge of the customs of high life; and to spare her feelings ate three large pieces of seed cake, with a placid, ruminative expression of countenance, not unlike a cow's.
>
> (Chapter vii)

The touch of irony over those 'Savoy biscuits' and that sparing of the ex-milliner's feelings is very much Gaskell's own, although speaking through the voice of her young narrator, Mary Smith – whose very name suggests a kind of 'Everywoman' observer, one who both participates in and identifies with the Cranford world, and yet who at the same time perceives its limitation and absurdities. As Mary herself remarks (chapter xvi), 'I had vibrated all my life between Drumble and Cranford' – Drumble being Manchester and the great world outside.

Gaskell's treatment of the same society in *Wives and Daughters* (1865) is more dispassionately rigorous, the shallow, vain and sentimental Mrs Gibson being the kind of character to attract the satirical gaze of a Jane Austen or George Eliot. In Gaskell's case one's laughter is participatory rather than detached; though the shrewd account of the seduction of the impatient Dr Gibson by this softly purring widow (who embodies everything that irritates him and which he most despises) amounts to an instance of ironic wit in its most morally perceptive form. Gaskell's humour is not so cosy as at first sight it might appear. But her satire in these domestic stories is at the expense of character rather than at that of the religious and social outlook that helps to determine character. For such analysis one turns to George Eliot and, when combined with a comedic viewpoint, Samuel Butler.

Where Eliot is concerned, a character such as Mrs Gibson would have been subjected both to a keener moral analysis and to an account of her social conditioning: she would not have been enjoyed in the purely humorous manner that Gaskell's demurely malicious strategy encourages. And even in the ironical account of the Dodson family in *The Mill on the Floss* (1861), their nature and outlook are clearly meant to serve as a critically relevant and representative instance of the social and moral forces that produced them:

> there was in this family a peculiar tradition as to what was the right thing in household management and social demeanour, and the only bitter circumstance attending this superiority was a painful inability to approve the condiments or the conduct of families ungoverned by the Dodson tradition. A female Dodson, when in "strange houses", always ate dry bread with her tea, and declined any sort of preserves, having no confidence in the butter, and thinking that the preserves had probably begun to ferment from want of due sugar and boiling. There were some Dodsons less like the family than others – that was admitted; but in so far as they were "kin", they were of necessity better than those who were "no kin". And it is remarkable that while no individual Dodson was satisfied with any other individual Dodson, each was satisfied, not only with him or her self, but with the Dodsons collectively. (I:vi)

Against this background the formally 'humorous' characters of the gruff Aunt Glegg and the twittering Aunt Pullett become less two-dimensional, less monolithic.

None the less, Eliot's satire remains concerned mainly with morals and manners in the traditional humorous sense; it is controlled by the need for charity and compassion. Its intellectual quality, however, helped to educate the public that was in due course to respond to *The Way of All Flesh* (1903). Samuel Butler's definitive moral and social critique of nineteenth-century commercialised piety was indeed a landmark: 'For the first time in the Victorian age a comic work is partially concerned with underlying causes as well as systematic abuses.'[4] Begun in 1873, it drew extensively upon the author's own experience, displaying a clean-cut savagery and mordant sarcasm which were to influence novelists as diverse as Elizabeth, E.M. Forster, Ivy Compton-Burnett, Aldous Huxley, Evelyn Waugh and Sylvia Townsend Warner. It is one of those seminal works whose effect is more on literary expression than on literary form.

Its autobiographical nature determines both its perspective and its structure. The narrative portrays four generations of the Pontifex family, moving from eighteenth-century rationality through Evangelical piety into the rebellious materialism of Butler's own day. The names of the three principal Pontifexes – George, Theobald, Ernest – carry their own resonances. The book is, among other things, an evolutionary enquiry into the origins of its own point of view; and its attempt at detachment is furthered through the use of a narrator. This narrator (whose access to family papers offers yet another instance of novelistic attempts at plausibility) makes every effort to be fair to the people whose history he describes, and certainly the young Ernest Pontifex, the book's 'hero', is in no way indulged by this fictional godfather.

The Way of All Flesh attacks the monolith's moral concomitant – humbug, that businesslike approach to spiritual matters exemplified here in the advertisement for a religious book entitled *The Pious Country Parishioner*, which provides 'directions how a Christian may manage every day in the course of his whole life with safety and success'. (Chapter v) It is that 'success' which is the give-away. The cool suavity of Butler's prose serves him well as he analyses the inextricability of the connection between the urge to power and a reluctance to admit to it. His advice to parents displays him at his most incisive.

> Tell your children that they are very naughty – much naughtier than most children; point to the young people of some acquaintances as models of perfection, and impress your own children with a deep sense of their own inferiority. You carry so many more guns than they do that they cannot fight you. This is called moral influence and it will enable you to bounce them as much as you please; they think you know, and they will not have yet caught you lying often enough to suspect that you are not the unworldly and scrupulously truthful person which you represent yourself to be; nor yet will they know how great a coward you are, nor how soon you will run away, if they fight you with persistency and judgement. (Chapter vi)

But *The Way of All Flesh* is not satirical in one key only. Some of its funniest passages describe the contortions of religious scrupulosity. Here is the ordinand Ernest, worrying about smoking.

> [He] admitted that Paul would almost certainly have condemned tobacco in good round terms if he had known of its existence. Was it not then taking rather a mean advantage over the Apostle to stand on his not having forbidden it? On the other hand, it was possible that God knew Paul would have forbidden smoking, and had purposely arranged the discovery of tobacco for a period at which Paul should be no longer living. This might seem rather hard on Paul considering all he had done for Christianity, but it would be made up to him in other ways. (Chapter l)

But Ernest is his mother's child in such mental muddle.

> Christina said the will was simply fraudulent, and was convinced that it could be upset if she and Theobald went the right way to work. Theobald, she said, should go before the Lord Chancellor, not in full court, but in chambers where he could explain the whole matter; or perhaps it would be even better if she were to go herself – and I dare not trust myself to describe the *reverie* to which this last idea gave rise. I believe in the end Theobald died and the Lord Chancellor (who had become a widower a few weeks earlier) made her an offer, which however she firmly but not ungratefully declined; she should ever, she said, continue to think of him as a friend – at this point the cook came in saying the butcher had called, and what would she please to order. (Chapter xxxvii)

But here the author's personal bias lets him down. The narrator's account can only be supposititious and *parti pris*, and the reader's confidence is lost. Moreover, to reproduce, as Butler does elsewhere, a close approximation to his own mother's posthumous message to her children is scarcely justified on the grounds of its use of moral blackmail. The letter is simply not comical in the way that Christina's reveries are comical; and even those fantasies are obviously the product of authorial manipulation, and thus offend against the comic spirit. The author does not trust the inherent absurdities in the situation to correct themselves.

Theobald and Christina are products of a monolithic attitude to life, of which they are the victims and through which they victimise their offspring. Butler anatomises it with care.

Theobald considered himself, and was generally considered to be, and indeed perhaps was, an exceptionally truthful person; indeed he was generally looked upon as the embodiment of all those virtues which make the poor respectable, and the rich respected. In the course of time he and his wife became persuaded, even to unconsciousness, that no one could even dwell under their roof without deep cause for thankfulness [...] There was no road to happiness here or hereafter, but the road that they had themselves travelled, no good people who did not think as they did upon every subject, and no reasonable person who had wants, the gratification of which would be inconvenient to them – Theobald and Christina. (Chapter xxvi)

The Way of All Flesh, cruelly satirical though it is, does not however proceed beyond the anatomy of Ernest's saga. His emergence from captivity as a clergyman into what turns out to be liberation through a spell in gaol, is a neat piece of irony; but the novel's analytic procedures do not permit a strong enough dramatic presentation to make his subsequent career of interest. Ironically it is the two 'villains', his parents, who dominate the book. To that extent *The Way of All Flesh* is comedic at its own expense, though as a matter of theory rather than of dramatic realisation. There remains, however, an awareness of what comedy does involve, expressed (as always in this writer's case) with economy and force. Life for Butler has to be approached with 'a charitable inconsistency', since it is 'like a fugue, everything must grow out of the subject, and there must be nothing new [...] there being a unity in spite of infinite multitude, and an infinite multitude in spite of unity'. (Chapter xlvi)

Non-conforming consciences: E.M. Forster, D.H. Lawrence

Later novelists owe much to Butler for exposing the basic human instincts that determine ethical beliefs. Rose Macaulay, for example, was inspired by his revival of the concept of enlightenment to subtitle her popular post-war novel *Potterism* (1920) 'A Tragi-Farcical Tract'. For a tract it is, a tract for its times in the sense that the prefaces to the plays of Bernard Shaw (let alone the plays themselves) are tracts for theirs. *Potterism* is a plea for right reason, honesty and common sense in the face of that proliferation of linguistic and emotional clichés which was among the many deleterious legacies of the First World War; and it is motivated by the brisk, not wholly ill-humoured impatience which is the hallmark of its author's style.

'Potterism' itself is the generic term applied by its young opponents to the pervasive spirit of self-serving slipshod idealism which in this particular novel finds expression and endorsement through the Pinkerton newspapers – the creation of the press mogul Lord Pinkerton, formerly Mr Percy Potter of Potter's Bar. Potterism is based on fear.

> The other bases are ignorance, vulgarity, mental laziness, sentimentality, and greed. The ignorance which does not know facts; the vulgarity which cannot appreciate values; the laziness which will not try to learn either of these things; the sentimentality which, knowing neither, is stirred by the valueless and the untrue; the greed which grabs and exploits. But fear is worst; the fear of public opinion, the fear of scandal, the fear of independent thought, of loss of position, of discomfort, of consequences, of truth. (II:ii:1)

That indictment still has force. This is the society so subtly exposed by E.M. Forster in his early novels, and which is the perennial target for the satirical novelist, before and since.

Forster's own methods as a satirist are deceptive. He has a knack of establishing an intimate rapport with the world he castigates, so that when he does speak out against it he avoids the portentous solemnity of the outsider. He prefers to work at close quarters with his subject, burrowing like a mole in the infrastructure of accepted norms of feeling, and then emerging with the work of potential demolition almost out of sight. Of his six novels, only two can in any sense be described as comedies; and of these, *Where Angels Fear to Tread* (1905) is akin to the gallows humour of later writers in its account of the violent outcome of applying rigid monolithic standards of propriety to a society that fails to understand them. Much of the novel is amusing, especially in its portrayal of the effect of Italy upon English visitors; but there is no comedic transmutation in the movement of the plot. A situation is laid bare and issues stated, nothing more.

In returning to the Italian theme for his one genuine comedy, *A Room with a View* (1910), Forster was helping to found a literary tradition. The effect of Mediterranean sunshine on the strict Protestant work-ethic of the English middle classes, especially with regard to sexual behaviour, was to become a recurring subject for early twentieth-century novelists, and produced a number of entertaining, and on occasion mordant, satires, among them being Norman Douglas's

South Wind (1917), *The Enchanted April* (1922) by Elizabeth, Compton Mackenzie's *Vestal Fire* (1927) and T.H. White's *They Winter Abroad* (1932). But it is Forster who may be said to have fathered the tradition, and his two 'Italian' novels have a toughness and sense of social responsibility that the others lack. Lucy Honeychurch, the innocent young heroine of *A Room with a View*, returns from Florence with a fresh perspective upon her Surrey home and neighbours.

> In this circle one thought, married and died. Outside it were poverty and vulgarity, for ever trying to enter, just as the London fog tries to enter the pine-woods, pouring through the gaps in the northern hills. But in Italy, where anyone who chooses may warm himself in equality, as in the sun, this conception of life vanished. Her senses expanded; she felt that there was no one whom she might not get to like, that social barriers were irremovable, doubtless, but not particularly high. You jump over them just as you jump into a peasant's olive-yard in the Apennines, and he is glad to see you. She returned with new eyes. (Chapter x)

But this being a Forster novel, even the vision of Italian freedoms, though a shade sentimental (one is not so sure about that peasant), is not a monolithic vision; we are next told that 'Lucy had consecrated her environment by the thousand little civilities that create a tenderness in time, and [...] though her eyes saw its defects, her heart refused to despise it entirely.' Nor does the reader: the description of Lucy's home life is one of the most winning features of the book. It also enhances one's sense of what Christopher Gillie calls her 'virginality', the state of being 'unaware of and unconcerned with intrusion by the world which involves the individual in its anxieties and responsibilities and the complexities and corruptions that attend on them'.[5] In Forster's novel it is the rôle of satire to expose those corruptions for what they are.

But *A Room with a View* is an instance of almost perfect comedy. Its plot is the well-nigh monolithic one of the girl caught between two suitors. The contrast between Cecil Vyse and George Emerson is so sharp as to amount to parody – Cecil all talk and æsthetics and histrionics and inhibitions, George silent, a man of action, passionate and, when he does speak, incoherent: neither man is without a touch of the ridiculous. Lucy's struggle for her own soul and to know her own mind is furthered by a series of accidents that belong properly to the realm of farce – the kisses that George steals, the kiss that Cecil bungles, the impromptu larking in the woodland pool. And the plot is rich in ironies, both of action and of presentation. Cecil's arrogant caprice in bringing the Emersons to Summer Street costs him his betrothed. 'He would tolerate the father and draw out the son, who was silent. In the interests of the Comic Muse and of Truth, he would bring them to Windy Corner'. (Chapter x) And of course the Comic Muse betrays him to the Truth.

The book's satire on propriety is delightfully but acutely sustained, particularly in the person of the cheerless, aggressively apologetic Charlotte Bartlett, whose repeated catch-phrase is 'Grant me that, at all events.'

> "My own wishes, dearest Lucy, are unimportant in comparison with yours. It would be hard indeed if I stopped you doing as you liked at Florence, when I am only here through your kindness. If you wish me to turn these gentlemen out of their rooms, I will do it. Would you then, Mr Beebe, kindly tell Mr Emerson that I accept his kind offer, and then conduct him to me, in order that I may thank him personally?"
>
> She raised her voice as she spoke; it was heard all over the drawing-room [...] The clergyman, inwardly cursing the female sex, bowed and departed with her message.
>
> "Remember, Lucy I alone am implicated in this. I do not wish the acceptance to come from you. Grant me that, at all events."
> (Chapter i)

The sheer troublesomeness of strict propriety has rarely been more desolatingly exposed.

Burlesque is never a prominent feature of Forster's work, but here there is a touch of it in the portrayal of the rancorous, monolithically censorious Mr Eager and of the fatuous novelist Miss Lavish, so proud of her 'emancipation' (yet who, by the neatest of ironies, precipitates the 'unsuitable' marriage between George and Lucy). On the verbal wit there is no need to comment: this is a novel which conveys its message through every nuance of dialogue and interplay of thought with feeling. Authorial comment slips in and out of Lucy's consciousness, so that the characters and action form part of a single web.

But even *A Room with a View* falls short of total celebration. Lucy's salvation from the deadening constrictions of a social code of propriety which would doom her to a loveless union and to the acting of a lie, is achieved at the cost of estrangement from her friends: this novel, if a positive affirmation of common sense and the romantic conscience, is never monolithically so. As George declares in his lugubrious manner,

> There is a certain amount of kindness, just as there is a certain amount of light [...] We cast a shadow on something wherever we stand, and it is no good moving from place to place to save things; because the shadow always follows. Choose a place where you won't do harm – yes, choose a place where you won't do very much harm, and stand in it for all you are worth, facing the sunshine. (Chapter xv)

To which Lucy's mother replies, 'Oh, Mr Emerson, I see you're clever!'

But the comedic triumph of the book is achieved in the rôle played by Charlotte Bartlett. Her excessive sense of what is proper makes Lucy self-conscious about the Emersons; but it is Charlotte who in the end makes it possible for her to be alone with George's father and thus susceptible to understanding her own heart. The young couple may speculate as to how deliberate that action was; but an alert reader will have realised already that, in freeing Lucy, Charlotte is making good some error of her own that has made her life the wilderness it is.

> Miss Bartlett [...] had really been neither pliable nor humble nor inconsistent. She had worked like a great artist; for a time – indeed, for years – she had been meaningless, but at the end there was presented to the girl the complete picture of a cheerless, loveless world in which the young rush to destruction until they learn better – a shame-faced world of precautions and barriers which may avert evil, but which do not seem to bring good, if we may judge from those who have used them most. (Chapter vii)

That Charlotte has herself resisted a lover's approach is suggested by her instant suspicion of George. 'Unfortunately I have met the type before. They seldom keep their exploits to themselves.' But in discussing Lucy's predicament the author lets fall a stronger hint. Lucy 'pretended to George that she did not love him, and pretended to Cecil that she loved no one. The night received her, as it had received Miss Bartlett thirty years before'. (Chapter xvii) It is the precision of that 'thirty years' which is significant. 'It was a family saying that "you never knew which way Charlotte Bartlett would turn"'. (Chapter v) In *A Room with a View* the monoliths of false sentiment, of sexual rôle-playing, of class distinctions, of token religious orthodoxy, comedically become the means towards their own transcending. In contrast to Forster's work, that of D.H. Lawrence confronts those monoliths linguistically, as a matter of tone rather than of action. His own declaratory insights and intuitive dissection of the workings of industrialised society are too dialectical, too self-involved, to be critical in a comic manner – either of their subject-matter or of their own literary methodology. Yet there is a snapping bite to Lawrence's prose that lends his various critiques an air of jauntiness. He may not proceed from mental certitudes, but he is fired by emotional ones: as a satirist he is not so much a detached observer as a fox upon a scent. This particular tone is recognisable throughout his work, from the portrayal of sexual antagonism in 'Tickets, Please' to that of sexual attraction in *Lady Chatterley's Lover*. It is at its most light-hearted in the first part of the unfinished novel *Mr Noon* (1984)[6] and at its most mordant in *St Mawr* (1923). The former pounces with hilarious ferocity upon the relaxation of Victorian notions of sexual propriety and its mollifying compromise with idealistic sentimentalism.

> There are only spooners now, a worldful of spoons. Those wicked young society people, those fast young aristocrats, ah, how soft as butter their souls are really, tender as melted butter their sinfulness, in our improved age. Don't talk of lust, it isn't fair. How can such creamy feelings be lustful! And those Oxfordly young men with their chorus girls – ah God, how wistful their hearts and pure their faces, really! – not to speak of their minds. Then look at young colliers and factory lasses, they fairly reek with proper sentiment. (Chapter ii)

Lawrence here mimics, yet adopts for his own purposes, a mode of sensibility that is linguistically induced: one senses an anger half-turned against itself in its very anxiety to expose the object of its contempt; while a positive loathing for the bourgeois world saturates such later stories as the fable of *The Virgin and the Gypsy*. More good-humoured and closer to the comedic is the novel that preceded *Mr Noon*, the undervalued, and only minimally parabolic, essay in social realism, *The Lost Girl* (1920).

Its account of the Midlands town from which Alvina Houghton escapes to the dubious liberation of life as the partner of an Italian farmer in the Abruzzi is characteristically sardonic, even in the spirited nicety of its opening descriptions.

> A well-established society in Woodhouse, full of the fine shades, ranging from the dark of coal-dust to grit of stone-mason and sawdust of timber-merchant, through the lustre of lard and butter and meat, to the perfume of the chemist and the disinfectant of the doctor, on to the serene gold-varnish of bank-managers, cashiers for the firm, clergymen and such-like, as far as the automobile effulgence of the general manager of all the collieries.

The jubilant reification of social hierarchies is inherently comedic in its transmuting quality. The succeeding paragraph, however, replaces this playfulness with a more soberly analytic summing-up, only to revert at the end to metaphor – with clinching comical effect.

> Here we are then: a vast substratum of colliers; a thick sprinkling of tradespeople intermingled with small employers of labour and diversified by elementary school-masters and non-conformist clergy; a higher layer of bank-managers, rich millers and well-to-do ironmasters, episcopal clergy and the managers of collieries: then the rich and sticky cherry of the local coal-owner glistening over all.

It is the incorrigible human urge to social elevation which is the real target for the author's scorn. But his insight into causes never allows him simply to contemplate an absurdity: he must analyse it.

> [Arthur] was keen and sly in business, very watchful and slow to commit himself. Now he poked and peered and crept under the sink. Alvina watched him half-disappear – she handed him a candle – and she laughed to herself seeing his tight, well-shaped hind-quarters protruding out from under the sink like the wrong end of a dog from a kennel.

The sharp, intimate descriptive humour lends force to the subsequent anatomising of a psychological trait.

> He was keen after money, was Arthur – and bossy, creeping slyly after his own self-importance and power. He wanted power – and he would creep quietly after it till he got it: as much as he was capable of. His "h's" were a barbed-wire fence and entanglement, preventing his unlimited progress. (Chapter v)

The Lost Girl is also full of brilliant mimetic comic observation: at times Lawrence's skill resembles that of Dickens, as in the description of a trio of acrobats,

> the Baxter brothers, who ran up and down each other's backs and up and down each other's fronts, and stood on each other's heads and on their own heads, and perched for a moment on each other's shoulders, as if each of them was a flight of stairs with a landing, and the three of them were three flights, three storeys up, the top flight continually running down and becoming the bottom flight, while the middle flight collapsed and became a horizontal corridor. (Chapter vi)

However, such surrealistic humour is less in evidence in Lawrence's writing than is a sensuousness which sometimes gets the better of his moral convictions and intellectual doubts. But for the most part he is in too much of a hurry to dynamite the monolith for him to savour its absurder aspects. A sense of urgency is no friend to comedic observation. Lawrence's satire, like that of his contemporaries, suffers from having to engage with a period of weakening convictions and corresponding social flux.

Satirists, as much as ironists, owe a debt of gratitude to Swift. For if *Gulliver's Travels* is a masterly piece of irony where its literary methodology is concerned, it also satirises that hyper-rationality on which irony depends. As well as being a piece of biting comedy, the fourth book is a warning against taking Gulliver's assessment of humanity too seriously. The point is made with characteristic subtlety when he says farewell to his equine master. 'But as I was going to prostrate myself to kiss his Hoof, he did me the Honour to raise it gently to my Mouth.' Gulliver is overwhelmed by the conferred distinction. The incident is both comical and audaciously expressive. It is the extreme gravity of the Houyhnhnms which enables it to be both, for they embody the monolithic rationality which this book is designed to call in question. In forswearing his humanity, Gulliver has failed the challenge presented by the Yahoo nature; he has lost his nerve through disgust, and has surrendered to the idolatrous worship of pure reason. However lofty the imposture, he has been deluded by a horse.

Satire here satirises itself as Swift lays down the moral position underlying it – the affirmation of the human norm as material for transmutation, as something not to be rejected but to be set in order through a discernment of its possibilities for growth and change. If irony is a state of mind, satire is an activity that needs an object; and as the nineteenth and twentieth centuries pass, those objects become ever more fragmented, the moral perspectives of Forster and Lawrence narrowing to personal idiosyncracies and dreams.

But the weakening of the satiric impulse has another side to it: if it betokens the collapse of moral and judgemental certainties, it also reflects a growth in compassionate empathy where individuals are concerned, and reflects that impatient tolerance of misfortune which gives rise to the realism of gallows humour. This is an aspect of comedy to which twentieth-century writers have been especially prone.

> I remember that once when my brother and a comrade had gone horse-back riding, one of the horses returned riderless to the hotel, the mother of the other boy began to make a terrible scene. Be calm, madam, said my father, perhaps it is my son who has been killed.

Rational morality could go no further than this story told in the mendaciously entitled *Autobiography of Alice B. Toklas* which Gertrude Stein wrote on her behalf and in her name. The ambiguities of fictive discourse are here comedically rebuked by human stoicism in the teeth of fate.

7
Subversive Comedy: the Infernal Marriage

> I believe in no justice on earth except poetic justice; and neither, I believe, does God.
>
> Peter Levi, *The Flutes of Autumn*

Lawrence's relationship with Aldous Huxley was no less uneasy than was his relationship with E.M. Forster: though endorsing the younger man's clear-sightedness he questioned his negative conclusions. The dancing shepherds of Huxley's *Antic Hay* (1923) are not at all like Lawrentian grooms and gamekeepers, being uprooted individualistic drifters; while the nymphs in this shoddy inter-war pastoral are self-deluded, their couplings as joyless as any depicted by Eliot in *The Waste Land*. *Antic Hay* exhibits its characters' emotional sterility with a distaste that both energises and cripples its credentials as a social satire. 'Ah, if only there were a ditch, a crevasse, a great hole full of stinking centipedes and dung, how gleefully I should lead you all into it!'. (Chapter v) In the succeeding novel, *These Barren Leaves* (1925), the glee is more oblique. Francis Chellifer refuses to repine, cultivating a gallows humour that takes an active pleasure in the enormities, however petty, which a sophisticated consciousness is forced to undergo. For him the gulfs of existential despair are a pleasure to be sought on the most ordinary occasions.

> "So naice, I always think, these Corner Houses," says Mrs Cloudesley. "And the music they play is really quite classical, you know, sometimes."
>
> "Quite," says Mr Chellifer, savouring voluptuously the pleasure of dropping steeply from the edge of the convivial board into interstellar space. (II:iii)

Chellifer contends with a sense of futility by relishing the banality which precipitates it. In Huxley's world the sheer pressure of physical existence is a challenge to the comedic sense; yet the vitality that impinges draws out the vitality that responds, and the close connection between the two has been the material of fictive humorists from earliest times. Comedy among other things is the art of bouncing back.

Egotistical sublimities: *Humphrey Clinker*

If in his disgust at human nature Huxley echoes Swift, his preoccupation with physicality resembles that of Tobias Smollett, a novelist whose work is much concerned with the impact of character in terms of characteristics, rendered in his case with a delight in grotesque exaggeration. In *Humphrey Clinker* (1771) a typically jaunty letter from the young spark Jeremy Melford begins with 'In my last I treated you with a high flavoured dish, in the character of the Scotch lieutenant, and I must present him once more for your entertainment'. (Chapter l) Lismahago, one of his creator's more renowned inventions, is a 'character' – a highly individual mass of quirks and oddities served up for the amusement of a readership the author assumes to be normative and ordinary. The robust extravagance of the delineation is, in Melford's culinary metaphor, something to be 'savoured and enjoyed'; but that particular pleasure arises from the fact that Lismahago is the kind of person better kept between the pages of a book. No less than Squire Western or Sir Pitt Crawley, he would be intolerable to live with. Unforgettably amusing though they are, all three are reminders of the overpowering pungency of a life lived beyond the confines of an organised civility. Accordingly they are figures not of satire but of burlesque.

Burlesque is an aspect of comedy more attuned to the relative grossness of Smollett's sensibility than it is to that of the more benevolent and discriminating author of *Tom Jones*. It focuses on the disorderly, grotesque and generally ungovernable elements in human circumstances and behaviour. There are passages in *Roderick Random* (1748), *Peregrine Pickle* (1751) and even in *Humphrey Clinker* that can make one flinch: Smollett's unquestioning acceptance of human brutality, and the coarseness of speech attendant on it, separates him from the more deliberate and ultimately fastidious exploration of iniquity embarked on by twentieth-century writers. For there is a bitterness in our own outraged gallows humour that his laughter lacks, just as, for all our ready acceptance of sexual peculiarities, we recoil from his cloacal preoccupations.

Like *Clarissa*, *Humphrey Clinker* is a polyphonic novel, conducted through the narratives of various letter-writers; but these correspondents are not in tension with each other as they are in Richardson's tragic story. Instead, they represent five different 'types', revealing themselves with the consistency belonging to a portrayal of humours. Young Melford provides the most detached and self-critical of these voices; that of his sister, the endearingly soft-hearted Liddy, the most innocent and straightforward of them. Her aunt Tabitha Bramble is a caricature of the old maid desperate for a husband (a type who is the butt of too much masculine – and feminine – humour in both eighteenth- and nineteenth-century writers); but she has a tart and disagreeable quality that lends her a certain dignity. Her Welsh maid, Winifred Jenkins, provides the verbal comedy: her letters are an exuberant cross-fertilisation of malapropisms with *doubles entendres*, conveyed in misspellings that result in a positively Joycean richness of ambiguities and puns.

> O Mary! the whole family have been in such a constipation! Mr Clinker has been in trouble [...] He was tuck up for a rubbery, and had before gustass Busshard, who made his mittamouse; and the pore youth was sent to prison upon the false oaf of a willian, that wanted to sware his life away for the looker of cain. (Chapter xliii)

Such exuberance is the affirmative aspect of burlesque; it induces enjoyment of limitation and distortion. But, as with all major comic works, *Humphrey Clinker* subjects its own procedures to scrutiny. In this respect the fifth letter-writer, Squire Matthew Bramble, controls the novel's tone. Himself a mass of idiosyncratic humours, he is also generous and kindly; of the five correspondents he is the one with whom a twentieth-century mind can most readily associate itself, his testiness and incipient valetudinarianism especially. His interest in cultivating his estate, his common sense and belief in order, knit the topographical aspects into the novel's fabric. He is the controlling, normative figure by whose light the antics and attitudes of the others are assessed. Bramble presides over the book as he does over his household, crusty but adaptable, and anything but monolithic in his proprietorial benevolence.

Humphrey Clinker is more spectacle than action: its plot is minimal, and it has none of the structural elegance of *Tom Jones*. It neither speculates on human origins and destiny, nor engages in any wrestling with social or cosmic injustice, concentrating instead on manners and achievements, measuring their potential absurdity by the rationalistic philosophy of the time. Its employment of burlesque is thus creatively satirical and celebratory: Lismahago, in his contrariness and touchiness, in his sense of personal dignity and forlorn singularity of situation, is a subject both for mockery and for compassion. And if he scarcely deserves to be married off to the scratchy Tabitha, there is evidence that he can tame her.

This is amusingly provided in the episode where he turns the tables on Squire Bulford, that gouty instigator of practical jokes and of the undermining of Lismahago's dignity through raising a false fire alarm: the latter's retaliation (he tricks him into fleeing, gout and all, from a non-existent mad dog) disposes in action of Bramble's assertion that he lacks a sense of humour. Smollett subjects that particular concept to sardonic scrutiny, and is scarcely more indulgent to those people who would exploit it at the expense of others.

His own peculiar sense of humour can be seen in the grisly moment when Lismahago, having outlined in sickening detail the tortures inflicted by his Red Indian captors, goes on to describe his enforced taking of a squaw.

> The description of poor Murphy's sufferings, which threw my sister Liddy into a swoon, extracted some sighs from the breast of Mrs Tabby: when she understood he had been rendered unfit for marriage, she began to spit, and ejaculated "Jesus, what cruel barbarians!" and she made wry faces at the lady's nuptial repast; but she was eagerly curious to know the particulars of her marriage-dress; whether she wore high-breasted stays or boddice, a robe of silk or velvet, and laces of Mechlin or minionette; she supposed, as they were connected with the French, she used *rouge*, and had her hair dressed in the Parisian fashion. (Chapter I)

Gallows humour of the 'Apart-from-that-Mrs-Lincoln-how-did-you-enjoy-the-play?' variety could hardly be extended further. Behind this particular instance is a rasping and agonised insistence on not only the cruelty, but also the levity, of which the human race is capable.

A further species of humour in which Smollett anticipates twentieth-century comedic strategies occurs in his incorporation of real-life characters in fictitious situations. Thus he presents that political buffoon the Duke of Newcastle (to be immortalised likewise in the letters of Horace Walpole),[1] an appearance in which the author's gifts of burlesque and mimicry are activated to the full.

"Mr Bramble – your servant, Mr Bramble – how d'ye, good Mr Bramble? Your nephew is a pretty young fellow – faith and troth, a very pretty fellow! His father is my old friend – how does he hold it? Still troubled with that damned disorder, ha?" "No, my lord (replied my uncle), all his troubles are over: he has been dead these fifteen years." "Dead! how! Yes, faith! now I remember: he is dead, sure enough. Well, and how – does the young gentleman stand for Haverford West? or – a – what d'ye? My dear Mr Milfordhaven, I'll do you all the service in my power: I hope I have some credit left." (Chapter xxxv)

But the author can mock himself as well, as in the portrait of Mr S— and his extraordinary tableful of guests, and in the introduction of his own cousin, with whom Johnson and Boswell were to stay in their turn during a visit to Loch Lomond. Smollett's kinsman had erected a monument to his memory, and in the course of their visit Johnson helped to compose a Latin inscription for it – a measure of the esteem in which Smollett's writing was held. Firbank and Beerbohm were not the first writers to resort to playful authentification of this kind.

Perhaps the ultimate joke in the book lurks in its title: *The Expedition of Humphrey Clinker*. For our five correspondents are here subordinated to their servant, the impulsive, Methodistical innocent whom they pick up on their travels and who turns out to be Squire Bramble's son. Clinker's good intentions get him into perpetual scrapes; but if he constantly upsets the company's plans and progress, he is equally the means of saving and rescuing them: he is a kind of holy fool. In this connection the word 'expedition' takes on a richness of meaning that on the title-page it cannot have. And in the final letter Melford, having announced that 'the comedy is near a close', goes on to describe the conversion of Lismahago from a skeleton at a feast into a merry Andrew. 'His temper, which has been soured and shrivelled by disappointment and chagrin, is now swelled out, and smoothed like a raisin in plumb-porridge.' In *Humphrey Clinker* the redemptive process is less a matter of dramatic contrivance than a case of everyone finding what is, in relation to everyone else, their proper place and function. The expedition has terminated in good fortune for them all – good fortune, not merely luck. The term implies a benevolent, or at any rate an ordering, providence against which apparent hardships and injustices are to be measured. But it was precisely the sense of such protection which the following century was to see withdrawn. The shadow of the gallows grows ever larger on the scene of English humour.

Fixed principals: *Martin Chuzzlewit*

There are plausible reasons for the poor sales of Dickens's *Martin Chuzzlewit* (1844) when it began to appear in serial form in 1843 – there was a slump in the book-trade, nor had his historical novel, *Barnaby Rudge* (1841), enjoyed the popularity of its predecessors. But it is also likely that this initial distrust on the part of its readers derived from the story's peculiarly grim and enigmatic atmosphere and from the absence of an immediately engrossing plot. The author himself saw the book as being more purposeful than his early successes, analysing as it did the nature of selfishness, most especially as this affects family life; and indeed there are very few sympathetic or even likeable characters in *Martin Chuzzlewit*. It is arguably the bleakest of all Dickens's novels.

Yet it is also among the funniest, and it is this juxtaposition of an unsparing darkness of content with an outlandish linguistic extravagance and a ribaldry of presentation which gives it its peculiarly astringent quality. It is in no sense a 'nice' book, and develops that line of gallows humour which the author had already realised in the person of the malignant Daniel Quilp, who does so much to establish the sado-masochistic tone of *The Old Curiosity Shop* (1841). This quality is present in much of the narrative, the descriptions, and the characterisation in *Chuzzlewit*, and is even apparent in those American scenes which Dickens introduced in a successful bid to win back his waning readership.

These chapters, indeed, have a crazed excessiveness that amounts to fantastic caricature: Hannibal Chollop, Eliza Pogrom, Mrs Hominy and the rest seem to belong to a region scarcely of this earth (though Martin's experiences at the hands of the press certainly anticipate the excesses of late twentieth-century journalism). And the purgatorial place where he dies to his monolithic self-centredness is that abomination of desolation that is advertised as 'Eden'. These American scenes are written with the specificity and contemptuous extravagance of Swift in the Third Voyage of *Gulliver's Travels*; nor is Dickens far behind in his disgust at the folly and pretentiousness of the unrooted self-referential intellect. These chapters not only galvanised their original readers; their wild humour underwrites the effect of *Martin Chuzzlewit* as a discouraging moral fable.

Dickens himself would seem to have recognised that the book was something of an oddity, defending his use of exaggeration (disingenuously where America was concerned) as being no distortion of the reality, and, more persuasively, as a portrait of character that highlights what people make of both their own and of each other's lives. He emphasises that what is reaped is also sown. The physical setting of much of this novel serves as a metaphorical expression of a spiritual wilderness. In this respect not even *Our Mutual Friend* (1865), with its dust-heaps and mortuary river, presents a darker view of human life, and the first genuinely comfortable domestic scene in *Chuzzlewit* is encountered in the home of Mr Mould the undertaker. Nowhere is there a sense of a presiding benevolent providence. The embodiments of virtue are inadequate to confront this world of darkness: as John Westlock tells the meek and virtuous Tom Pinch, 'You haven't half enough of the devil in you'. (Chapter ii) The concept of comedy as remedial transmutation is challenged and tested to the utmost.

It is in this connection that one can appreciate the rôle of the resolutely cheerful Mark Tapley. 'Resolute' is the vital word, since Tapley embraces hardship and adversity for positive ends. He interprets 'being jolly' as a redemptive activity and seeks out the repellent in order to transfigure it. Finding his job at the Dragon Inn too comfortable, he thinks of becoming a grave-digger, since 'It's a good, damp, wormy sort of business [...] and there might be some credit in being jolly, with one's mind in that pursuit, unless grave-diggers is usually given that way; which would be a drawback'. (Chapter v) If this jollity is not to be viewed as mere sentimentality it must be seen as having a metaphysical context, for it is an assertion and recognition of the subordination of evil to the good: it is an act of faith, and serves the good. It is not so much comical or comic as comedic: it is not to be laughed at or analysed reductively; it is to be respected. And when at the novel's close Mark Tapley settles down with Mrs Lupin at the Dragon he has, figuratively, transcended mere dualism and entered paradise.

The behaviour of Mark Tapley enacts the literary technique of *Martin Chuzzlewit*: it engages with 'horror' through exaggeration and relish. This novel raises burlesque to the status of a philosophical and moral agent. A good instance occurs when Mr Pecksniff observes that

> it is always satisfactory to feel, in keen weather, that many other people are not so warm as you are. And this, he said, was quite natural, and a very beautiful arrangement; not confined to coaches, but extending itself into many social ramifications. "For" (he observed), "if every one were warm and well-fed, we should lose the satisfaction of admiring the fortitude with which certain

conditions of men bear cold and hunger. And if we were no better off than anybody else, what would become of our sense of gratitude; which," said Mr Pecksniff with tears in his eyes, as he shook his fist at a beggar who wanted to get up behind, "is one of the holiest features of our common nature." (Chapter viii)

Pecksniff, the very embodiment of cant, raises cant to architectural heights – he is absurd; but if the absurdity cloaks the nastiness within, it never hides it. The burlesque exposes the theory implicit underneath the verbiage. As Chesterton observes, 'the instant [Pecksniff] ceases to be laughable he becomes detestable'.[2]

Dickens underlines this by burlesquing conventional metaphor, exaggerating it and thus making it repellent, as when he remarks that Pecksniff

> looked at this moment as if butter wouldn't melt in his mouth. He rather looked as if any quantity of butter might have been made out of him, by churning the milk of human kindness, as it spouted upwards from his heart. (Chapter iii)

He can likewise modulate simile to grotesque effect, depicting with exaggerated irony the agent of the fraudulent Eden Settlement as

> no doubt a tremendous fellow to get through his work, for he seemed to have no arrears, but was swinging backwards and forwards in a rocking-chair, with one of his legs planted high up against the door-post, and the other doubled up under him, as if he were hatching his foot. (Chapter xxi)

Dickens is a master of the rhythms and pacing of individual speech, working up to a climax, even when this is whirled away on the wind of a *non sequitur*. Here is the glossy and sycophantic Dr Jobling discoursing *à propos* of the whereabouts of Mr Crimple's stomach.

> "There was a patient of mine once," touching one of the many mourning rings upon his fingers, and slightly bowing his head, "a gentleman who did me the honour to make a very handsome mention of me in his will – 'in testimony,' as he was pleased to say, 'of the unremitting zeal, talent, and attention of my friend and medical attendant, John Jobling Esquire, M.R.C.S.', – who was so overcome by the idea of having all his life laboured under an

erroneous view of the locality of this important organ, that when I assured him, on my professional reputation, he was mistaken, he burst into tears, put out his hand, and said, 'Jobling, God bless you!' Immediately afterwards he became speechless, and was ultimately buried at Brixton." (Chapter xxvii)

Martin Chuzzlewit is full of jokes about graves, corpses, bodily organs: it describes an overwhelmingly tactile world. Mrs Gamp, supreme instance of Dickens's grotesquerie, twice has her discarded garments likened to a hanging body. She is the familiar spirit of the world of poverty, of resignation and an eye to the main chance; and like Pecksniff, if she were not so funny she would be too horrific to be borne. But she transcends the rôle of mere comic relief, insinuating herself as the story proceeds into more and more of its crucial situations. She may make us laugh with her denunciation of Betsey Prigg's disbelief in the mythical Mrs Harris, which 'lambs could not forgive [...] nor worms forget'; but by a marvellous stroke integrating the comedy of burlesque with the climax, the poetic justice of the drama when Jonas Chuzzlewit is denounced as his father's murderer, it is Mrs Harris whom she invokes as guardian of the potential witness for the prosecution, the senile Chuffey. Even here, extravagant humour is juxtaposed with horror, in order to evince the ironic workings of the moral law.

Both Pecksniff and Mrs Gamp generate language that soars well beyond its immediate occasion; but whereas he does not so much speak for himself as is himself being spoken by the inflationary attitudinising verbiage of cant, Mrs Gamp's speech is thick with the experience of a real world. Angus Wilson describes it graphically, and in so doing also describes something of Dickens's own achievement in this novel as a whole.

The squalor, the greed and the brutality of Mrs Gamp are woven as closely into all the tag ends of religiosity, folk wisdom, macabrerie, coy salaciousness and sickly sentiment that make up her speech, as the brutality of the lives of the Victorian poor was blended with all their desperate attempts to evade it.[3]

Mrs Gamp speaks out of genuine experience: her vitality puts Pecksniff's false currency to the test, just as it puts to the test the religiosity that pervaded the society that he unconsciously burlesques. The gallows humour of *Martin Chuzzlewit*, like that in all of Dickens's work, is not reductive of its subject, but bracing and revivifying. As the American Literary Lady, Miss Toppit, rhapsodically declares,

> Howls the sublime, and softly sleeps the calm Ideal, in the whispering chambers of Imagination. To hear it, sweet it is. But then, outlaughs the stern philosopher, and saith to the Grotesque, 'What ho! arrest for me that Agency. Go, bring it here!' And so the vision fadeth. (Chapter xxxiv)

It is the definitive epitaph on cant, and also a perfect instance of that untrammelled extravagance which allowed Dickens to sustain the darker insights of his comic vision. It was his feeling for violence, rather than for self-protective cosiness, which was to fructify the imaginations of a later age.

Juvenile delinquents: Stalky and Saki

The contemporary popularity of Dickens's work, so pungent in its humorous relish for grotesquerie and the awful shocks and dislocations administered by what was officially accounted a benign and all-wise Providence, is a reminder of how robust, beneath the patina of Pecksniffian affectation, the Victorians really were. There was an element of disrespectfulness in popular humour that the early nineteenth-century writers cheerfully exemplified; and, as we have seen in *Rebecca and Rowena*, this disrespect lent itself readily to parody and to a kind of playful anachronism. The more facetious aspects of Thackeray's particular burlesquing of established literary tradition were to be a feature of later nineteenth and early twentieth-century popular fiction as well, achieving their happiest flowering in *The Sword in the Stone* (1939), T.H. White's account of the education of the future King Arthur. White's kind of humorous burlesque is designed to appeal both to children and adults, a comprehensiveness which Thackeray had anticipated in the comic fairy-tale of *The Rose and the Ring*, which appeared in 1855 as the last of his *Christmas Books*.

This has always been a favourite, and deservedly so; its continuous high spirits are contagious. The parody of romantic drama and of contemporary historical romance comes across as a joke to be appreciated as much by children as by their elders. Indeed, Thackeray addresses children with an absence of condescension that completely over-sets the contemporary notion as to the desirability of 'improving' literature, familiarly associated with the names of Maria Edgeworth and Mrs Sherwood; he is, indeed, mildly iconoclastic. These children are ill-treated by their elders and come out on top in a kind of domesticated Feast of Fools. (*The Rose and the Ring* looks ahead to the emancipated, unselfconscious humour of E. Nesbit.) Irreverence delights children; nor is Thackeray deficient in the kind of physical gusto that appeals to them still more.

> Rising up from the ground, he ground his teeth so that fire flashed out of his mouth, from which at the same time issued remarks and language, *so loud, violent, and improper,* that this pen shall never repeat them! "R-r-r-r— Rejected! Fiends and perdition! The bold Hogginarmo rejected! All the world shall hear of my rage; and you, madam, you above all shall rue it!" And kicking the two negroes before him, he rushed away, his whiskers streaming in the wind. (Chapter xiii)

It is '*loud, violent, and improper*' which strikes the distinctive note. The author suddenly speaks in the tone of the repressive adult world under which the children suffer, while, by italicising the comment, at the same time mocks it for the amusement of the adults themselves.

The story is borne along throughout on a keen sense of absurdity – and this is matched by a sophisticated narrative technique which conveys all the familiarity of domestic scenes such as its readers know and share. Here is King Valoroso preparing to sign the document that will reprieve Prince Bulbo from imminent execution.

> "Confound it! Where are my spectacles?" the monarch exclaimed. "Angelica! Go up into my bedroom, look under my pillow, not your mamma's; there you'll see my keys. Bring them down to me, and – Well, well! what impetuous things these girls are!" Angelica was gone, and had run up panting to the bedroom, and found the keys, and was back again before the King had finished a muffin. "Now, love," says he, "you must go all the way back for my desk, in which my spectacles are. If you *would* but have heard me out— Be hanged to her. There she is off again. Angelica! ANGELICA!" When His Majesty called in his *loud* voice she knew she must obey, and came back.
>
> "My dear, when you go out of a room, how often have I told you, *shut the door*. That's a darling. That's all." At last the keys and the desk and the spectacles were got, and the King mended his pen, and signed his name to a reprieve, and Angelica ran with it as swift as

the wind. "You'd better stay, my love, and finish the muffins. There's no use going. Be sure it's too late. Hand me over that raspberry jam, please," said the monarch. "Bong! Bawong! There goes the half-hour. I knew it was." (Chapter xi)

That Bong! Bawong! was bound to elicit children's laughter; but the streak of gallows humour is a perennial item in the equipment of comic writers, from Abhorson's 'He will profane our mystery' in *Measure for Measure* to the appalling physical afflictions endured by the Lynch family in Samuel Beckett's *Watt*.

Ideally, *The Rose and the Ring* should be read with the author's illustrations and rhyming page-headings to adorn the text: they emphasise the essentially ironic tone of the story, with its echoes of *Hamlet* complementing the motifs of magic rose and magic ring, benevolent fairy and outcast princess. The occasional ferocity adds an hysterical note to the humour and even a touch of cynicism when 'the great, fierce, rushing lions' who were supposed to devour Rosalba 'were grown as fat as pigs now, having had Hogginarmo and all those beefeaters, and were so tame, anybody might pat them.' (Chapter xvi) The fairy-tale romantic adventure is consistently, but genially, cut down to size. Nevertheless, were burlesque to be as reductive a literary enterprise as this suggests, it would not have the comedic potential that it does. The high spirits of *The Rose and the Ring* inform all such stories which deal with the overthrow of the oppressors by the weak: while requiring parental rule for their protection, the young also need to rebel against it for the sake of their own growth and capacity to exercise authority in adult life.

This is the message of a very different book for children, published some 45 years later. In *Stalky & Co.* (1899) Rudyard Kipling drew on his own years at the United Services College at Westward Ho! in Devon, producing an account that is full of recklessness and energy and which yet describes a living hell – or so it would appear to most sensibilities half a century later. It is the obverse of the idyllic childhood world of Arthur Ransome's fiction, where children are almost entirely free from adult supervision.

At the heart of the book is what T.R. Henn describes as 'the classical device of all comedy, the reversal of the situation, "the engineer hoist with his own petard", the rejoicing in a victory, however temporary, over authority'.[4] In all but the last of the book's nine chapters victory over the authorities is achieved by the enterprising Stalky, the saturnine M'Turk and the literary Beetle (Kipling himself): in the words of the Chaplain to his fellow masters, 'every time that any one has taken direct steps against Number Five study, the issue has been more or less humiliating to the taker' ('The Impressionists'). The humour of these stories is not as infectious as the author seems to think it is, despite his ability to convey stylistically the animal hurly-burly of school life (one can all but smell the carbolic); but what gives *Stalky & Co.* its extraordinary interest is the wedding of its occasionally hysterical high spirits with an underlying sense of the cruelty endemic in the human situation as such. As Stalky says to Beetle, 'My Hat! You've been here six years, and you expect fairness. Well, you *are* a dithering idiot' ('An Unsavoury Interlude'). But the remark receives no authorial underlining.

The stories are narrated with all Kipling's elliptical concentration, which at its most effective can induce the feeling that one is being oneself most intimately involved in what is happening. This technique yields to a more overt appeal to the reader in the most subtle and interesting chapter, 'The Flag of their Country', in which an unpopular act of interference by external authority (the imposition of a 'voluntary' cadet corps) is taken up by the boys for their own purposes – only to be discarded in disgust at an exhibition of inflated patriotic rhetoric by an opportunist politician.

> In a raucous voice he cried aloud little matters, like the hope of Honour and the dream of Glory, that boys do not discuss even with their most intimate equals; cheerfully assuming that, till he spoke, they had never considered these possibilities. He pointed them to shining goals, with fingers which smudged out all radiance on all horizons. He profaned the most secret places of their souls with outcries and gesticulations. He bade them consider the deeds of their ancestors in such fashion that they were flushed to their tingling ears. Some of them – the rending voice cut a frozen stillness – might have had relatives who perished in defence of their country. (They thought, not a few of them, of an old sword in a passage, or above a breakfast-room table, seen and fingered by stealth since they could walk.) He adjured them to emulate those illustrious examples; and they looked all ways in their extreme discomfort.

Any danger of inflated emotion is averted by the succeeding comment that

> Their years forbade them even to shape their thoughts clearly to themselves. They felt savagely that they were being outraged by a fat man who considered marbles a game.

This is one of Kipling's most bitterly ironical pieces of writing, characteristically converting a potential piece of hilarious satire into an indictment of spiritual vulgarity. And the point is driven home in the final tale, which shows Stalky and his schoolmates implementing their lessons with their lifeblood as they exert authority in their turn, far away in India. *Stalky & Co.* really does present school life as the world in miniature.

A variant on this theme can be found in a markedly different book, Saki's novel *The Unbearable Bassington* (1913), published on the eve of the First World War, when the authoritative structures of society were beginning to display signs of decay. Saki (Hector Herbert Munro) was already established as a sophisticated subversive comic writer through his short stories, in which an intent to shock the bourgeoisie is but a stage removed from a child's desire to shock grown-ups. In this novel Comus Bassington is a portrait, if not of Munro the writer, then of the author of Saki's fictive world:

> fate had fashioned him with a certain whimsical charm, and left him all unequipped for the greater purposes of life. Perhaps no one would have called him a lovable character, but in many respects he was adorable; in all respects he was certainly damned. (Chapter ii)

Earlier he has been likened to a Lord of Misrule, and to one on whom Fate has the last laugh. Incurably a charming, frivolous wastrel, he is despatched to West Africa to make his living, only to die there in despair of his ever being able to endure a way of life in which individual oddities have no place. The novel appears to question the very nature of the comic sense, for it proclaims the insufficiency of its own imaginative procedures.

The Unbearable Bassington has most, if not all, of the elements which make Saki's short stories so entertaining. It displays his gift for the witty character-sketch. Mrs Goldbrook

> did not share her sister's character as a human rest-cure; most people found her rather disturbing, chiefly, perhaps, from her habit of asking unimportant questions with enormous solemnity. Her manner of enquiring after a trifling ailment gave one the impression that she was more concerned with the fortunes of the malady than with oneself, and when one got rid of a cold one felt that she almost expected to be given its postal address. (Chapter xv)

The book is also full of Saki's particular brand of humorous nomenclature: Ada Spelvexit, Courtenay Youghal and Lady Veula Croot take their place alongside Loona Bimberton, Octavian Ruttle, Mrs Bebberly Cumble and others who people the short stories. And it even contains a whiff of the supernatural when, on the eve of his departure, Comus glimpses the same black dog he has seen before his father's death.

Animals indeed play a prominent part in Saki's world, highlighting the essential savagery and subversive nature of his comic sense. One of the tales is called 'The Feast of Nemesis', and many others could have shared that title. Story after story exemplifies the turning of the tables – on bores, for example (as in 'The Romancers'), on bullies, on pretentious snobs, on oppressive authority-figures, often embodied in the persons of aunts similar to the two who had oppressed the author in his childhood. In every case the monolith is tracked down, burlesqued, and laughed out of court. This rebelliousness sometimes manifests itself in verbal farce.

> "We've lost Baby," she screamed.
> "Do you mean that it's dead, or stampeded, or that you staked it at cards and lost it that way?" asked Clovis lazily.
> "He was toddling about quite happily on the lawn," said Mrs Momeby tearfully, "and Arnold had just come in, and I was asking him what sort of sauce he would like with his asparagus—"
> "I hope he said hollandaise," interrupted Clovis, with a show of quickened interest, "because if there's anything I hate—"
> "And all of a sudden I missed baby," continued Mrs Momeby in a shriller tone. "We've hunted high and low, in house and garden and outside the gates and he's nowhere to be seen."
> "Is he anywhere to be heard?" asked Clovis. "'If not, he must be at least two miles away."
>   'The Quest', *The Chronicles of Clovis* (1911)

The particular curtness which blackens Saki's humour also serves him well when in more responsible vein. Here is his comment on a wealthy social reformer.

When she inveighed eloquently against the evils of capitalism at drawing-room meetings and Fabian conferences she was conscious of a comfortable feeling that the system, with all its inequalities and iniquities, would probably last her time. It is one of the consolations of middle-aged reformers that the good they inculcate must live after them if it is to live at all.

'The Byzantine Omelette', *Beasts and Super-Beasts* (1914)

But the poise of Saki's style always involves a holding-back. Beneath it there lurks a jungle of violence, nowhere more tellingly apparent than in 'The Strategist' with its vivid portrayal of bullying at a children's party. And in 'The Recessional' his most typical spokesman, Clovis Sangreal, voices the epigraph for his entire *œuvre*.

The tawny tigress 'mid the tangled teak
Drags to her purring cubs' enraptured ears
The harsh death-rattle in the pea-fowl's beak,
A jungle lullaby of blood and tears.

The last recorded words of that quatrain's composer were heard in the trenches: 'Put that bloody cigarette out!'[5] It seems an appropriate epitaph for one who saw all too clearly that to subdue the beast it might be necessary to become a super-beast oneself.

Animal crackers: Gulley Jimson and Mr White

Knockabout farce and slapstick are a controlling element in burlesque; they assist in the channelling of anger into laughter. What is adapted for children in *The Rose and the Ring* becomes a veritable shaping element in a far more ambitious piece of fiction, one avowedly for adults – *The Horse's Mouth* (1944) by Joyce Cary. In this exuberant self-portrait of a disreputable painter the line between burlesque and something far more serious is hard to draw.

Gulley Jimson belongs to that suspect and potentially sentimental class, the lovable rogue. An artist obsessed with his own need to paint, he is oblivious of advancing years, failing health and a chronic need for money. Earlier perspectives on him are afforded by the book's two predecessors, *Herself Surprised* (1941) and *To Be A Pilgrim* (1942), whose narrators have their own very different interpretation of events in his career, Cary's conception of such a triptych of novels being yet another literary refutation of monolithic assertions as to absolute objectivity. Now Gulley tells his own story, and his view of those narrators reflects his imaginative and social priorities, the conscientious lawyer Tom Wilcher, so movingly portrayed in the second novel, becoming 'five foot of shiny broadcloth and three inches of collar […]

All eaten up with lawfulness and rage; ready to bite himself for being so respectable'. (Chapter xxviii) As for the warm-hearted, slapdash Sara Monday, she appears as a scheming egoist, good-natured but self-seeking, sentimental and deceitful. Cary's comic vision delights in the different ways in which people regard each other when conditioned by the way they see themselves: for him, each human being is an artist when it comes to living his or her own life. As he comments in his Preface to the Carfax edition of the novel, 'Every living soul creates his own world, and must do so.'

The Horse's Mouth is written throughout in a succession of mordant phrases, reading as much like a series of expletives as a piece of logically-developed prose. Although this technique can be exhausting, it permits the voicing of the tough gallows humour of working-class and under-privileged people. Gulley consorts with tramps, down-at-heel shopkeepers, the rag-tag-and-bobtail of the streets, cranky religionists and would-be artists, whose attitude to life is 'KEEP YOUR PECKER UP OLD COCK. HERE'S THE CHOPPER COMING'. (Chapter xvi) The chopper comes for Gulley himself when the wall on which he is painting a mural is demolished by the local council. But even so he is not resentful: his desire is more to be actively painting than to have produced a finished picture.

While disdaining the commercialising of art, he does not scorn the collectors, the critics and the dealers. As he remarks to his young promoter,

> It's all in the game. Hickson is a business man. And I'm a painting man. He makes money for fun and needs art to keep him alive. I paint pictures for fun, and need money to keep me alive. He wants to boost his pictures and get fun out of them, and I want to get some money and paint new pictures. And you want a job. (Chapter xxvi)

A disciple of William Blake, Gulley is at the same time well aware of the hard laws of economics. 'The history of civilisation is written in a ledger.' Yet his own life refutes any cynical endorsement of that text: if he is uncompromising about his vision as an artist, he knows it to be only his own vision. He declines to be acknowledged as a legislator for mankind.

Much of *The Horse's Mouth* is extremely funny, in its strenuous sardonic way. Cary has a good ear for Cockney speech-rhythms, and, indeed, for the patter of the music-hall comedian, combining them in this account of a sculptor friend's attempted suicide.

First time he jumped off Westminster steps, but it turned out very well. Because the chap who fished him out had no lobes to his ears, and gave him an idea for an abstract bit of stuff he was doing, an urn or something; and the second time he put all his hammers in his pocket and jumped off Waterloo Bridge, but as soon as he hit the water, he got such a strong feeling of the horizontal that he shouted for the police. And he went straight home and did a thing called Plane Surface, which everybody thought was a joke. And between you and me, so it was. But it kept him happy for six weeks. And made a nice pastry board afterwards. (Chapter xxxi)

The book is full of such comic turns, most effectively when Gulley is himself the speaker.

One time there was a dog that would rush at people's legs whenever they tried to get into Ikey's. Ikey was then a smart young man with long yellow hair and knotty fingers; a connoisseur of real Chinese china. Every time the dog barked he used to rush out and have hysterics. I put a *Times* down each leg, and when the dog nipped me, he got such a surprise that he couldn't believe his teeth. He staggered away in silence. He must have felt like a gourmet who bites on a stick of asparagus and finds it solid drainpipe. (Chapter xviii)

Appropriately enough, the book is full of a larger-than-life feeling for physical objects – as so often, it is Dickens who lurks behind many passages in Gulley's saga. For all his love for Blake, he rejects Blake's metaphysic, as leading to high-falutin posturing. But the artist knows the relativity of all human experience, the impossibility of attaining absolute truth: '... when you tell the truth, you kill it. And it changes into something else'. (Chapter xvii)

The Horse's Mouth is an exacting book: there are no dull passages and the pace does not let up. At times the high cockalorum tone grows wearisome, especially in Gulley's descriptions of Sara and the barmaid Coker; but the exuberance is bound up with pain, the joy of living with its anguish. There is a beautifully judged note of wry sympathy in the account of a disgruntled adolescent.

Frank was having trouble with boils. He had a plaster on his neck and was carrying his head all on one side. I like Franklin. He's about nineteen, and is just getting his first real worries. The girls he fancies don't fancy him; the ones he fancied last year and doesn't fancy any more are lying in wait for him with kisses and hatchets. Made a bit on the pools and lost a lot on the dogs. And his best friend did him out of a good job, because he wanted to get married. Three years ago he was a happy corner boy, living like a hog in his dirty little mind. Now he's been stabbed alive. He's seeing things. The old woman of the world has got him. Old mother necessity. (Chapter xii)

Compared with Franklin, Gulley considers himself fortunate: he knows that 'Being alive was enough – to contemplate God's magnificence and eternity'. (Chapter xvii) As he remarks to a fellow inmate of the Doss House 'Elsinore', 'it saves a lot of trouble between friends to swear that life is good, brother. It leaves more time to live'. (Chapter xxxiv)

Gulley himself, however, is a potential monolith. His need to create puts him outside the law. He is a thief, a swindler, a scrounger, a con-man, undependable, reckless, a liar and a drunk. He is the embodiment of subversion, a threat to the monolith of social order, to the reverence for wealth and material achievement – but no less a threat to sentimental spirituality, hyper-refinement and transcendental idealism. He laughs at pretension, at 'market-forces', cultural snobbery, 'domestic values', at every cliché of twentieth-century bourgeois standards of behaviour. It is Cary's triumph that this demonic harlequin should also be pantaloon, a humorous, quirkily compassionate old man whose very frailty witnesses to the strength of his imaginative life. In the person of Gulley Jimson and the portrayal of his surroundings and interior world *The Horse's Mouth* draws burlesque and gallows humour as close to pure celebration as they can get.

In this respect it has something in common with another comic *tour de force*, T.H. White's *The Elephant and the Kangaroo* (1948). Here the protagonist 'Mr White' is clearly a self-portrait, just as Burkestown is the Irish farm where the author spent the years of World War II. The premiss of the plot is insolently outrageous. The Archangel Michael comes down the kitchen chimney and announces the impending arrival of a flood, ordering Mr White and his hosts to build an ark. Such blatant fictionalising is not even rendered plausible by any attempt to rationalise it, to theologise it, or to make it imaginatively acceptable. All we are told of the visitant is that 'It hung against the dark background of the range in a nimbus of Its own light, looking straight between his eyes, with awful splendour'. (Chapter iii) But the author is good enough at his job for this to do the trick. Mr White and his companions are not being deluded.

None the less, what they make of the given, inexplicable event is in keeping with their individual characters. Ironically it is the rational atheist Mr White who most readily accepts the miracle: the devout (to him, maddeningly devout) O'Callaghans preserve a certain scepticism. Although it is Mrs O'Callaghan who first suggests that the apparition might be the Archangel, and thus puts the idea into Mr White's head, she is still prepared to be cautious: 'She could be the Devil'. (Chapter ii) By the end of the story one is inclined to feel that this time her supposition was correct.

Mr White, following the dictates of his fussily practical nature, duly constructs an ark out of an inverted hay-barn; the process is described with the particularity of a *Robinson Crusoe*. In due course the flood takes place. Mr White, his dog Brownie, and the O'Callaghans all embark. But the ark does not get far on its journey down the swift-flowing river: Mr White's calculations have left out of account the incidence of bridges. In the end the voyagers are rescued, revolving in three water barrels far out in Dublin Bay. The farcical extravaganza then concludes with the apparition of a perfect rainbow.

These accumulating absurdities embrace a variety of comic modes. There is a riot of Joycean parody as the unhappy travellers sweep through Dublin; there is Swiftian rage and disgust in the numerous satirical invectives against Irish self-deception and incompetence; there is burlesque in the portrayal of Mikey O'Callaghan, that catastrophically lazy farmer. And there is genuine wit in the account of the tangled but fundamentally loving relationship between the exasperated Mr White and the endlessly, deviously, acquiescent Mrs O'Callaghan, humbly resigned to a life that offers her nothing but the livelihood which at the story's close she presumably has forfeited at his behest.

The faces these two present to each other, and in turn to the reader, keep revolving as dizzily as do the barrels in the river. The process is enacted in miniature as he misguidedly attempts to teach her to do conjuring tricks.

> They had stood opposite each other, like image and object in a mirror, manhandling the corks, matches, and fountain pens which were Mr White's materials, and when he had treated her as an image, she had treated him as an object – lifting the opposite hand – while, when he had quickly switched over to being the object,

she, as quickly, had caught up with the original intention and had treated him as the image. She had said how silly she was, how wonderful it was, what a head Mr White had, and would you believe it? She had poured with sweat, dropped things, became entangled with her fingers, and laughed with wild propitiation, like some elderly Ophelia forced to hand out rosemary, rue, matches, corks and fountain pens. [...] Suddenly – and how strangely, in this world, comedy verges on tragedy at a clap – Mr White had seen that her hands were trembling. The poor, long, red fingers, which had scrubbed for so many years so many kitchen tables so inefficiently, had been trembling with fear and misery and humiliation. In another minute, she would have begun to cry.

It was things like this that made him love her so much. (Chapter viii)

The satire is more at the expense of the officious, omniscient Mr White than it is at that of the O'Callaghans; but neither he nor they have succeeded in growing up.

The Elephant and the Kangaroo is a comic novel entirely enclosed within the conditions of its making, a telling piece of authorial self-projection, the do-it-yourself man carrying out an exercise in satirical self-scrutiny. The book is self-sufficiently, though not exclusively, comical: there is no comedic transmutation in the action of the story, only the creation of a particular fantasy Irish world which distils learning and wit in a kind of loving anguish at the sight of human muddle, good intentions and stupidity.

> The rain pattered against the window of the playroom, slithered and skittered down the kitchen window, hummed on the galvanized Ark. It did not drum on the Ark, for that would not have been in character. Everything at Burkestown happened obliquely, by stealth. It sighed and moaned and gently roared on it, ceaselessly, by sunless day and moonless night. The ooze of the muck heap filled into a broad lake of cascara-coloured misery; the beech trees showed dark patches of bad drainage in their bark; the walls of the farmhouse sucked in the saturated air like blotting paper, and transferred it, in the form of mildew, to the various pictures of the Sacred Heart. (Chapter xv)

One feels that there is nothing further to be said. Here is a marriage of pain and pleasure, of beauty and discomfort, which is only not infernal because it is so wet. But *The Elephant and the Kangaroo* is a true burlesque, floating free of normal critical measurements and procedures. It is that rare thing, an instance of purely comic writing which admits suffering as well as joy into its fictive world and yet thereby enhances rather than diminishes the pleasure to be derived from it. White's linguistic skills ensure that its quality of gallows humour amounts to a potential act of comedic celebration.

Gulley Jimson and Mr White may stand for the artist and the artificer respectively, the one in his unending celebration of life and the other in his battle against chaos. The comedies in which they take part (and up to a point initiate) subvert any notion that chaos and creation can either of them be ultimately controlled: the storm can be ridden out, not quelled. Burlesque's insistence on the injustice of the world's affairs involves a genuine acceptance of that which it recognises as hostile or undesirable: it is a more integral marriage of opposing forces than one finds in irony.

It could be argued that the very juvenility of response that erupts in the kind of rough justice exemplified in *Martin Chuzzlewit* and repeatedly elsewhere in Dickens, as in Kipling, is a necessary accommodation to the rigours of the human lot. There is nothing sanitised about the comedic process: it must embrace everything, the shit with the wit, the slop-pail with the fan. In all its angry sardonic vigour, burlesque is an infernal conjunction of contrasting elements which through sheer power of differentiation regenerate each other.

8
Intellectual Comedy: the Distillation of Elements

> It is as pleasant as unusual to see thoroughly good people getting their deserts.
>
> Charles Williams, *James I*

It is characteristic of the comic unpredictability of English fiction that its two most enduringly popular writers for children should approach their material in an adult manner. The appeal of Lewis Carroll and Beatrix Potter spans the generations, for in addition to respecting their readers and displaying imaginative inventiveness, they exercise an intellectually astringent wit. It is an unusual quality to find in children's literature.

From the beginning of *Alice in Wonderland* (1865) we are uncertain as to time and space. 'Either the well was very deep, or she fell very slowly, for she had plenty of time as she went down to look about her, and to wonder what was going to happen next.' This intellectual quality is sustained throughout the book, which is full of encoded references, and has a meta-text that an adult reader can enjoy deciphering. It may be for this reason that some children find the two Alice books unsympathetic and even faintly frightening. Tenniel's illustrations too, as much part of Carroll's text by now as Beatrix Potter's are of hers, have a grotesquerie which disturbs because of its obvious derivation from an adult world.

Potter's pictures have the reverse effect: their delicate beauty and sturdy innocence complement a crisp and frequently ironic prose that treats the child as an adult, not through intellectual game-playing but through a confidentiality of tone. 'Tabitha Twitchit was disdainful afterwards in conversation'; 'Alexander was hopelessly volatile'; 'And when Mr John Dormouse was complained to, he stayed in bed, and would say nothing but "very snug"; which is not the way to carry on a retail business.'[1] The last phrase, like many others of Potter's, seems to be as applicable to an adult narrative as to one set in a childhood world.

Both she and Carroll are prepared to be witty in a way that concentrates the child's perception.

> "Well!" thought Alice to herself. "After such a fall as this, I shall think nothing of tumbling downstairs! How brave they'll all think me at home! Why, I wouldn't say anything about it, even if I fell off the top of the house!" (Which was very likely true.)
>
> *Alice in Wonderland*, Chapter i

Potter goes one better than this in *Ginger and Pickles* (1909), by incorporating her mordant comment in a piece of dialogue. Pickles the terrier and the tom-cat Ginger keep the village grocery shop; and the implications are followed through with unflinching logic.

> The shop was also patronised by mice – only the mice were rather afraid of Ginger.
>
> Ginger usually requested Pickles to serve them, because he said it made his mouth water.
>
> "I cannot bear," said he, "to see them going out at the door carrying their little parcels."
>
> "I have the same feeling about rats," replied Pickles, "but it would never do to eat our own customers; they would leave us and go to Tabitha Twitchit's."
>
> "On the contrary, they would go nowhere," replied Ginger gloomily.

It is that 'gloomily' which is so satisfying: the verbal wit is reinforced by an encompassing sense of irony. Beatrix Potter's total absence of nostalgic sentiment makes her a Jane Austen among children's writers.

Quite the thing: *Emma*

Jane Austen is a novelist for whom wit is less a matter of verbal adornment than one of structuring and plot. In this respect (and, as many would argue, in all others) her masterpiece is *Emma* (1816). In celebrating 'the beauty of truth and sincerity in all our dealings with each other' (III:xv) it interfuses satire with irony, keeps farce under control, refutes burlesque and makes of parody the subject-matter of what is a flawless instance of pure comedy. Comedy is also its subject-matter. The dominance of thematic material in Jane Austen's three early novels, and the potentially tragic overtones of *Mansfield Park*, are here replaced by a portrayal of the positive aspects of human discordances and relativities. *Emma* is full of surprises, for the reader as for the characters: it is a game in which all alike take part, so that the dignity of the players in the comedic process is preserved. Every one is treated with respect, and there is no collusive patronage by author and reader at the expense of persons who depend for their existence upon both. Good manners govern the exposition of the story, just as they form the subject-matter of the plot. And in this most geographically restricted of novels the self-discipline involved in the practice of courtesy and in concern for others takes on heroic qualities that are the fruit of foresight and imagination. Not for nothing is the term `to pay attention' used so frequently, for it denotes both social amenity and unflagging moral rigour.

It is her capacity for self-scrutiny and amendment – ultimately her capacity for love – which justifies the ascription to Emma Woodhouse of heroic qualities. The author may have described her as 'a heroine whom no one but myself will much like',[2] but modesty rather than judgement must have motivated that foreboding, since it applies more to Fanny Price than to one whose powers of mimicry and of composing scenarios for other people's lives reflect the superior intelligence and restricted scope for creative talents which were her creator's own. Jane Austen, like Emma Woodhouse, was the cleverest member of her circle, and here displays an awareness of the moral pitfalls such supremacy entailed.

For Emma's story is a parody of novelistic readings of communal affairs, describing as it does the imposition of one particular viewpoint upon the interlocking diversities of autonomous subjectivities. Emma herself is a far more sophisticated creation than is Catherine Morland; but she shares with her a tendency to impose preconception upon actuality. The prescriptive model, the monolith, is not in this case the result of too much reading, but of a will to power. Emma will matchmake; she will arrange. But the comedic process sees to it not only that she constantly mistakes the true nature of affairs (as in Mr Elton's matrimonial aspirations and in Frank Churchill's apparent absence of them), but is compelled to see herself parodied, burlesqued even, in the person of the pretentious Mrs Elton (the one odiously monolithic person in the book) and to recognise her own potential likeness to

Miss Bates, the garrulous old maid it is her abuse of privilege to mimic. Yet ironically, while learning her lesson, she is rewarded at the end, being not only Miss Woodhouse of Hartfield but the future Mrs Knightley of Donwell Abbey also:

> for as to any of that heroism of sentiment which might have prompted her to entreat him to transfer his affection from herself to Harriet, as infinitely the most worthy of the two – or even the more simple sublimity of resolving to refuse him at once and for ever, without vouchsafing any motive, because he could not marry them both, Emma had it not. (III:xiii)

The smile here is at the expense of moralistic readers who would be ready with their own monolithic verdicts and their regulations of the various comic misunderstandings of the plot.

The celebrated opening sentence is a perfect example of Austenian artistry and balance.

> Emma Woodhouse, handsome, clever, and rich, with a comfortable home and happy disposition, seemed to unite some of the best blessings of existence; and had lived nearly twenty-one years in the world with very little to distress or vex her.

Had 'handsome, clever, and rich' been 'beautiful, talented and wealthy' the effect would have been entirely different, and the faintly reductive quality of the words been lost. The sentence is a plain statement of fact, yet contains the seeds of its rebuttal: something is indeed going to distress and vex our heroine, though not very much and not for long. She is subjected, briefly, to farcical indignity on the occasion of Mr Elton's proposal; she is patronised by his insensitive and vulgar wife; she is rebuked by the man she truly loves. But in his subsequent words to her, she has 'borne it as no other woman in England would have borne it'. (III:xiii) At the conclusion of the story we are invited to appreciate her all the more.

The book's ironies are legion, all of them based on a sense less of dramatic reversal than on that of things being as they are and not what they may seem. Thus Harriet Smith's obtuseness repeatedly and by its very nature frustrates Emma's seeming perspicacity. Infinitely suggestible, Harriet none the less remains drawn to her natural affinity, so that her eventual marriage to the farmer Robert Martin is a matter not of fickleness to the suitors whom Emma, whether intentionally or not, has encouraged her to think aspire to her, but of an intuitive knowledge of what will suit her best. Harriet, so frequently portrayed as being absurd, in her innocent stupidity is wise at heart.

Nor are the ironies all at Emma's expense: not only is George Knightley prejudiced in his judgements, but the reader likewise can be implicated. Mr Woodhouse may be an affectionate satire on invalidism, and as such potentially risible and monolithic. Valetudinarians are frequent objects of mockery in fictional narratives. Compared with Scott's company in *St Ronan's Well* (1823) or Frederick Fairlie in Wilkie Collins's *The Woman in White* (1861), however, Mr Woodhouse is a subtle and rounded portrait. He invites both mockery and irritation, yet when his own standards of kindness and compassion are infringed, the effect is daunting. His verdict on Frank Churchill, 'That young man is not quite the thing', strikes home.

Similarly, the 'comical' character of the insufferably loquacious Miss Bates does not permit a simplistic response. She only makes her appearance at the start of Volume II, and has been anticipated in references by the other characters, references which tend to blur one's recollection of the author's own initial account of her as

> a happy woman, and a woman whom no-one named without good-will [...] The simplicity and cheerfulness of her nature, her contented and grateful spirit, were a recommendation to everybody and a mine of felicity to herself. (I:iii)

When she does appear, her garrulity is as excessive as Emma has declared it to be; but with each appearance and each outpouring it becomes more exuberant, attaining a kind of airborne velocity worthy of comparison with the verbal flights of Dickens's Mrs Nickleby. But Miss Bates has her feet firmly on the ground; unlike Emma, she makes no mistakes. She is indeed Emma's complement: they both look after, and are endlessly patient with, an elderly parent; but the one is rich, the other poor. Hetty Bates is what Emma Woodhouse might have become (for she too speculates, though without Emma's self-will); but she has a greater sense of her limitations.

> I do not think I am particularly quick at these sort of discoveries. I do not pretend to it. What is before me I see [...] but one never does form a just idea of any body beforehand. One takes up a notion, and runs away with it. (II:iii)

When Emma derides her at the disastrous picnic on Box Hill, it is a turning-point in the former's comedic process of self-knowledge; thereafter she is able to repent. Once that repentance is complete and she is affianced to George Knightley, Miss Bates fades out of sight. Only Mrs Elton remains to remind Emma of what she might so much less worthily have been.

Mrs Elton is a figure from the early novels and sketches. One cannot but speculate, with critical impropriety, as to what might have been the effect upon his career had she, and not Charlotte Lucas, become the wife of Mr Collins. Mrs Elton's portrait, indeed, is the novel's nearest approach to burlesque, her patronage of Jane Fairfax being a wicked mimicry of Emma's attitude to Harriet Smith. More characteristic of the essential wittiness of *Emma* is the treatment of the extrovert Mr Weston with his 'unmanageable good-will', and of Mr Woodhouse's being stampeded into accepting his daughter's marriage by the necessity of having a man about the house, following the robbery of a neighbour's hen-coop. In *Emma* the monolithic dichotomies are overturned – and even the monolith of absolute delightfulness. We are made well aware of the monotony of daily life in Highbury, and there is a chilling reference to the small change of everyday which both accounts for, and in part excuses, Emma's propensity to organise and rearrange the lives of those about her:

> The children came in, and were talked to and admired amid the usual rate of conversation; a few clever things said, a few downright silly, but by much the larger proportion neither the one nor the other – nothing worse than every day remarks, dull repetitions, old news, and heavy jokes. (II:viii)

Yet against this bleak exactitude of observation, the novel as a whole is suffused with a contented awareness of 'all those little matters on which the daily happiness of private life depends'. (I:xiv) It is this underlying normality which provides the ground-base for the play of wit.

The action is largely transmitted through Emma's eyes and consciousness: indeed, such is the coincidence of sensibility between protagonist and author that the novel itself might be the retrospective work of Mrs Knightley of Donwell, as when, in a disputation with her husband-to-be, Emma 'to her great amusement, perceived that she was taking the other side of the question from her real opinion, and making use of Mr Weston's arguments against herself'. (I:xviii) Emma's ability to laugh at herself gives the comedy its peculiarly intimate tone. It portrays a community tested by its various divisive elements and restored through each discordant movement being resolved and by each person within it discovering their proper level. Even Mrs Elton has to be accommodated: *Emma* is the most sociable of comedies. Every one in it is dependent upon others for the expression of themselves. It is because of this that the secret engagement between Jane Fairfax and Frank Churchill is such a serious offence, for it involves not only a failure of candour but also an undisclosed manipulation of other people's characters and purposes. However understandable and innocently intended, it remains not quite the thing.

This vision of necessary harmony is furthered by the book's immaculate sustaining of its mood and its succession of appropriate balances and couplings. It begins with Miss Taylor's departure from Hartfield to marry Mr Weston, and ends with Mr Knightley's taking up residence there upon his marrying Emma. And for each turn of the plot there is a corresponding twist. Emma, misunderstanding Mr Elton, unwittingly deceives Harriet; Harriet, misunderstanding Mr Knightley, unwittingly deceives Emma. And each apparent elucidation until the final one (that Emma and George Knightley love each other) becomes a means of further misunderstanding. Although the author plants abundant clues as to the true state of affairs, it is only on successive readings that one is able to appreciate the density of the design. Although it is Emma's version that we primarily receive, there are enough pointers to provide material for a parallel interpretation of the same pattern of events: indeed, Mr Knightley has to undergo nearly as much self-chastening in order to meet Emma as she does to meet him. The monolithic statement of objective fact composed for deciphering is here distilled into a comedic conjugation of a whole variety of perspectives and corrective insights, one which involves as much readerly participation as it does a display of the characters' personalities and motives. The qualifying aspects of comedy – parody, irony, satire, burlesque – are subsumed into that pure distillation of the comic spirit which we know as wit. It is because *Emma* so triumphantly exemplifies this unifying process that it remains the quintessential English comedic novel, 'as profound as pure comedy can be'.[3]

Feasts of reason: Thomas Love Peacock

The quiet meals at Hartfield under Mr Woodhouse's gently dictatorial supervision are in marked contrast with the bibulous, endlessly talkative ones attended by the opinionated characters of Thomas Love Peacock. Headlong Hall, Crotchet Castle, Gryll Grange – within these hospitable walls any number of embodiments of the monolith collide, argue, quarrel, are reconciled, while remaining to the end of each little story as solidly themselves as when they entered it. In Peacock's fiction the comedic action is discovered in the benevolent oversight of the author rather than in any transmitting agency within its plots; and it is this oversight which makes the novels so enjoyable. Their intellectual high spirits, their genuine and essential wittiness, are transmitted through a technique that accepts the artificiality of fiction as a vitalising part of the game.

Five of them give expression to their author's prejudices and immutable opinions, through satirising (for the most part in dialogue form) the various monolithic fads and opinions of the day; while *Maid Marian* (1822) and *The Misfortunes of Elphin* (1829) are comic updated versions of traditional romantic stories. Neither of them, however, pokes fun at the legends they adapt: rather it is the modern world that is the object of the author's good-humoured scorn. Indeed much of the humour resides in the disparity between picturesque subject-matter and lucid rational tone. Peacock does not modernise his ancient sources, but none the less he treats them with the uncondescending respect due to a contemporary one.

> Medicine was cultivated by the Druids, and it was just as much a science with them as with us; but they had not the wit or the means to make it a flourishing trade; the principal means to that end being women with nothing to do, articles which especially belong to a high state of civilisation.
>
> *The Misfortunes of Elphin*, Chapter vi

However, irony and satire are no more than contributory elements in the general good humour of these two narratives. *Elphin* in particular is rich in Peacock's peculiar blend of poetry and learning, with a sense of pleasure in the processes of the physical world. His robust presentation of the forces of nature and the life of the body offsets the more cerebral flights of his wit, and enables him to create in this legend of Arthurian Wales a figure such as Seithenyn ap Seithyn, that rarest of creatures – an habitual drunkard who is not a bore.

For Peacock's fiction embodies a critique of the wilder excesses of the cult of personality. He has a genuinely comic perspective, one which views individuals as belonging to a society in which they have a part to play. His various satirical attacks on monolithic points of view are content to remain as that; each holder of such views is left to take part in the same social dance, irrigated by good wine and nourished on untrammelled discourse. Mental presumption is combated by physical exuberance. In *Headlong Hall* (1816), for example, the Squire's hospitality and abounding energy ride rough-shod over the potential prickliness of his various guests. Peacock has an enjoyable ability to evoke a sense of physical movement.

> Squire Headlong, in the mean while, was quadripartite in his locality; that is to say, he was superintending the operations in four scenes of action – namely, the cellar, the library, the picture-gallery, and the dining room – preparing for the reception of his philosophical and dilettanti visitors. His myrmidon on this occasion was a little red-nosed butler, whom nature seemed to have cast in the genuine mould of an antique Silenus, and who waddled about the house after his master, wiping his forehead and panting for breath, while the latter bounced from room to room like a cracker, and was indefatigable in his requisitions for the proximity of his vinous Achates, whose advice and co-operation he deemed no less necessary in the library than in the cellar. (Chapter ii)

Peacock handles classical allusions and Latinate circumlocutions with an injection of homely imagery peculiarly his own – witness that 'like a cracker'. And the theme of combustion is developed as the landscape gardener Mr Milestone blows up a rock with gunpowder just as two of his fellow guests emerge on the summit of a nearby ruined tower.

> Mr Milestone had properly calculated the force of the explosion; for the tower remained untouched: but the Squire, in his consolatory reflections, had omitted the consideration of the influence of sudden fear, which had so violent an effect on Mr Cranium, who was just commencing a speech concerning the very fine prospect from the top of the tower, that, cutting short the thread of his observations, he bounded, under the elastic influence of terror, several feet into the air. His ascent being unluckily a little out of the perpendicular, he descended with a proportionate curve from the apex of his projection, and alighted, not on the wall of the tower, but in an ivy-bush by its side, which, giving way beneath him, transferred him to a tuft of hazel at its base, which, after upholding him an instant, consigned him to the boughs of an ash that had

rooted itself in a fissure about half-way down the rock, which finally transmitted him to the waters below. (Chapter viii)

'Descended ... alighted ... transferred ... consigned ... transmitted' – the ludicrous descent is enacted in the rhythms of the prose, the dapper gravity of its phraseology serving only to enhance the comicality of such a (fortunately harmless) detonation.

In *Headlong Hall* the landscape of North Wales plays an influential rôle in determining the beneficial effect of pleasure upon its various cantankerous disputants. The importance of this unity of place in Peacock's scheme of things is evident in the comparative failure of its successor, *Melincourt* (1817), in which the various characters part company, to wander through a series of picturesque scenes bearing but a vague relation to their alleged Cumbrian original. This mobility means that the comedic action is diffused and thus (to employ a pun surely permissible in such a context) defused. *Melincourt* is less like a comedy as such than a loose collection of jokes and humorous set-pieces. Among the former is the introduction of the longest word in the English language, while set-piece and joke combine in the use made of Sir Oran Haut-Ton, Peacock's mischievous embodiment of an amateur anthropologist's contention that the orang-outang was no monkey but primitive man – itself a potential joke at the expense of Rousseau's doctrines of original innocence. As David Garnett observes, *Melincourt* contains more statements of the author's own beliefs than do the other novels.[4] Perhaps because of this, it is less good-humoured: Coleridge (Mr Mystic), Southey (Mr Feathernest) and Wordsworth (Mr Paperstamp) all three receive a drubbing. Altogether there is too much serious conviction for the book's comic good. None the less it does contain some of Peacock's most insouciant asperities, as in Mr Sarcastic's exposition of his own modes of ironical entrapment, whereby he aims 'to show a man his own picture, and make him damn the ugly rascal'.

> ... it is a habit, I believe, peculiar to myself, and a source of inexhaustible amusement [...] I ascertain the practice of those I talk to, and present it to them as from myself, in the shape of theory: the consequence of which is, that I am universally stigmatised as a promulgator of rascally doctrines. (Chapter xxi)

Such a self-satisfied exposition of the methodology and upshot of ironic statement is entrapped in its turn by Peacock's intellectual wit.

A vivid sense of place is resumed in *Nightmare Abbey* (1818) and integrated thematically into the story. The latter being a satire at the expense of self-conscious, self-induced romantic pessimism, it is appropriate that it should be set against a desolate landscape; and it is typical of Peacock that he should resist the temptation of wild moors and mountains in favour of the dead flat fens of Lincolnshire. The gothic dwelling of the atrabilious widower Christopher Glowry is described with a precision that belies its romantic pretensions, and the effect is furthered by its owner's comment that it 'was no better than a spacious kennel, for every one in it led the life of a dog'. (Chapter i) Among his guests are Mr Flosky, the transcendentalist philosopher (Coleridge again), Mr Cypress (Byron on a flying visit before leaving England) and young Scythrop Glowry (Shelley). All of them represent various self-deluded manifestations of excessive monolithic mental preoccupations of a negative variety. The place and its temporary inhabitants are illustrative of each other.

Scythrop's dilemma at being in love with two young women simultaneously is familiar subject-matter for farce. But it enables the author to embroil his other characters in the ridiculous situation that ensues, and thus prevents them from becoming mere mouthpieces of their several eccentricities. At times the dialogue achieves a simple terse absurdity that anticipates the work of Evelyn Waugh. Here is Scythrop giving his orders to Raven the butler, before his intended suicide. Quoth the Raven,

"Shall I bring your dinner here?"
"Yes."
"What will you have?"
"A pint of port and a pistol."
"A pistol!"
"And a pint of port. I will make my exit like Werter. Go. Stay. Did Miss O'Carroll say anything?"
"No."
"Did Miss Toobad say anything?"
"The strange lady? No."
"Did either of them cry?"
"No."
"What did they do?"
"Nothing."
"What did Mr Toobad say?"
"'He said, fifty times over, the devil was come among us.'"
"And they are gone?"

"Yes; and the dinner is getting cold. There is a time for everything under the sun. You may as well dine first, and be miserable afterwards." (Chapter xiv)

This last remark could well stand as the epigraph for this particular novel. It is the very quintessence of its author's witty common sense. Whereas in *Nightmare Abbey* the excesses of romanticism are mocked in a farcical plot and a parody of Byronic gloom, irony is the predominant mode of *Crotchet Castle* (1831). This 'unconquerable fortress of wit and scholarship'[5] is built up of the clash and complementariness of opposites. The talkative guests at Mr Crotchet's Thames-side villa pair off neatly. Thus the romantic liberal Mr Chainmail, with his love of the Gothick, is contrasted with the hyper-rationalist Mr MacQuedy, not least when the party is disturbed at the former's house by a rabble of discontented peasantry.

> MR CHAINMAIL: The way to keep the people down is kind and liberal usage.
> MR MACQUEDY: That is very well (where it can be afforded), in the way of prevention; but in the way of cure, the operation must be more drastic. (*Taking down a battle-axe*) I would fain have a good blunderbuss charged with slugs.
> MR CHAINMAIL: When I suspended these arms for ornament I never dreamed of their being called into use.

But the dilemma is then by-passed by a transcendentalist philosopher.

> MR SKIONAR: Let me address them. I never failed to convince an audience that the best thing they could do was to go away. (Chapter xviii)

Poor Coleridge!

But Peacock is capable of a more subtle arraignment of the illogicality of stubbornly held opinion. A memorable instance occurs in the heated discussion between Mr Crotchet senior and the Reverend Dr Folliott concerning nudity in art. By the time they have reached the virtuous wives of Athens it is going completely off the rails.

> THE REV. DR FOLLIOTT: ... the Athenian virgins [...] grew up into wives who stayed at home, – stayed at home, sir; and looked after the husband's dinner, – his dinner, sir, you will be pleased to observe.

Intellectual Comedy: the Distillation of Elements   161

MR CROTCHET: And what was the consequence of that, sir? that they were such very insipid persons that the husband would not go home to eat his dinner, but preferred the company of some Aspasia, or Lais.

THE REV. DR FOLLIOTT: Two very different persons, sir, give me leave to remark.

MR CROTCHET: Very likely, sir; but both too good to be married in Athens.

THE REV. DR FOLLIOTT: Sir, Lais was a Corinthian.

MR CROTCHET: 'Od's vengeance, sir, some Aspasia and any other Athenian name of the same sort of person you like.

THE REV. DR FOLLIOTT: I do not like the sort of person at all: the sort of person I like, as I have already implied, is a modest woman, who stays at home and looks after her husband's dinner.

MR CROTCHET: Well, sir, that was not the taste of the Athenians. They preferred the society of women who would not have made any scruple about sitting as models to Praxiteles; as you know, sir, very modest women in Italy did to Canova: one of whom, an Italian countess, being asked by an English lady, "how could she bear it?" answered, "Very well; there was a good fire in the room."

THE REV. DR FOLLIOTT: Sir, the English lady should have asked how the Italian lady's husband could bear it. The phials of my wrath would overflow if poor dear Mrs Folliott – : sir, in return for your story, I will tell you a story of my ancestor, Gilbert Folliott. The devil haunted him, as he did St Francis, in the likeness of a beautiful damsel; but all he could get from the exemplary Gilbert was an admonition to wear a stomacher and longer petticoats. (Chapter vii)

The passage needs to be quoted at such length if the wonderfully deft rhythms and shifts of mood and allusion are to be appreciated.

For such exchanges are always benignly resolved in Peacock's world: the festive, not to say gastronomic, delights of his novels are transmuting solvents. And even in its rarest flights his wit remains in touch with the world from which its atmosphere has been distilled, as when Mr Chainmail, gazing in rapture at a young lady asleep above a waterfall, found that for him to hear her breathing was 'out of the question: the noses of a dean and chapter would have been soundless in the roar of the torrent'. (Chapter xiv) The book here achieves that fusion of what the monolithic mind would regard as being exclusive opposites, and in doing so transcends the divisions which Mr Crotchet has invited his company to debate.

> The sentimental against the rational, the intuitive against the inductive, the ornamental against the useful, the intense against the tranquil, the romantic against the classical; these are great and interesting controversies, which I should like, before I die, to see satisfactorily settled. (Chapter ii)

The comedy of *Crotchet Castle* exposes the impossibility of such a resolution, but in that spirit of happy scepticism which is one of wit's progenitors.

After a gap of nearly thirty years there appeared the only one of Peacock's novels to be named by him a comedy. *Gryll Grange* (1860) is also the most conventional of them. Quirks and oddities and opinionated discourse no longer exclude detailed characterisation, and for the first time the two heroines have personalities of their own. Nothing else in Peacock's work is so touchingly humanised as the account of the developing relationship between the reserved Alice Niphet and the impetuous, over-confident Lord Curryfin, who

> invented a new sail of infallible safety, which resulted, like most similar inventions, in capsizing the inventor on the first trial. Miss Niphet, going one afternoon, later than usual, to her accustomed pavilion, found his lordship scrambling up the bank, and his boat, keel upwards, at some little distance in the lake. For a moment her usual self-command forsook her. She held out both her hands to assist him up the bank, and as soon as he stood on dry land, dripping like a Triton in trousers, she exclaimed in such a tone as he had never before heard, "Oh! my dear lord!" (Chapter xvi)

This is the kind of humorous eroticism that one finds in E.M. Forster's novels, and like them this one portrays a world in which the cure for human troubles is to be found in common sense, toleration, and a generous heart. Its tone and vision of life is in perfect keeping with its beautifully-evoked New Forest setting. *Gryll Grange* shows the fruit of the comedic process, and is a communication from a fictive world that is basically happy, physically romantic, intellectually bracing, full of absurdities and incongruities, and lovingly indulgent to the young: it is an old man's book in which wit is unsheathed for the sheer pleasure of it. But Peacock's son-in-law was to wield it to more warlike purpose.

Striking attitudes: *The Egoist*

It seems appropriate that such a sociable novelist as Peacock should have acquired the author of *The Egoist* (1879) as a member of his family circle. This masterwork of George Meredith, the first English novelist to attract a self-consciously intellectual readership, is unusual among nineteenth-century English novels in being the product of the prescriptive rather than the pragmatic imagination. Like George Eliot, Meredith had ideas as to what a novel should aim to do, and sought to elucidate his fictive methodology by means of propagatory theory. However, the book's `Prelude' on the nature of comedy disowns itself. Its self-description as 'A chapter of which the last page only is of any importance', undermines any serious intent either in the preceding analysis of the comic spirit or in the decisive opening sentence, 'Comedy is a game played to throw reflections upon social life, and it deals with human nature in the drawing room of civilised men and women.' Such a definition encourages the distillation of the rough and tumble of flesh-and-blood humanity into a world of artifice and wit. But that world is not necessarily heartless, while the stress on social relationships indicates the inadequacy of any monolithic aspirations towards self-sufficiency.

As to Meredith's *Essay on Comedy*, published two years earlier, it remains more a series of comments on the workings of comedy, and of discriminations between differing kinds of comedic methodology, than a systematically-argued intellectual analysis. What it stresses lies more in the domain of morality – the essentially generous nature of the comic spirit.

> You may estimate your capacity for comic perception by being able to detect the ridicule of them you love without loving them less; and more by being able to see yourself somewhat ridiculous in dear eyes, and accepting the correction their image of you proposes.

The *Essay* proceeds to argue for the separation of the *idea* of comedy from its *manifestations* in ironic, satiric and farcical (which Meredith calls 'humorous') forms.

> If you detect the ridicule, and your kindliness is chilled by it, you are slipping into the grasp of satire.
> If, instead of falling foul of the ridiculous person with a satiric rod, to make him writhe and shriek aloud, you prefer to sting him

under a semi-caress, by which he shall in his anguish be rendered dubious whether indeed anything has hurt him, you are an engine of Irony. If you laugh all round him, tumble him, roll him about, deal him a smack, and drop a tear on him, own his likeness to you, and yours to your neighbour, spare him as little as you shun, pity him as much as you expose, it is a spirit of Humor that is moving you.

Above all, Meredith insists on the imperfection of popular thinking about humour. He tilts against obvious jocularity, against 'the pursuit of the grotesque, to the exclusion of the comic', against what George Eliot refers to as 'fun obligato'[6] – as in the 'case of poor relatives' where 'it is the rich, whom they perplex, that are really comic; and to laugh at the former, not seeing the comedy of the latter, is to betray dullness of vision'. Such dullness is characteristic of the monolithic temperament, one which Meredith anatomises without mercy.

Insufficiency of sight in the eye looking outward has deprived them of the eye that should look inward. They have never weighed themselves in the delicate balance of the comic idea, so as to obtain a suspicion of the rights and dues of the world; and they have, in consequence, an irritable personality.

In *The Egoist* the monolith is the subject of the novel. Sir Willoughby Patterne's betrothed, Clara Middleton, 'conceived the state of marriage with him as that of a woman tied not to a man of heart, but to an obelisk lettered all over with hieroglyphics, and everlastingly hearing him expound them, relishingly renewing his lectures on them'. (Chapter x) Yet Willoughby is no obvious target for satire (as is, for instance, the character of Wemyss in Elizabeth's *Vera*). He is talented, athletic, quick-witted (where his own interests are concerned) and with a handsome presence that ensures him the automatic devotion of his maiden aunts and the more susceptible local ladies; as the epigrammatical *grande dame* Mrs Mountstuart Jenkinson sums up, 'Rich, handsome, lordly influential, brilliant health, fine estates'. (Chapter xxxv) It sounds like a masculine equivalent of Emma Woodhouse. And the likeness is itself a warning. The inherent absurdity of such apparent perfection is neatly pin-pointed by Mrs Jenkinson at Willoughby's coming-of-age with the cryptic observation that 'He has a leg'. At once he becomes mere posture. But he is acute enough to scent danger in the ascription, just as he does in her designation of his bride-to-be as 'a dainty rogue in porcelain'. Why 'rogue'? The word catches the spirit of independence in Clara which is to lead her to find Willoughby's egoism and overbearing self-will asphyxiating. She tries to escape from her engagement, but honour is involved as well as life.

In reality the two are one: for Clara, the keeping of her vow becomes the surrender of a deeper integrity.

> The cage of a plighted woman hungering for her disengagement has two keepers, a noble and a vile; where on earth is creature so dreadfully enclosed? It lies with her to overcome what degrades her, that she may win to liberty by overcoming what exalts. (Chapter x)

Such a situation is the raw material of tragedy; and for all its high spirits, *The Egoist* runs as close to pain as does *Twelfth Night*. Sir Willoughby at one point seems like first cousin to Malvolio; yet where women are concerned the indictment of him is damning, since

> the devouring male Egoist prefers them as inanimate overwrought polished pure-metal precious vessels, fresh from the hands of the artificer, for him to walk away with hugging, call all his own, drink of, and fill and drink of, and forget that he stole them. (Chapter xi)

The tension between comedy and tragedy in this novel is so taut as to beget a species of witty appreciation that vibrates equally through its moments of lyrical beauty and its appalled contemplation of Willoughby's self-referential consciousness.

As in *Emma*, this witty atmosphere is distilled within a unity of place out of comings and goings, the motive of which the various characters misunderstand, and out of the reversal of expectations. Lætitia Dale's refusal of Willoughby's offer of marriage, so unbelievable to him, is not so unlike Mr Elton's aspirations towards Emma, so unbelievable to her. But Meredith's comedy is poised above an abyss at which Jane Austen only momentarily glances. Lætitia's final acceptance of her unrelenting suitor is the exhausted, clear-sighted rational decision of one who has ceased to love. The comedy lies in the gloss the novel stylistically applies to this lugubrious solution. To Willoughby's attempt to alleviate matters, 'But you are the only woman of all the world who knows *me*, Lætitia', she can only reply,

'Can you think it better for you to be known?' (Chapter xlix) The termination of *The Egoist* has the foreclosing conclusiveness of stage drama; and yet, intellectually, even its ironic ending is comedic in its nature. The monolith can dictate its terms, and even the opposition to it is not absolute, since, where the future is concerned, Willoughby's self-serving tactics have already been adumbrated in a previous dilemma when we are told that 'His blind sensitiveness felt as we may suppose a spider to feel when plucked from his own web and set in the centre of another's'. (Chapter xxix) The action he takes then is action he can take again.

For Willoughby's battle is with himself, and it is a universal battle. He is fighting for his life-illusion. Once he recognises that Clara has rejected him (replicating the collapse of a previous engagement and thus duplicating the offence) it becomes essential for him to recompose the scenario so that he appears to be rejecting her, in order to bestow her graciously on his cousin – with whom, of course, she has been in love all along. But when Lætitia Dale also rejects him (she, the lovelorn exploited one) the script has to be rewritten yet again, and he has no choice but to resort to moral bullying in order to persuade her. This comedy of self-deception is underwritten by the misunderstandings bandied about between the chorus of county ladies (Mrs Mountstart Jenkinson and her rivals) and also by the bewilderment of Clara's father (a scholarly epicurean straight out of Peacock). But while the limitations of the characters are exposed, by methods both ironical and satiric, to a situation that increasingly amounts to farce, the verbal signalling indulged in by the author elevates his readers to his level as spectators who can appreciate the various self-deceptions as they are illuminated in the lucid air of his wit. Meredith is a novelist wise enough to flatter those readers whom the strenuous virtuosity of his style does not repel.

Family fortunes: Ivy Compton-Burnett

Although Meredith's verbal gymnastics have proved exhausting to readers nurtured on the comparative simplicities of James and Joyce, he did open up a field of linguistic and intellectual possibilities for later novelists to explore. If his stylistic influence was unfortunate, declining into the preciosities and mannerisms of lesser romantic and society novelists such as Maurice Hewlett or Henry Harland, his readiness to make his readers work and to disperse self-scrutiny as a stimulating tonic is to be seen not only in the plays of Bernard Shaw but also in the fiction of Ivy Compton-Burnett, who, if wit be regarded as a moral weapon, may well be considered the wittiest of English novelists. Her very technique amounts to a joke at the expense of readerly expectations and a game with the dictates of traditional fictive methodology. She largely dispenses with narrative and provides a minimum of authorial analysis and comment. Such physical portraiture as she provides is redundant to the stories and unmemorable in its effect. In the later novels dialogue alone sustains the plot; and in all of them this is a formalised dialogue, in which precise, almost legalistic, language is spiced with conventional social jargon and carried forward on a cadence often echoing the Bible. And yet, such is the author's skill in her eccentric medium, the progress of events is clear, people's voices are distinct, and clues as to motivation and personality adroitly placed. Close attentiveness is required in order to take part in the game; and a game it is, since, despite the sombre, not to say tragic, events which take place in most of these novels, the actual manner and technique of their narrational method is itself implicitly comedic. The tone, the sharp-eyed relish with which the interplay of personal talk with unspoken commentary (for the author records thought-processes as though they were articulated speech) allows for a readerly detachment which is at once highly pleasurable to those who have mastered the rules, and a source of bracing mental recreation. The sheer impersonality of Compton-Burnett's methodology is comic in its approach to its subject-matter, frequently comical in its effects, and comedic in its result. In this instance the juxtapositions of gallows humour are distilled as wit. The novels are borne up in a stream of polyphonic verbal dialectic.

Here is an example from *Daughters and Sons* (1937). A brother and two sisters are debating whether to visit a neighbour who has faked a suicide in order to disoblige her family.

> "I shall just be myself," said Evelyn, "as that is the truest tact. And I think it must be more awkward for them to be alone. To give people a lesson and live with them afterwards must be very awkward. And to have had a lesson must be awkward too."
>
> "I hope they have not learned the lesson,' said Stephen, 'That is the great mistake."
>
> "It would never do to reward people for causing us discomfort," said his sister, "and that is what a lesson always is."
>
> "Suffering may be wholesome," said Jane, "but we should not cause it to each other."

"Why is it wholesome?" said Stephen. "And, if it is, why should we not cause it?"
"We generally do, so it is all right, dear," said his sister. (Chapter xi)

Compton-Burnett's novels contain more villainy, outrageous behaviour and deliberate ill-doing than any other English novels of comparable seriousness: they are as full of dreadful deeds as a Jacobean drama – murder, forgery, incest, moral blackmail, physical and mental cruelty form the substance of their plots. Yet their unflinching stylistic formalism ensures that they never collapse into melodrama, the continuous play of verbal wit being directed at the stock response to such outraging of morally standardised behaviour. The violent happenings are merely so many occasions for the exposure and overthrow of cant, the cant that this author's master, Samuel Butler, attacks in *The Way of All Flesh* and in his *Notebooks* – a work which was to have a lasting influence on her.[7]

In this respect Ivy Compton-Burnett is a comedic artist; but where her plots are concerned this is not the case. Through them she evaluates the family dramas in which she confronts the monoliths of patriarchal and matriarchal tyranny, of self-righteousness and self-importance, and also that of the reader's own tendency to respond to these matters on their own terms. The unceasing moral dialectic that informs the conversation of her people is as much directed at the fictive material, both in relation to characters and readers, as it is to its own self-perpetuating celebration of the elusive agility of words and meanings.

In her major works (the ten novels beginning with *Men and Wives* (1931) and ending with *Darkness and Day* (1951)) the comedic aspect is incidental. There are amusing characters in all these books, and comical encounters and exchanges; but with the exception of the relatively mellow *Two Worlds and Their Ways* (1949), the cold-blooded ruthlessness of human egotism, lustfulness and greed are the predominating realities. But in the more pared-down later novels the movements of the plots suggest some kind of comedic resolution, almost some kind of transmutation, of what in the previous ones had been a grim acceptance of an apparently amoral *status quo*.

Good examples of this tendency can be found in both the first and the last of these later novels. *The Present and the Past* (1953) is full of entertaining ironies. The self-consequential and fussily tyrannical Cassius Clare precipitately welcomes back into his home his ex-wife Catherine, who wishes to resume contact with the two sons she has abandoned. The histrionic Cassius makes an emotional meal of the situation, at the expense of his second wife Flavia, who has been a devoted stepmother to the boys. But when the two women strike up a close friendship he feels excluded, and stages a suicide-attempt in order to recapture the family's attention. But his deceit recoils upon him: confronted later on with what is a genuine heart-attack they assume that he is once more shamming, and let him die. The plot is an instance of black comedy, almost of gallows humour; but its comedic element does not lie there.

For the impact of these events on Cassius's two elder sons and on Catherine and on Flavia is cruel and hard. As the latter comments,

> I knew he wanted flattery. I could have given it to him. Why cannot we serve each other? Why could I not meet his need? I knew he wanted too much sympathy, and I gave too little. I had my own standard and observed it as if it were absolute. And it was only mine. Cassius was alone. (Chapter xii)

The moral thrust of this offsets the comedy of the situation. Moreover, Cassius's 'suicide' having been comically presented, his death comes as a genuine shock: the reader is as much caught out by events as are the book's protagonists. The comedy is thus at our expense; as is the constant reciprocal unveiling of meaning and motivation in which the characters – servants, children, parents, bystanders – all indulge. The nearest we get to a formal comic device is the use of the servants' talk as a satirical gloss upon the rigid conventions of class and social structures which confine the seething passions of their employers within a social straitjacket. The toadying butler Ainger is here discussing Cassius's death with Mrs Frost, the cook.

> "Mrs Frost, had you no feeling for the master?" said Ainger.
> "I had as much as he had for me."
> "He estimated your skill in your line, and indeed gave voice to it. He was not conversant with your life in its other aspects."
> "He did not know it had any."
> "Now, Mrs Frost, how could he?"
> "He could not, as it had none."
> "Now, Mrs Frost, you cannot expect us to believe that."
> "I daresay the master would have believed it, if he had thought about me." (Chapter xii)

Truth-telling in Compton-Burnett's world is always in the name of doing away with emotional false pretences: it is a chastening, even a chastising, weapon.

Such plain-speaking attains a profounder depth in the disenchanted utterance of two of Cassius's younger children, especially in that of Henry, a doleful small boy with a faculty of coming to the point.

"What would have happened to us, if you had died?" said Henry.
"This house would have belonged to Fabian; so we should still have had a home. But would other things have been different? [...]"
"Would you not have found that losing me made a difference?" said Cassius, looking at his son.
"Yes, but I knew about that."
"So that is how you talked, when you thought I might be going to die?"
"Well, we couldn't have helped it, if you had," said Megan. "We shouldn't have had to feel ashamed about it. That is unfair when people haven't done anything. And when a thing is done on purpose, it isn't even sad." (Chapter xi)

Compton-Burnett is a morally unsparing writer, but her economy of means, precision of utterance, and adroit dissection of the motives underlying speech amount almost to a celebration of the conditions which make such anatomising possible.

And celebration is virtually what *A God and his Gifts* (1963) amounts to. Hereward Egerton is a best-selling romantic novelist with a dependent family. His self-confidence is overweening, yet not overtly tyrannical: he genuinely believes in his own good nature and godlike generosity. Indeed, he bestows himself in a very literal manner, begetting children on his sister-in-law, and, before her marriage, on his daughter-in-law as well; a further liaison comes to light at the novel's close. But as in so many other of Compton-Burnett's fictions, the victimised family accepts and puts up with the wrong-doer. In these novels the wicked are never punished either outwardly or by their own guilty consciences. Hereward succeeds in reconciling his family circle to his actions; the potential for tragedy is neutralised by a refusal of any response other than an acceptance that things and people are as they are, for better or for worse. *A God and his Gifts* may be described as a comedy that exists without containing any comedic process. The monolith remains unchallenged save by an amused contemplation of its bland impermeability. Ultimately the verdict on

Hereward is ironic. Transmutation is achieved through a species of moral bluff.

Compton-Burnett's novels, indeed, represent the furthest that wit can go in dramatising the struggles, contradictions, and perversities of human nature with a view to their resolution. On a superficial reading her books may all seem to be alike; but a closer acquaintance reveals a marked difference between them in emphasis and tone. The idiom may be identical, but what the author achieves with it varies from book to book. But in every case, through their verbal energy and 'rattling of the bones of grammar',[8] these novels reiterate comedy's insistent message that nothing is precisely what it seems to be. They remain, however, on the near side of comedic transmutation, and leave their world exactly as they found it. What has been transformed is the reader's capacity to enjoy and to endure that world.

All those novelists whose work is predominantly characterised by wit portray a stable world. They deal in fundamental assumptions as to social structures and priorities, and with human communities in which, because there are rules, it is possible to play a game. In some of them, Peacock most notably, the ludic quality can erupt in farce – intellect is at once celebrated, evaluated and derided; in others, such as Compton-Burnett, the game is played in tight-lipped earnest. For these writers, for all their outward artificiality, are dealing in the passions.

Wit encourages an appreciation of dangers as much as of delights: its function is to maintain balance by articulating ambiguities. Whereas, in the twentieth century, burlesque has become increasingly serious, wit has become more abstract. It includes the other aspects of comedy within its essentially indulgent grasp; but it is not comedy in itself. Its comprehensiveness is measured by its possessors' capacity to comprehend. Meredith may declare that 'Folly is the natural prey of the Comic [...] and it is with the springing delight of a hawk upon heron, hound after fox, that it gives her chase';[9] but the metaphor of the hunt belies that total acceptance even of folly which is the inclusive comic vision so definitively enshrined in *Emma*. Wit is as near allied to charity as it is to madness; yet it is too entirely sane to be confused with either. It is an essentially adult form of play – it appreciates the humour of farce, burlesque and parody, but like irony it remains predominantly a state of mind, one which provides a tool with which to shape an attitude to life more comprehensive even than itself.

9
Celebratory Comedy: the Accomplished Work

"You won't make yourself a bit realler by crying," Tweedledee remarked: "there's nothing to cry about."
Lewis Carroll, *Through the Looking Glass*

As in so many Victorian novels, at the end of Henry Kingsley's *Ravenshoe* (1861) there is a wedding. Appropriately enough in this most good-natured story, with its confiding style so redolent of friendship and the joys of rural sports and of the Turf, the crowning celebration is disturbed by the misbehaviour of two naughty children. They virtually take the book over at the moment of its formal closure when bride and groom are at the altar.

> Gus had crawled up, on all fours, under the seat of the pew, until he was opposite the calves of his sister's legs, against which calves, *horresco referrens*, he put his trumpet and blew a long shrill blast. Flora behaved very well and courageously. She only gave one long, wild shriek, as from a lunatic in a padded cell in Bedlam, and then, hurling her prayer-book at him, she turned round and tried to kick him in the face.

But it is all part of the celebration. At Gus's trumpet-blast the monolith of social propriety collapses.

The word 'celebration' is rich in meaning. It refers to the performance of solemn rituals in a context of rejoicing (the celebration of the Mass being the definitive fusion of tragic with comedic experience) and is essentially proclamatory in character, extolling its object and seeking to comprehend rather than to discriminate – with which it has as little to do as with incrimination. Novels embodying such an outlook are bound to be popular. J.B. Priestley's *The Good Companions* (1929), a best-seller of the inter-war years, is a case in point; but what makes this jolliest of jolly books additionally enjoyable is that here and there it secretes an element of gall. Not even conviviality can afford to become monolithic.

The complete consort: *Joseph Andrews*

The English novel's first best-seller is Samuel Richardson's *Pamela: or Virtue Rewarded*. Published in 1740, by the April of the following year it had gone into three editions and become the subject of the pseudonymous lampoon entitled *An Apology for the Life of Mrs Shamela Andrews*, which described itself as an exposure and a refutation of 'the many notorious Falsehoods and misrepresentations of a Book called *Pamela*'. This one aims to expose 'all the matchless Arts of that young Politician [...] The Whole being exact Copies of authentic Papers delivered to the Editor' and 'necessary to be had in all Families'. That injunction was seriously meant, for under the pen name of Mr Conny Keyber (the much-derided poet laureate, Colley Cibber).[1] Henry Fielding voiced his anger at Richardson's apparent reduction of the concept of virtue to the preservation of virginity for snobbishly calculating and commercial ends. To suggest that her employer's repeated efforts to seduce a servant could be made good by her triumphant marriage to him, appears to ignore the deeper moral issues involved in his behaviour; and Fielding satirically re-interprets Richardson's scenario by replacing the drawn-out titillations of attempted seduction by the rowdiness of bawdy farce, and by turning the original Pamela's desperate expedients to frustrate Squire B's attentions into the contrivances with which Shamela endeavours to ensnare him.

The exercise would be cheaply cynical were it not for the indignation and impatience with which the author chastises a readership gullible enough to find the original Pamela's story elevating. Through ridicule, *Shamela* demolishes its predecessor's claims to inculcate virtue. The merriment is at its most effective when most caustic – as when Shamela and the conniving Mrs Jewkes talk for a 'full hour and a half, about my Vartue' (Fielding's mocking substitution for a word which a 'refined' accent thus renders ridiculous). But anyone reading the pamphlet before coming to *Pamela* itself would tend to think that the latter cannot be as silly as all that. Nor is it: and when a year later the second part appeared, Fielding had a more formidably monolithic challenge to encounter.

For *Pamela* does not conclude with the heroine's triumphant marriage, but proceeds to demonstrate her successful career as wife and mother. The genuinely dramatic power of the first part of her story declines into a smug rehearsal of middle-class aspirations, which exclude the world outside the family circle. A monolithic propriety assumes the status of life in its totality; and this under the guise of an authentic record. One falsity is compounded by another in one of the perennial victories of cant, that 'currency of false opinion, a profession of belief in something which no one really believes, but which everyone finds convenient'.[2] To Fielding, in addition to the triumph of unscrupulous advertising methods (*Pamela's* first edition being accompanied by advance letters of approval, parodied in *Shamela* by letters *to* the Editor *from* the Editor, and from Mr Puff – a familiar figure to the present day) the book's reception represented the triumph both of a canting methodistical spirit and of a failure to distinguish between fact and fiction, a distinction deliberately blurred by Defoe in his fictive narratives and here inflated to the dimensions of self-parody. Fielding's new literary offensive was thus directed not only at an affectation of the spirit but at a manipulation of the truth.

Great fun though *Shamela* may be, *The History of the Adventures of Joseph Andrews and of his Friend Mr Abraham Adams* (1742) covers an altogether wider field of reference. It is a veritable gallimaufry of comedic effects and methodologies. From the outset its parodic intent is obvious; but rather than confronting *Pamela* head on in the manner of its predecessor, it subsumes that novel into its own world of discourse. Not the least amusing aspect of this strategy is the calm effrontery with which the anonymous author appropriates Pamela Andrews as a character in his own supposedly true book about her brother, in the process both ridiculing Richardson's pretence of factuality, and endorsing the morality of *Pamela* through the assertion that 'it was by keeping the excellent Pattern of his Sister's virtues before his Eyes, that Mr Joseph Andrews was chiefly enabled to preserve his Purity in the midst of such great Temptations'. (I:i)

But the attempted seduction of Joseph by Lady Booby is a parody which questions its own assumptions. If Joseph's resistance to the blandishments of this latter-day Potiphar's wife is initially absurd, it is because we see it in the light of Pamela's more provisional resistance to Lady Booby's nephew; but once *Pamela* is forgotten, Joseph as the hero of his own story can be seen as naturally loyal to his delectable true love Fanny. Instead of commending chastity in the abstract, the comedy directs us towards a living human relationship: Joseph has someone *for whom* to be chaste, and the comic reversal of rôles permits the assertion, where chastity is in question, of an equality between the sexes. The original humorous intention is outflanked.

By such means the parodic element in the novel opens out quite naturally into the shape of comic epic. The very naturalism with which the conversation between Lady Booby and her maid Slipslop, as to the form her attitude to the obstinately chaste young footman should now take, involves a different kind of attention than that aroused by the slapdash interchanges found in *Shamela*. And once Parson Adams comes on the scene a genuine comedic note is struck, for here we have a Quixote figure, whose very innocence and generosity are potentially damaging in a corrupted world. 'As he had never any Intention to deceive, so he never suspected such a Design in others'. (I:iii) But Adams's names are emblematic: the man of faith who is also Everyman is here matched with the wise, chaste, put-upon and ultimately vindicated Joseph, whose own surname, in the context of Fielding's (rather than of Richardson's) imagination, suggests festive celebration – a merry Andrew indeed. The journey of the two men back to their respective homes is an Odyssey that has its Homeric parallels; but Fielding prefers to set up random correspondences (such as that of Parson Trulliber and his pigs with the swine-herd Eumæus) rather than to establish a fixed frame of allegorical reference. These correspondences are endorsed by textual forms of parody, as in the various mock-heroic accounts of weather, of battles and of states of feeling: the result is to reverse Richardson's technique and to establish in the reader's mind the fictive and artificial nature of such literary undertakings.

The principal theme of the book, however, is anything but artificial. As against the stilted emotionalism and domestic preoccupations of *Pamela*, Fielding celebrates the world of mid-eighteenth-century England in all its vigour, diversity and lawlessness. Nothing is stable: we are forever on the move, judgements are modified or rescinded, expectations overthrown, rigidity of belief or opinion refuted, all with a continuous undertow of good humour which serves to make the sardonic commentaries still more lacerating. In this particular world the love of money is the prevailing source of evil, the lack of it the inevitable prelude to misfortune; but despite such vigilant attention to human venality and greed, it is the power of human kindness, what Fielding designates 'good nature', which calls the tune, the poor and unfortunate who are generous, the afflicted who are ready with help and consolation. *Joseph Andrews* celebrates the unexpected, confutes hardened attitudes, and exposes the stupidity of the morally inflexible as genuine comedy always does.

In addition to parody, the other faces of comedy contribute to the book's celebratory character. Where farce is concerned, one may turn to the episode when Adams ends up in Mrs Slipslop's bed, which forms a kind of saturnalia; while for irony, a classic instance can be found in the treatment of the robbed and naked Joseph when rescued by a coach-party after being beaten up. Having told how he 'absolutely refused, miserable as he was, to enter, unless he was furnished with sufficient Covering, to prevent giving the least offence to Decency', Fielding goes on poker-faced to comment,

> So perfectly modest was this young Man; such mighty Effects had the spotless example of the amiable *Pamela*, and the excellent sermons of Mr *Adams* wrought upon him. (I:xii)

The distinctive Fielding touch here is that the straight-faced mockery of Pamela is accompanied by a more straightforward compliment to Adams – a compliment, however, that is to be modified as the tale proceeds.

A different kind of irony, a dramatic one, occurs at the story's conclusion when Joseph and Fanny, confronted with the (fortunately incorrect) revelation that they are brother and sister, are hardly consoled by Adams's thankfulness that they have thus been spared a grievous sin. A further irony ensues when it is discovered that they have been exchanged as children and that Joseph is not therefore Pamela's brother at all. By removing its initial *raison d'être*, the novel has finally cut loose from its parodic opening.

There is plenty of satire, a good instance being the exchange of amenities between Slipslop and Miss Grave-airs when the latter declines to allow a footman to ride with her in the coach.

> "Madam," says *Slipslop*, "I am sure no one can refuse another coming into a Stage-Coach." "I don't know, Madam," says the Lady, "I am not much used to Stage-Coaches, I seldom travel in them." "That may be, Madam," replied *Slipslop*, "very good People do, and some People's Betters, for aught I know." *Miss Grave-airs* said, "some Folks, might sometimes give their Tongues a liberty, to some People that were their Betters, which did not become them: for her part, she was not used to converse with Servants." *Slipslop* returned, "some People kept no Servants to converse with: for her

Part, she thanked Heaven, she lived in a Family where there were a great many; and had more under her own Command than any paltry little Gentlewoman in the Kingdom." Miss *Grave-airs* cry'd, "she believed, her Mistress would not encourage such Sauciness to her Betters." "My Betters," says *Slipslop*, "who is my Betters, pray?" "I am your Betters," answered Miss *Grave-airs*, "and I'll acquaint your Mistress." – At which Mrs *Slipslop* laughed aloud, and told her, "her Lady was one of the great Gentry, and such little paultry Gentlewomen, as some Folks who travelled in Stage-Coaches, would not easily come at her." (II:v)

Game and set, one feels. The theme of snobbery is to recur again and again in English fiction, but seldom is it expounded at such a spanking pace and with such twirls and volleys as are executed here. (The embedding of the dialogue in a single paragraph furthers the effect of imminent combustion.)

The more involved, conniving and graphic methods of burlesque are illustrated in scenes such as Adams's dowsing with a bucket of pig's blood, and more purposefully in the account of Parson Trulliber. Despite one brief appearance, he makes all the impact of a sacred monster.

The Hogs fell chiefly to his care, which he carefully waited on at home, and attended to Fairs; on which occasion he was liable to many Jokes, his own Size being with much Ale rendered little inferior to that of the beasts he sold. He was indeed one of the largest Men you should see, and could have acted the part of Sir John Falstaff without stuffing. Add to this, that the Rotundity of his Belly was considerably increased by the shortness of his Stature, his Shadow ascending very near as far in height when he lay on his Back, as when he stood on his Legs. His Voice was loud and hoarse, and his Accents extremely broad; to complete the whole, he had a Stateliness in his Gate, when he walked, not unlike that of a Goose, only he stalked slower. (II:xiv)

The touch about the shadow might have come from Dickens, the humour being remarkable for its visually analytic quality; but there is an avoidance of rhetoric, save for the masterly rhythmic deployment of 'only he stalked slower'. Had the passage ended on 'goose', Trulliber would have been a comical object merely; but by that masterly transference of 'walk' into 'stalk' he becomes a subject with whom one is going to have to deal.

But it is the wit that flickers from page to page which keeps the book alight with a gaiety that is never whimsical or merely superficial. Consider the treatment of the theme of vanity. Chapter Fifteen of Book One concludes with a sudden outburst, commencing 'O Vanity! How little is thy Force acknowledged, or thy Operations discern'd?' and proceeds in the finest palpitating manner to wind up with 'The Bully Fear, like a coward flies before thee, and Joy and Grief hide their Heads in thy Presence.' One can almost hear the preacher smack his lips before lowering his voice to drive the point more intimately home.

> I know thou wilt think, that whilst I abuse thee, I court thee; and that thy Love hath inspired me to write this sarcastical Panegyrick on thee: but thou art deceived, I value thee not a farthing; nor will it give me any Pain, if thou shouldst prevail on the Reader to censure this Digression as errant Nonsense: for know to thy Confusion, that I have introduced thee for no other Purpose than to lengthen out a short Chapter; and so I return to my history.

The neatness of the reversal chastises both complacent vanity and the complacent reader.

The joke is resumed with variations during Mr Wilson's story of his life, in the course of which he remarks that vanity is the worst of passions. This causes Adams to fumble in his pocket

> after a Sermon, which he thought his Masterpiece, against Vanity. "I would read it, for I am confident you would admire it: Indeed I have never been a greater Enemy to any Passion than that silly one of Vanity." (III:iii)

Adams's pride in his sermons is a weakness which makes his humanity the more winning.

The whole tenor of *Joseph Andrews* is to vindicate normality and to rebut pretence – and vanity. The Preface makes this clear: 'The Ridiculous only [...] falls within my province in the present work.' And the object of ridicule is affectation, the fruit of vanity and cant. The display of discrepancies between appearance and reality pervades the book; but what makes it truly comedic, rather than merely satirical, is the universality of those discrepancies – not only Parsons Barnabas and Trulliber are exposed, but also Parson Adams himself; nor does the deception inherent in appearances necessarily tend towards the uncovering of evil: the good may equally lie hidden where it is least expected.

Perhaps the most telling scene is that of the 'smoking' or 'flyting' of Adams by the hunting squire and his cronies. It is a criticism of humour in itself. The monolithic, insensitive and unimaginative mind delights in crude practical jokes; and Adams's dignified rebuke of the assembled party for their discourtesy towards a guest has a Johnsonian ring. Even so, the author will not allow matters to stop at that: Adams has still to endure a ducking before he can retaliate in kind. Fielding is always wary in his usage of the high moral tone. But his trouncing of cheap humour, insinuation, and facetiousness is unrelenting: the twelfth chapter of Book One contains a succession of lewd puns presented in *oratio obliqua* – a method that should shame any reader who might have been betrayed into a snigger had it been recounted at first hand.

Indeed, humorous pretensions are anatomised no less than are religious, cultural or literary ones; and in the last chapter of all, the balance between true and false comedy is established at the wedding of the lovers,

> at which nothing was so remarkable as the extraordinary and unaffected Modesty of *Fanny*, unless the true Christian Piety of *Adams*, who publickly rebuked Mr *Booby* and Pamela for laughing in so sacred a Place and so solemn an Occasion [...] It was his Maxim, that he was a Servant of the Highest, and could not, without departing from his Duty, give up the least Article of his Honour, or of his Cause, to the greatest earthly Potentate. Indeed he always asserted, that Mr *Adams* at Church with his Surplice on, and Mr *Adams* without that Ornament, in any other place, were two very different Persons.

The distinction between the sacred office and the character of the person holding it is not only fundamental to the concept of priesthood, but also a theological refinement of that distinction between appearance and reality which underlies the dissective and analytic proceedings of the comedic process, and which it is the nature of the monolithic outlook to deny.

Innocence abroad: *The Pickwick Papers*

In the fourth chapter of *David Copperfield* Dickens attributes to his young protagonist his own boyhood delight in *Don Quixote*, *Gil Blas* and the eighteenth-century English novelists, 'a glorious host, to keep me company. They kept alive my fancy and my hope of something beyond that place and time'. It is a function of comedy to do so; and Dickens's first – and indeed only – systematic essay in comedic fiction certainly owes much to Fielding and Smollett, and still more to Cervantes. *The Posthumous Papers of the Pickwick Club* (1837) began as a projected series of comic sporting sketches, to follow in the wake of the recently successful *Jorrocks' Jaunts and Jollities* of R.S. Surtees. Such sketches were popular at the time, and these were designed to accompany drawings by the sporting artist Robert Seymour; but by a series of mishaps, culminating in the latter's suicide, they ended up as a picaresque romance not far off a comic epic.

The first chapter is pure parody and the fruit of journalistic observation. Its relentless facetiousness is lowering to the spirits of a later age, and the Samuel Pickwick who reads to his admirers his 'Speculations on the Source of the Hampstead Ponds, with some Observations on the Theory of Tittlebats' is a very different man from the dispenser of material blessings who presides over the story's conclusion. Tupman, Snodgrass and Winkle each have their separate monolithic speciality, and the book's constituents seem set to be as systematic as are the researches of the Pickwick Club's Corresponding Society. Only Mr Blotton of Aldgate sounds off a warning gong that such pretensions are all vanity and will go for nothing.

Indeed the derivative humour and its occasions disperse like fog: the 11 chapters that follow are the most carefree and uncomplicated that Dickens ever wrote. Parody gives way to playfulness, a morning light suffuses the comic action. Two things at the start effect this change. The first sign is the contrast between the parodic account of the dawn ('The punctual servant of all work, the sun, had just risen ...') with the essentially Dickensian description of the wind 'like a distant giant whistling for his house-dog'. The second and more significant is Pickwick's note-taking, in conformity with his status in the self-consciously 'literary' first chapter. This arouses the suspicions of his cab-driver and nearly aborts the expedition at its outset; then, as Pickwick deliberately takes down the outrageous lies of Mr Jingle, the absurdity of the enterprise and of the literary machinery which contains it becomes obvious. Both Jingle and the cab-driver assert their autonomy of the bookish context, the former striking the first note of grisly humour to sound in his creator's fiction.

> "Heads, heads—take care of your heads!" cried the loquacious stranger, as they came out under the low archway, which in those

days formed the entrance to the coach-yard. "Terrible place—dangerous work—other day—five children—mother—tall lady, eating sandwiches—forgot the arch—crash—knock—children look round—mother's head off—sandwich in her hand–no mouth to put it in—head of a family off—shocking, shocking! ... " (Chapter ii)

Such comical grotesquerie dogs all the adventures of the Pickwickian foursome. But in this opening section it is high spirits which predominate, and a stress on misadventure, misunderstanding, and incompetence upon which the fast-talking Jingle plays with a virtuoso's skill. The Pickwickians are innocents abroad and the victims of their own respective vanities – Pickwick as antiquary, Tupman as Lothario, and Winkle, most spectacularly, as sportsman. (Snodgrass the poet, however, reminds one more of Mary Bennet in *Pride and Prejudice*, who 'wished to say something very sensible, but knew not how'.)

The climax of the first section, the elopement of Jingle with Miss Wardle, serves to introduce the character of Sam Weller, who is among other things to be the story's ironical mouthpiece. Sam and his father, the coachman Tony Weller, are true Cockneys in their good-humoured disenchantment with the world, their capacity for endurance and their capacity for pleasure. Sam's recurrent verbal tic of the 'as-the-so-and-so-said-to-the-whatsit' variety provides a gruesome undertone of realism, exemplified by 'I only assisted natur', ma'am; as the doctor said to the boy's mother, arter he'd bled him to death'. (Chapter xlvii) It is the more appropriate that his engagement as Pickwick's servant should be the origin of Mrs Bardell's suit for breach of promise, which precipitates the entry into a world of savage actuality. For now the story moves from ludic to satirical comedy as the group sets off to view the Eatanswill election.

The satire, however, is broad and too exaggerated to be really telling; and despite the delights of Mrs Leo Hunter's *fête champêtre*, it is a relief to go to Ipswich in quest of Jingle and his servant Job Trotter, whose outwitting of Sam Weller introduces a touch of comedy within comedy: the latter's being himself taken in humanises him and enhances his stature. As to Pickwick, at this stage he is much put-upon, victimised in a burlesque manner by Trotter and later by the Ipswich magistrate; and this prepares us for the crueller victimisation he undergoes in the third portion of the book when the comical surface is disturbed by eruptions from below.

The breach of promise case of Bardell *versus* Pickwick has its origin in wishful thinking on her part and wilful blindness upon his: Dodson and Fogg play a demonic rôle in stirring up their evil brew from such beginnings. As soon as Dickens starts to describe the Inns of Court the tone changes.

> These sequestered nooks are the public offices of the legal profession, where writs are issued, judgements signed, declarations filed, and numerous other ingenious machines put in motion for the torture and torment of His Majesty's liege subjects, and the comfort and emolument of the practitioners of the law. They are, for the most part, low-roofed, mouldy rooms, where innumerable rolls of parchment, which have been perspiring in secret for the last century, send forth an agreeable odour, which is mingled by day with the scent of the dry rot, and by night with the various exhalations which arise from damp cloaks, festering umbrellas, and the coarsest tallow candles. (Chapter xxxi)

Only Dickens could have dreamed up 'festering umbrellas'; and indeed here the narrator himself takes over, no longer transmitting through the Pickwickians' reactions but speaking in his proper person. Significantly, Pickwick has just suffered what comes to look like a ritual immersion beneath the ice at Dingley Dell; and following the mild satirical diversions at Bath, the trap closes and, armoured in his own integrity, he is in the Fleet Prison for declining to pay what he considers to be unjust costs. Here the comic protagonist is forced into close contact with his fellow men – and in so doing almost breaks the unspoken contract of comedic fiction, the contract that the comic world shall subsist within its own territory and preserve innocent and entire its fictive nature. Pickwick himself accepts his limitations.

> "I have seen enough," said Mr Pickwick, as he threw himself into a chair in his little apartment. "My head aches with these scenes, and my heart too. Henceforth I will be a prisoner in my own room." (Chapter xlv)

The fatal knowledge that despair is possible has knocked upon the door, and it is the function of Sam Weller's comic ironies to keep it out.

It is the author's responsibility as well; and Dickens achieves his hero's release by a neat piece of dramatic irony, whereby Mrs Bardell is imprisoned in her turn for her failure to make good the costs of Dodson and Fogg which Pickwick has refused to pay. But the devil must have his due. Pickwick's release is a necessary compromise with principle – he too has been in danger of becoming monolithic. Thereafter the comedy turns celebratory; thoughts run to marriage; Pickwick disposes largesse, the Wellers, retribution; and the Pickwick Club dissolves. Pickwick himself has moved through light-hearted exploration of contemporary England, by way of the abyss of the Fleet prison, to the re-establishing of justice and a bestowal of blessings – a classic comedic structure.

As much as *Joseph Andrews*, *The Pickwick Papers* is a compendium of comic themes and motivs. In places one is aware of parallels – Pickwick himself can be as luckless and gullible as Parson Adams, witness his accidental intrusion into Miss Witherfield's bedroom in The Great White Horse at Ipswich. The coarse vigour of Fielding's portrayal of Adams getting into bed with Slipslop is replaced by the demure impropriety of the night-capped Pickwick peeping out between the curtains: the tyrannous world of ladylike decorum is always a butt and an avenger in this kind of masculine comedy. As a writer of slapstick Dickens lacks Fielding's panache and unselfconscious boisterousness (one is always conscious of a family readership requiring euphemisms to prevent embarrassment) but none the less the following is both neat and characteristic of its author.

> There are very few moments in a man's existence when he experiences so much ludicrous distress, or meets with so little charitable commiseration, as when he is in pursuit of his own hat. A vast deal of coolness, and a peculiar degree of judgement, are requisite in catching a hat. A man must not be precipitate, or he runs over it; he must not rush into the opposite extreme, or he loses it altogether. The best way is, to keep up gently with the object of pursuit, to be wary and cautious, to watch your opportunity well, get gradually before it, then make a rapid dive, seize it by the crown, and stick it firmly on your head: smiling pleasantly all the time, as if you thought it as good a joke as anybody else. (Chapter iv)

It is such incongruous occasions which provide material for the comic sense. The monolithic person is affronted by them.

One of the strengths of *The Pickwick Papers* lies in its accommodation of individual people's notions of humour as an element within comedy itself. Dickens is alert to the cruelty in much that is considered humorous, no less than he is to the cruelty in anything else. Sam Weller's various sick jokes are one case in point, as are the numerous misfortunes of the hapless Winkle, which are farcical in the best Fielding manner. More subtle is the account of the humourless Peter Magnus, a beautifully observed portrait of a self-consequential fusspot.

> Peter Magnus—sounds well, I think, sir. [...] You will observe—P.M.—post meridian. In hasty notes to intimate acquaintances, I sometimes sign myself 'Afternoon'. It amuses my friends very much, Mr Pickwick. (Chapter xxii)

Mr Leo Hunter is a further instance of the comedy inherent in solemnity: his wife, superbly fatuous though she may be, with her 'Ode to an Expiring Frog', would not be half so funny without his acting as her impresario. Indeed, Dickens's comic effects here are less amusing when presented frontally than when observed obliquely through the eyes of someone who does not find them funny at all. Joe, the fat boy, is never so risible as when pounding on Mr Perker's office door: the reader is party to a joke to which those inside the office are not. The fat boy is but one of many figures of the comedy of humours to crowd the book. Such characters are designed to be wheeled on and to sound off on a single note, predictable, stagey, and amusing to the extent that their entrances and exits are. Dickens was to develop these figures to more telling effect in later novels, and in this one he allows Tupman and Winkle to become three-dimensional and pathetic through acting not exclusively in character. Snodgrass is left undeveloped, but even he has his immortal moment when, on the morning of the breach of promise trial, he speculates, 'by way of keeping up a conversation', 'I wonder what the foreman of the jury, whoever he'll be, has got for breakfast'. (Chapter xxxiv) It is one of those occasions when a fictional character seems to speak for innumerable human beings at such times of embarrassment and tension.

Dickens's humour is frequently companionable in this way. His account of the Pump Room at Bath is a loaded description which in every turn of phrase assumes a knowing readership.

> There is a large bar with a marble vase, out of which the pumper gets the waters; and there are a number of yellow-looking tumblers out of which the company gets it; and it is a most edifying and satisfactory sight to behold the perseverance and gravity with which they swallow it. There are baths near at hand, in which a part of the company wash themselves; and a band plays afterwards, to congratulate the remainder on their having done so. There is another pump-room, into which infirm ladies and gentlemen are

wheeled, in such astonishing variety of chairs and chaises, that any adventurous individual who goes in with the regular number of toes, is in imminent danger of coming out without them; and there is a third, into which the quiet people go, for it is less noisy than either. There is an immensity of promenading, on crutches and off, with sticks and without, and a great deal of conversation, and liveliness and pleasantry. (Chapter xxxvi)

The humour here is a matter of tone, with an indulgent softening at the end that marks the difference between the eighteenth- and nineteenth-century attitudes to human nature: the effects of the Evangelical revival, with its emphasis on domestic virtue and family cohesiveness, are already being felt, and were to have powerful support in Dickens's more sentimental celebrations, such as those robustly set forth in the Christmas scenes at Dingley Dell. The excesses of Evangelical religion, however, are contemptuously portrayed in the character of the Reverend Mr Stiggins, though one has to wait until *Bleak House* and Mr Chadband, with 'a good deal of train oil in his system', to see what Dickens could really do in this department. In *Pickwick* anger forces the pace, and the exposure scene when the coachmen get Stiggins drunk in public most disappointingly falls flat.

As against this emphasis on geniality, *Pickwick* also displays a troubling vein of misogynistic rancour. Practically every woman to appear is either a ninny or a shrew. The roll-call of nagging wives is formidable – Mrs Weller, Mrs Potts, Mrs Nupkins, Mrs Raddle, all of them resorting to fainting-fits with a pertinacity worthy of the heroines of Jane Austen's juvenilia. Silly women also are legion – the pathetic old maiden aunt, Miss Wardle, or the more opportunist Mrs Bardell. The young women, whether servants or daughters of the employer class, are good for little else than roguish gallantry and a stolen kiss. This is a book for bachelors – the Pickwick Club is confined to men (as it would be at that time) and the stress on male bonding glows with warmth, most notably in the affectionate, sparring relationship between the Wellers, father and son, or, more obliquely, in the scapegrace comradeship of the medical students Ben Allen and Bob Sawyer, delightfully captured in the following exchange concerning Arabella Allen's preference for Nathaniel Winkle.

"You loved her when we were boys at school together, and, even then, she was wayward, and slighted your young feelings. Do you

recollect, with all the eagerness of a child's love, one day pressing upon her acceptance, two small caraway-seed biscuits and one sweet apple, neatly folded into a circular parcel with the leaf of a copybook?"
"I do," replied Bob Sawyer.
"She slighted that, I think?" said Ben Allen.
"She did," rejoined Bob. "She said I had kept the parcel so long in the pockets of my corduroys, that the apple was unpleasantly warm."
"I remember," said Mr Allen, gloomily. "Upon which we ate it ourselves, in alternate bites." (Chapter xlviii)

Dickens has a great appreciation of boys and their ways; and there is a whole gallery of others like them, from the fat boy to Tommy Bardell: they flash on the scene and off again, given momentary life characteristic of the overall comic vision of the book, which is alight with a vivacity the author never quite displayed again.

For the carefree world of pure comedy is menaced by the social realities of the Fleet prison, and although Pickwick himself turns his back on them, certain rifts in the fabric make themselves felt early on in such an officious comment on Mrs Leo Hunter as 'Minerva with a fan!', in which the exclamation-mark gives an uncomfortable effect of authorial self-distancing from his creation. A similar misjudgement occurs when Joe is knocking at Mr Perker's door and Pickwick remarks on it 'as if there could be the smallest doubt of the fact!' Again that tell-tale exclamation-mark: one senses a shepherding authorial intrusion. The comedy is not allowed to speak for itself.

More serious are the weakening effects of sentiment, anticipated in the hortatory introduction to the Christmas scenes at Dingley Dell (a favourite with Victorian readers) and quite disastrously at the conclusion of the story, when the buoyant vitality of Jingle, which got the entire adventure off to such a rousing start, is rendered flaccid with remorse. The failure of comic nerve at this point anticipates the split between sentiment and moral indignation which is a feature of the Victorian consciousness, and which is to be exemplified most conspicuously in the fiction of Dickens's contemporary and rival, Thackeray.

However, the predominating mood of *Pickwick* is celebratory, expressive of the comic process in all its aspects, even if some of them, that of burlesque especially, await their full development. In this world-picture the enemies are the monolithic aspects of Evangelical religion and the Law, vindictiveness, hypocrisy and greed. Pickwick himself learns his lesson in the world: nowhere is innocence better shown and distinguished from gullibility than when he permits himself to be carried in a wheelbarrow at Mr Wardle's shooting party. But it is Sam whose sense of irony holds the two poles of optimism and disenchantment in balance. And his humour is but one aspect of the verbal wit which pervades the book, as when Peter Magnus is said to have 'conjugated himself into the imperative mood', or in the extended metaphor (to him perfectly natural) in which Tony Weller likens his wife's demise to the last journey of a mail coach. To adapt Chesterton's comment on Sam Weller, it is Dickens's achievement in *The Pickwick Papers* that 'the reader cannot go on being content merely with people to laugh at when he has found someone he can laugh with'.[3]

Clerical errors: *Barchester Towers*

A hallmark of celebratory comedy is the sense of liberation it induces. Unshackled by rebellious or revolutionary principle, disrespectful towards established institutions that take themselves for granted, yet declining to identify the sinner with the sin, it reveals an attitude of resolute but not undiscriminating tolerance. That it is not afraid to scrutinise dark places, both *Joseph Andrews* and *The Pickwick Papers* attest; that it is not afraid to make light of treasured spiritual projections is exuberantly demonstrated in one of the breeziest and, implicitly, most radical of nineteenth-century novels, *Barchester Towers* (1857).

Having opened up a mine of unexplored fictive material in *The Warden* (1855), Anthony Trollope now exploited it in what is still the most popular of his 47 novels. But the cosy cathedral-close setting which renders the book so delightful to a later age was not at the time of its appearance the occasion for nostalgia or for gentle satire that it since became. As *Barchester Towers* itself makes clear, theological divisions within the Church of England were at the time taken with consuming seriousness. Although Trollope crystallises them into seemingly trivial particularities (Mrs Proudie's obsession with 'Sabbath Day Schools', for instance, or Mr Slope's attacks on the cathedral's musical tradition) the gap between the Evangelicals and the supporters of the Catholic-orientated Oxford Movement did represent serious questions as to the nature of a metaphysical institution in which the nation officially believed. In making fun of these divisions and these personalised embodiments of authorised religion, Trollope was being more challenging to established attitudes than he perhaps intended. For whereas previous novelists had satirised, even attacked, the characters of individual priests and ministers, none of them had played with the institutionalised religion of their day as he does here. It is the rocking of a communal boat that interests and amuses him; it is the fallibility and confused motivation of his clerical personages which his novel demonstrates. They are personalities rather than mere types; but they are personalities who express themselves through their clerical functions, and who are related to people through those functions.

The comedy in *Barchester Towers* derives from the fragmentation of the monolithic ecclesiastical establishment as a social structure. The force of the dominance of the imperious Mrs Proudie, the references to her as 'Bishopess', have the effect of diminishing the male characters – for she confronts not only the hen-pecked Bishop but also the recalcitrant Archdeacon and the insinuating Mr Slope. Even if she is playing the traditional masculine rôle, it is the female principle in her which triumphs. The customary hierarchies of fictive presences are also lacking in the book. Gone are the divisions between protagonists and supporting cast: Eleanor Bold and Mr Arabin may be the official hero and heroine, but their story is subordinate to that of the social organism as a whole. *Barchester Towers* is an exercise in the assertion of dramatic relativities – as witness the portrayal of the raffish Stanhope family, who are worldly in a context which makes that worldliness amount to a critique. They provide an anti-Victorian voice, and their charm exposes the limitations of their surroundings. But the author has their measure.

> The great family characteristic of the Stanhopes might probably be said to be heartlessness; but this want of feeling was, in most of them, accompanied by so great an amount of good nature as to make itself but little noticeable to the world. They were so prone to oblige their neighbours that their neighbours failed to perceive how indifferent to them was the happiness and well-being of those around them. (Chapter ix)

Trollope's own good-natured tone is both the conductor of the comedy and the assertion of a personal authorial freedom. He plays his own games of intertextuality, borrowing a character from Disraeli's *Coningsby* (1844) and accounting for the name of his odious clerical conspirator by references to a writer more distinguished still.

> I have heard it asserted that he is lineally descended from that eminent physician who assisted at the birth of Mr T. Shandy, and

that in early years he added an 'e' to his name, for the sake of euphony, as other great men have done before him. If this be so, I presume he was christened Obadiah, for that is his name, in commemoration of the conflict in which his ancestor so distinguished himself. (Chapter iv)

No less than Sterne does Trollope blatantly refer to his own authorial manœuvres, arguing against keeping his readers in the dark as to his characters' future (since he has after all invented them himself), announcing the commencement of each separate volume, and above all by cynically intervening when Eleanor and Arabin, so close to an understanding, are prevented from reaching it through her powers of self-restraint.

Had she given way and sobbed aloud, as in such cases a woman should do, he would have melted at once, implored her pardon, perhaps knelt at her feet and declared his love. Everything would have been explained, and Eleanor would have gone back to Barchester with a contented mind. How easily would she have forgiven and forgotten the Archdeacon's suspicions had she but heard the whole truth from Mr Arabin. But then where would have been my novel? (Chapter xxx)

No wonder Henry James threw up his hands at Trollope's casual attitude to the novelist's veridical responsibilities.[4]

But worldly-wise though Trollope is, he is not a cynic about people: if where womanly subordination is concerned he can weaken his effects by playing along with contemporary sentiment, he can also deepen them by articulating a serious charge against the monolithic attitudes of the clergy of whom he makes such indulgent fun.

It had always been taken for granted by those around her that they were indubitably right, that there was no ground for doubt, that the hard uphill work of ascertaining what the duty of a clergyman should be had been already accomplished in full; and that what remained for an active militant parson to do, was to hold his own against all comers. (Chapter xxi)

But this serious note only sounds from time to time; more often in *Barchester Towers* it is a case, as with Mr Slope's disastrous proposal to Eleanor at the Ullathorne sports, of champagne breaking forth. It remains the most high-spirited of Trollope's books because of the sheer pleasure it takes both in the absurdities and the securities of the world it so lovingly yet disrespectfully describes. No one in the story is faultless; the handling is uniformly naturalistic. But the sense of abounding vitality is as omnipresent as is the author's own presiding voice. *Barchester Towers* is among other things a celebration of fictive freedoms, one that is based on a certainty as to the underlying soundness of the material on which novelists embroider. It may cast a wary eye on ecclesiastical institutions, but it enhances one's sense of the multiplicity of human opportunities for modifying potential criticism. The monolith is left as tattered as were Mrs Proudie's flounces by the wheels of the Signora Vesey-Neroni's sofa.

A pack of cards: Evelyn Waugh

Regardless of time and fashion, certain novelists will always appeal to certain kinds of reader. Admirers of Thomas Hardy will probably be admirers of Walter Scott; those of Jane Austen, of Henry James. And those who enjoy Trollope are likely to appreciate the work of Evelyn Waugh, even though the two writers differ drastically in several ways. Waugh is witty, Trollope is not; Trollope is leisurely, discursive, fundamentally benign, where Waugh is economical, fast-moving, waspish and belligerent. But both are worldly-wise and are preoccupied with organisations and political affairs (in Trollope's case, parliament, in Waugh's, the army). Both have a sharp eye for the absurd, both are intolerant of cant and self-deception, and both are endlessly and undemandingly re-readable.

Where Trollope mocks the ecclesiastical establishment,[5] Waugh makes game of the life of fashionable society; and he does so with the assurance of one who had the entry to it – without, however, being conditioned by it as were two novelists who benefited from his literary example, Anthony Powell and Nancy Mitford. Avoiding in his early novels their use of first person narrative, he achieves an authorial inconspicuousness which allows one to move unchaperoned within his world. There is a self-sufficiency about his comic vision that transcends the savagery and bitterness of some of its constituents. But if his work displays an eighteenth-century callousness, it is also full of an infectious ribaldry, a sense of mischief that is singularly liberating: 'often one can sense behind [his] writing the presence of a schoolboy who knows to a hair's breadth how to keep his impudence out of the reach of retribution ...'.[6] It is an engaging quality, and one which enables Waugh to defy the monolithic definitions of what is and is not a permissible subject for a jest. For all its element of satire and burlesque, his work is celebratory in its overall effect.

If they do not readily lend themselves to systematic appraisal, his novels remain susceptible to a degree of methodological analysis. There is, for example, the fact of their comprehensive comedic strategies. Waugh is able to turn his hand with equal effectiveness to parody, to farce, to irony, to satire and burlesque. Where parody is concerned, he pounces joyfully on the distortions and frivolities of the popular press, most notably in *Vile Bodies* (1930) and, more systematically, in *Scoop* (1938). His gift of mimicry, so evident in his mastery of dialogue, serves him well in this respect: in *Work Suspended* (1941) there is a perfectly judged take-off of the belle-lettrist manner affected by his father, the publisher Arthur Waugh. When it comes to farce, few writers have such perfect mastery of timing as he displays in the account of how, following an all-night party three days long, the Honourable Agatha Runcible, apparelled in Hawaiian garb, emerges by accident through the front door of Number Ten Downing Street, to encounter the jubilant attentions of a crowd of waiting journalists. Or, as an instance of his mastery of phraseology, one can turn to *Scoop*, with its description of the come-uppance of a bully who, after delivering his parting threat, 'rose with dignity and swaggered into the yard'.

> The milch-goat looked up from her supper of waste paper; her perennial optimism quickened within her, and swelled to a great and mature confidence; all day she had shared the exhilaration of the season, her pelt had glowed under the newborn sun; deep in her heart she too had made holiday, had cast off the doubts of winter and exulted among the crimson flowers; all day she had dreamed gloriously; now in the limpid evening she gathered her strength, stood for a moment rigid, quivering from horn to tail; then charged, splendidly, irresistibly, triumphantly; the rope snapped and the welter-weight champion of the Adventist University of Alabama sprawled on his face amid the kitchen garbage. (II:iv:5)

Slapstick and elegance are triumphantly combined, the effect only enhanced by the pastiche of grandiose descriptive prose.

But anger can energise Waugh's comic effects no less than can high spirits and his delight in incongruity: there is the whole of *A Handful of Dust* (1934) to demonstrate the truth of that contention. This lean and understated novel resembles a fist prepared to strike. The conclusion of Tony Last's matrimonial tragedy, when he is trapped, seemingly for life, reading Dickens aloud to a madman in the Amazonian jungle, serves as a reflection of what has gone before, rather than as a continuation of it: only thus could the author's poker-faced mask remain unfrozen before the cold-hearted frivolity of the world he so effectively despises. In *A Handful of Dust* the comedy implodes.

Waugh's sense of satire is closely bound up with his aptitude for burlesque. The two gifts are exercised in harness in *The Loved One* (1948), a novella which uses bad taste to castigate the very follies that bad taste ensures. This account of Californian funeral rites is the kind of exercise that Aldous Huxley might have undertaken; but Waugh is blessed with a jauntiness that avoids the squeamish quality which compromises Huxley's brand of satire.

> With a steady hand Aimée fulfilled the prescribed rites of an American girl preparing to meet her lover – dabbed herself under the arms with a preparation designed to seal the sweat-glands, gargled another to sweeten the breath, and brushed into her hair some odorous drops from a bottle labelled: 'Jungle Venom' – *From the depth of the fever-ridden swamp,* the advertisement had stated, *where juju drums throb for the human sacrifice, Jeanette's latest exclusive creation* Jungle Venom *comes to you with the remorseless stealth of the hunting cannibal.*

The Loved One is carried through with a bravado that would have delighted Swift.

Burlesque predominates in *Black Mischief* (1932), the one of Waugh's comedies to present the greatest challenge to subsequent taste. It contains in the person of Basil Seal (a latter-day version of Saki's Comus Bassington) a Lord of Misrule who, besides influencing the comic novelists of the 1950s, also turns the attack upon the phonier aspects of the culture his creator deeply loved: his hawking of the three appalling evacuee children in *Put Out More Flags* (1942) abounds in sadistic glee. Waugh creates his own species of sacred monster – individuals of ungovernable ineptitude who disturb as much as they amuse – Captain Grimes in *Decline and Fall* (1928), Apthorpe in *Men at Arms* (1952) come instantly to mind. Anthony Blanche in *Brideshead Revisited* (1945) is a monster of a more familiar sort. His method of dealing with bullies is as effective, albeit more subtle, than that of Frau Dressler's goat in *Scoop*.

"Dear sweet clodhoppers, if you knew anything of sexual psychology you would know that nothing could give me keener pleasure than to be manhandled by you meaty boys."

But Waugh is not prepared to indulge in mere camp extravagance: Blanche is a tough customer, and morally so as well. He forestalls his tormentors by entering the college fountain of his own accord.

"When they're all married to scraggy little women like hens and have cretinous, porcine sons like themselves, getting drunk at the same club dinner in the same coloured coats, they'll still say, when my name is mentioned, 'We put him in Mercury one night,' and their barnyard daughters will snigger and think their father was quite a dog in his day, and what a pity he's grown so dull. Oh, *la fatigue du Nord*!" (Chapter ii)

The satire flickers back and forth, no more at the expense of Blanche's victims than at his own.

More characteristic is the portrayal of Attwater in *Work Suspended*, one of the finest instances of Waugh's analytic wit. A commercial traveller who has run down and killed the narrator's father, he voices an uncertainty and a brashness that both pinpoints a psychological and social type, and personifies the slipshod irresponsibility and spiritual illiteracy that Waugh by implication castigates as the besetting sins of the contemporary world.

"Mr Attwater," I said, "have I misunderstood you, or are you asking me to break the law by helping you to evade your trial and also give you a large sum of money?"

"'You'll get it back, every penny of it."

"And our sole connection is the fact that, through pure insolence, you killed my father."

"Oh, well, if you feel like that about it ... "

"I am afraid you greatly overrate my good nature."

"Tell you what. I'll make you a sporting offer. You give me fifty pounds now and I'll pay it back in a year plus another fifty pounds to any charity you care to name. How's that?" (I:v)

An instance of the author's gift for conversational exchange, the passage conveys an appreciation of effrontery that epitomises his particular comic outlook. As an artist he is too responsive to be judgemental: all his characters condemn themselves out of their own mouths, to their creator's sardonic relish.

Waugh's comic personages range from the young lady in 'Cruise', with her offhand reiteration of 'Goodness how sad', to the fire-eating Ritchie-Hook of *Men at Arms* and, in *Black Mischief*, the ineffably frivolous Sir Samson Courtenay, Envoy Extraordinary to the African kingdom of Azania.

> The Bishop [...] knew all about native law and customs and the relative importance of the various factions at Court. He had what Sir Samson considered an ostentatious habit of referring by name to members of the royal household and to provincial governors, whom Sir Samson was content to remember as "the old black fellow who drank so much Kummel" or "that what-do-you-call-him Prudence said was like Aunt Sarah" or "the one with glasses and gold teeth". (Chapter ii)

But the supreme instance of parody slipping joyously into caricature occurs in *Scoop*. The decrepit country household at Boot Magna forms the background to Waugh's satirical attack on the newspaper magnate Lord Copper, the motto of whose *Daily Beast* is 'Self sufficiency at home, self assertion abroad'. The luckless William Boot refuses to abandon the self-sufficient leisureliness of home, and in the process becomes inconveniently, if unintentionally, absurd because he cannot adapt to the newspaper world; but his very failure makes that world appear ridiculous itself.

The real joker in Waugh's fictive pack, however, is *Helena* (1950), a historical tale as disconcerting to his readers as *Romola* was to George Eliot's. Waugh makes a tactful use of contemporary vernacular in order to achieve what one might call an analogical plausibility; there is nothing facetious about the humour that results. *Helena* offers as bleak a picture of the perennial double-dealing of politicians and aspiring socialites as do any of the previous novels; but it reserves its satire for the wilder flights of metaphysical speculation. For Helena, the Empress, wants facts, not theories: she looks for, and she finds, the actual cross on which Jesus of Nazareth was crucified. Her triumph is the triumph of the literal mind in quest of a monolithic certainty; and in presenting her case Waugh appears to be bent on confounding his own sophisticated readership. But this is in the name of the physical reality against which every form of purely mental speculation is, in Helena's schoolgirl terminology, mere 'bosh'. In this she voices her creator's authentically Catholic imagination. No less than the robustly humanistic Fielding, Waugh accepts that things are as they are: but he has none of a later humanism's plaintive disappointment at the spectacle of evil. For him human life is irrevocably fallen, though simultaneously redeemed: comedy is an affirmation of that simultaneity. Waugh's fictive world is therefore paradoxical, alert to evil but undismayed by it. If *Helena* is his ironic testament (even opposition to the monolith must not be monolithically absolute) it is a testament to the finality of the comedic process.

Speaking through the narrator of *Work Suspended*, Waugh permits himself to articulate his enthusiasm for domestic architecture 'in the classical tradition, and more particularly, in its decay'. (II:i) This balance of wildness and constraint, the blend of admiration for solid structures and clean lines with nostalgia for lost graciousness, forms a distant parallel to the theme and technique of a very different imaginative work by a Catholic writer, one which was appearing in the last decade of Waugh's life. J.R.R. Tolkien's *The Lord of the Rings* (1954–55) is a masterly piece of narrative architecture, a carefully pondered and worked out design which satisfies even more through its coherence and imaginative logic than through its surface detail. Its underlying theme is that of the inevitable nature of mortality and decay, and the inescapable passing, with the destruction of the Ring of Power, of the deathless and enlightened Elves. The Ring is both an agent and a symbol of a monolithic authoritarianism: the tragedy of the story is that to confront it on its own terms is to be absorbed by it; the triumphant comedic irony is that the one being whom the Ring has all but devoured and turned into itself should, through the very craving which it has induced, be the means of its destruction. This irony is a perfect instance of comedic justice, so consistent and self-sufficient as to be well nigh monolithic in its turn.

But there is one significant loose end in Tolkien's scheme of things in this imagined world. Early on in their mission to destroy the evil Ring, the Fellowship encounter a jovial being named Tom Bombadil. He lives in what appears to be a nursery-tale world; yet when he puts on the Ring, its power to confer a dangerous invisibility is helpless, and he fails to disappear. He would thus appear to be all-powerful, yet at first sight he is merry, careless, carefree, supremely unimpressive. A singer of songs and teller of riddles, he is the most mysterious figure on Middle Earth. Not even Elrond, the High Elf, can account for him, knowing him only as 'the same that walked the woods and hills long ago, and even then was older than the old'. The Ring has no power over him because, as Gandalf the wizard remarks, 'He is his own master [...] and if he were given the Ring he would soon forget it, or most likely throw it away. Such things have no hold on his mind.' (II:ii)

Bombadil, oldest of all and at the heart of all, is outside the dualistic conflict which is the subject of Tolkien's story. It is tempting to see in him a figure analogous to the celebratory function of comedy in a world riven by good and evil, whether these be accorded a metaphysical dimension or not. Comedy too is self-sufficient, oldest of all, bound up with the nature of affirmative consciousness itself. And it resembles Bombadil in being forever on the move. The very fact that he himself is so unimpressive, so unportentous, only goes to enhance his credentials as its image. When transmuted into gold the *prima materia* transcends the dichotomies and distinctions that give rise to the alchemical experiment.

10
Comedic Stylistics

> I wish it wasn't real life, our life, my life. Then I would find it a trifle more amusing.
>
> William Gerhardie, *Futility*

In the course of Nancy Mitford's *The Pursuit of Love* (1945) there occurs an exchange of literary amenities. Settling down to dinner beside her host, the 'dumpy little fluffy' Lady Kroesig, 'in bits of georgette and lace', purely by way of conversation asks the ferocious Uncle Matthew whether he has read a book called *Brothers*?

"What's that?"
"The new Ursula Langdock – *Brothers* – it's about two brothers. You ought to read it."
"My dear Lady Kroesig, I have only read one book in my life, and that is *White Fang*. It's so frightfully good, I've never bothered to read another ..." (Chapter ix)

Slam bang! Uncle Matthew is a monolithic reader. The book exists for *him*. His wants are satisfied, and that is that. Yet the same is true of Lady Kroesig. If he wants nothing else, she merely wants more of the same; if he is stationary in space, she is stationary in time. Fiction, for her, is a means of social exchange; to have read a contemporary novel simply because it is popular is quite enough. The comical collision of two non-readers is achieved with all this author's characteristic gaiety and verve.

'The new Ursula Langdock' – a degree of productiveness is called for to raise such expectations, and regularity of theme; but by 1950, whereas 'the new Angela Thirkell' (say) suggested one kind of readership, 'the new Graham Greene' suggested quite another. Those writers who, in their lifetime, had been accorded systematic critical attention were in the position of suppliers for more than a booksellers' market, each new work being liable to contribute to the promotion of yet another academic thesis. And today the author of *White Fang*, Jack London, has himself become grist for the literary industrial mills.

The moral standing of a novel has been transformed since distrust of the effects of reading one was endemic in eighteenth and early nineteenth-century religious circles. That unease arose from the suspicion, nurtured by a Biblically-based Protestantism, that even verbally to imitate God's works was tantamount to manufacturing idols. One attempt to deal with such an accusation was to evade the issue by disguising fictions as historic documents, following the procedures adopted by the Elizabethan Thomas Deloney and his seventeenth-century successors, Daniel Defoe and Aphra Behn. Such an illusion is most readily worked by combining text and commentary within a single voice: events are vouched for by a narrator who has experienced them at first hand, and problems of unorthodox or disturbing interpretations are subsumed into the portrayal of an exemplar, from whose life-story a lesson can be learned. The unity between events and their interpretation reflects the absolutism of Calvinistic teaching as to Biblical inerrancy, whereby every jot and tittle of the sacred scriptures were uncompromisingly accepted as being the word of God. In this respect an analogy may be drawn between the materialistic absolutism of the purely naturalistic novel and the dictates of Biblical fundamentalism. In both cases we are called upon to admire, and to respond to, what is effectively a closed book – a monolith.

Ironically, this reluctance to regard overt fiction as morally improving was to give rise to literary strategies that were themselves morally questionable. An insistence on documentary plausibility could lead to ingenuous, not to say ludicrous, methods of mendacious verification in order to establish a story's authenticity. In *Pamela*, for instance, the narrator is made to account for her possession of sufficient paper on which to write the enormously long letters that form the novel's text; while in *Clarissa* Lovelace can interrupt an impassioned confrontation with his victim to inform his correspondent that

> though this was written afterwards, yet (as in other places) I write it as it was spoken and happened, as if I had retired to put down every sentence as spoken. I know thou likest this lively *present-tense* manner, as it is one of my peculiars. (Letter cclvi)

Had this occurred in *Tristram Shandy* one would have said that Sterne was making his novel comment on its own technique, and that it was an instance of his involvement of the reading process in the deciphering of the text; but Richardson's scrupulosity signifies a literal-minded adherence to naturalistic theory. (In terms of Protestant theology, however, it compounds the deceit still further.) It was Fielding's great achievement to have cut through this epistemological confusion. *Joseph Andrews* pokes fun at self-protective naturalism by taking Richardson's claims to truthfulness at their face value; the author's effrontery in appropriating the characters in *Pamela* for his own fictive ends, and in treating them with a freedom only excusable on the Richardsonian assumption that they are real people, amounts to a declaration of the necessary relativity of any fictive pretensions to convey objective truth.

No wonder, then, that prose fiction has been resistant to classification under monolithic categories; and even by the late eighteenth century, when Richardson, Fielding, Sterne and Smollett had produced their most substantial work, an uncertainty remained as to correct nomenclature. The terms 'romance', 'novel', 'history' were bandied about by contemporary journalists and critics without any sense of their referring to one specific fictive category; the confusion is to be found as late as Walter Scott's Prefaces to Ballantyne's *Novelists' Library* (1821–24).[1] Indeed, there would seem to be something comically ambiguous inherent in the fictive process as such. Philosophically considered, works as different as *Moll Flanders*, *Clarissa* and *Tom Jones* are empowered by their awareness of the discrepancy between human aims and their fulfilment, and between human pretensions and the actuality. Such a divergence, treated ironically by Defoe, tragically by Richardson, and satirically by Fielding, is the basic premiss of comedy of every kind. But the novel itself, as a literary form, rests on a comic discrepancy, since the art of fiction by its very nature involves deceit – though a deceit that, being palpable, is to that extent harmless. In every fictive undertaking there is an element of play, of an arbitrary 'let's pretend'.

Such a sense of happy superfluity is a basic element in the experience of comedy; but it is no less inherent in the fictive process as such. A game is set up between writer and reader: plausibility is offset by unpredictability, certainty as to space by uncertainty as to time. Predetermining authors confound the predetermining expectations of their readers, while their function as regulators plays upon and corrects those readers' responses. And from time to time a novelist will quite blatantly proclaim the artificial nature of the exercise. Thackeray's conclusion of *Vanity Fair*, for all its bittersweet whimsy, is a joke at the reader's expense which is in effect no less brutal than is Hilaire Belloc's abrupt disclaimer at the end of *The Green Overcoat* (1912).

> How the Guelph University looked when it found there was no Ten Thousand Pounds at all after Professor Higginsons' death none of us know, for the old idiot is not yet dead. How they will look does not matter in the least, for the whole boiling of them are only people in a story, and there is an end of them.

The paragraph follows one joke with another. The veridical pretensions of the first sentence are hopelessly compromised by its successor.

Indeed, the arbitrary nature of the fictive process shows itself most obviously in style: a tale and the manner of its telling are inseparable. The naturalistic ideal which would render the authorial voice inconspicuous, not to say inaudible, presupposes the possibility that language can transmit a pre-existent and apprehensible reality, that it functions as a verbal window (traditional romanticism might enrich that analogy by likening the window to a stained glass one). But twentieth-century linguistic studies would suggest that the glass, though clear, belongs to a mirror: we perceive what we are, and our surroundings are conditioned by the perception; our knowledge is self-reflexive, conditional upon our natures, and is only to be extended in relation to those of other people. There is no common impersonal language transmitted from a reality outside ourselves; the naturalistic ideal contains the seeds of its own refutation.

Comedy deals in the impossibility of unconditional communication: at one level it is invariably a comedy of errors. This is the point of departure for the linguistic procedures of fictive comedy, whose various elements and aspects express themselves not only in choice of material and in individual tones of voice, but also in the strategies of style and structuring. The presentation of a fictive comedy is itself subject to the comedic process, the verbal stylistics both contributing to the thrust of the comedic narrative, and interpreting it in a manner frequently at odds with its apparent content.

In the van: T.F. Powys

The amount of simple mockery a parody contains depends on the temperament of the parodist, on the nature of the parodied, and on the assumptions of the reader. Thus Beerbohm's 'The Mote in the

Middle Distance' is at once a discerning imitation of Henry James's later style and a salute to his achievement. That salute assumes an understanding of its methodology and purpose, and is directed towards a readership interested in the art of fiction as such. Beerbohm's parody of Hilaire Belloc,[2] on the other hand, pounces on mannerisms and laughs at affectations: there is no implied critique of the victim's choice of subject-matter. The same literary material can also evoke contrasting species of parodic treatment, and there is a world of difference between the way Beerbohm handles the story-telling style deployed by late nineteenth-century fabulists such as Oscar Wilde and the use made of it by the early twentieth-century writer T.F. Powys in his novels and stories about Dorset village life.

In Powys's case a sophisticated purpose is masked by a simplicity of style that deflates the claims both of literary magniloquence and of the implicit 'truthfulness' of fictive naturalism. In view of his reputation as contemplative and sage, and of the obvious derivation of his prose from the Authorised Version of the Bible and from Bunyan, it may seem perverse to consider his work in connection with that of such urbane sophisticates as Wilde and Beerbohm; and certainly it is doubtful in the extreme whether Powys himself was extensively acquainted with the work of either of them. But this particular mode of discourse is found fairly frequently in the decades prior to that in which Powys wrote and published his early books: one sees the misleading simplicity of a plain and apparently unevocative style (a reaction from the melodious orotundities of Walter Pater and George Santayana and their imitators) in the writings of E.M. Forster and Rose Macaulay likewise. It is a voice which addresses its audience as though they were children, while knowing them to be adults – the reverse of the methodology of Beatrix Potter, who writes for children as though they are as old as she is. But Powys appears to assume that his readers have already seen through the pretensions of stylistic elaboration and are thus willing to meet the author on confidential terms. He does not so much parody the style of fairy-tale as use it for a vehicle to parody beliefs and attitudes which that style's directness unerringly exposes.

An instance of his method occurs in his most celebrated novel, *Mr Weston's Good Wine* (1927). The field preacher Luke Bird feels 'convinced that it was the beasts of the field and the fowls of the air that God's Son came down to save'.

> To begin with, God's Son is called a Lamb a great many times in the Bible, and so, perhaps, He was really one. All through the Bible

> beasts are written of that show the utmost intelligence and virtue. Noah's dove, Balaam's ass, the ravens that fed the prophet, the bears that devoured the naughty children, are but a few of the many cases—and my readers may add to them—wherein the sense and discernment of the creature far exceeds that of his unjust tyrant and false master, man. (Chapter xxii)

The artlessness of the surface tone masks the mischievous collocation of the bears and ravens, as well as satirising the methodology of Biblical exegesis. Powys is prepared to subvert the monolith of organised religion itself.

Mr Weston's Good Wine is also an allegory, but an allegory that uses the parodic mode to comic effect. The effect is as much at the reader's expense as at that of the characters. For Powys eschews simple allegory, the one-to-one equation of signified with sign. The novel may describe the visit to a Dorset village by God and the Archangel Michael in the persons of an elderly wine-merchant and his assistant, who drive an old Ford van; but no coherent theological pattern lies behind the allegory, no structural presentation of the workings of Divine Providence. Rather, the narrative parodies both the nature of stories that purport to convey this kind of simple message, and also the simplistic credulity which an addiction to such writing demonstrates. The book might even be said to parody the allegorical method itself; one is constantly teased and surprised by humorous and ironic hints that subvert any tendency to improve the occasion with the attributes of the divinity that conventional piety likes to worship.

Thus the traditional version of God as creating the world *ex nihilo* is depicted in terms appropriate to his embodiment as a wine-merchant.

> Mr Weston, for a common tradesman—and the most princely of merchants is only that—possessed a fine and creative imagination. And, although entirely self-taught—for he had risen, as so many important people do, from nothing—he had read much, and had written too. He possessed in a very large degree a poet's fancy, that will at any moment create out of the imagination a new world. (Chapter vi)

(Here, Powys could have had Philip Sidney's *The Defence of Poesie* (1595) in mind, though Genesis is more likely; but it is worth noting that the Elizabethan poet's aspiration towards creating a golden imaginative world has affinities with the premisses of alchemical theory.) Biblical echoes and parallels appear constantly in Powys's text, frequently to stylistically humorous effect, as when Michael, speaking of Luke Bird, tells Mr Weston that 'He is despised, and I will add, if you have no objection, he is rejected of men'. (Chapter vii) The sly parenthesis delicately mocks the fundamentalistic application of Biblical texts.

Everyone in the village of Folly Down seems to have met Mr Weston before, but only the grave-digger dares to tell him so.

"Thee bain't John Weston, be 'ee?" he enquired, "me wife's brother, who did court twelve maidens in woon year, and all were mothers by the next? There be a photograph of John, hung up in cottage, who were chief singer in church choir, and thee do exactly resemble him."

"I am glad to hear it," said Mr Weston. (Chapter xx)

Mr Grunter's question parodies the equation of God with any particular person or quality or cause; yet since the strict allegorical identification of Mr Weston with Almighty God is left unasserted, the point is made simply as a matter of comic indirection. Even Mr Weston's announcement of his (second) coming is made through an arrangement of electric lights that write his name in the sky – a parody of the literal-minded reading of apocalyptic literature. Similarly, simple allegory does not illuminate the story's spiritual issues, since its monolithic nature confines the understanding of God to a formula. As Neville Braybrooke observes,

> In the story's framework, these echoes from the New Testament are of no more than subsidiary interest; they [...] do not add one cubit to Mr Weston's stature, since only a recognition of him (as Mr Grunter experiences) can explain who he *is*, and what he *means* by his Good Wine.[3]

At one point the villagers gathered at the inn hear words which each man thinks that someone else has spoken: the words define the inscrutability of God, the reluctance to accept it being the object of Powys's satire through his use of parody. 'I form the light, and create darkness: I make peace, and create evil: I, the Lord, do all these things.'[4]

The simplicity of Powys's language contains a curious ambivalence. Its mannered nature and frequent eccentricity serves to distance its subject-matter from the way in which it is set before us: the words display it without purveying it. The parodic element makes it clear that *Mr*

Weston's Good Wine is no straightforward allegory, but rather a story which uses Christian terminology and symbols in such a way that, through their humorous treatment, they put forward a very different view of life from the orthodox Christian one. It is the nature of the good wine, the twin vintages of love and death, which is the subject of the novel. It is not about the nature of God, but about that connection between love and death which gives rise to religious formulations in the first place. The use of parody, by dismantling false simplifications where language and popular belief are concerned, comedically reveals the nature of the truth that underlies them. It is a method which only a writer with Powys's combination of sensibility, sardonic ruefulness, and ability to call a spade a spade could have employed in quite this way.

Dungeons in Spain: Samuel Beckett

'He still loved her enough to enjoy cutting the tripes out of her occasionally'. (*Murphy*, Chapter viii) The ambiguous tone, the surgical imagery, the caustically observant laughter are typical of Samuel Beckett, whose first novel concerns an Irishman for whom most of the other characters are searching, but whose own longing is to live a life apart from them. Murphy's castle in Spain is a dungeon, a padded cell, a garret, where he can exist freely in his mind, away from social codes and pressures. He discovers the possibility of doing so by working as a nurse in a lunatic asylum, the Magdalen Mental Mercyseat; and attains his apotheosis by being virtually incinerated through the chance of someone else's mishandling of a gas appliance.

As a parody of fictive love stories, *Murphy* (1938) focuses on its protagonist's relationship with the prostitute Celia, whose inappropriately celestial name itself parodies all those virtuous fallen women with redemptive urges who conform to fictive prototypes. But the book also parodies the ideal of fictive naturalism. Its very opening sentence reads, 'The sun shone, having no alternative, on the nothing new.' As to love, the law of unrequital is inexorably operative.

> Of such was Neary's love for Miss Dwyer, who loved a Flight Lieutenant Elliman, who loved a Miss Farren of Ringsakiddy, who loved a Father Fitt of Ballinclashet, who in all sincerity was bound to acknowledge a certain vocation for a Mrs West of Passage, who loved Neary. (Chapter i)

Goodness how sad.

Beckett makes enlivening comedy out of sadness. His humour – sardonic, wry, grotesque – is true gallows humour, closely responsive to the inequitable indignities which attend the human lot. As the blinded Pozzo cries out in *Waiting for Godot* (1952), 'They give birth astride of a grave, the light gleams an instant, then it's night once more.' On which Vladimir comments, 'Down in the hole, lingeringly, the grave-digger puts on the forceps. We have time to grow old. The air is full of our cries'. (Act II) Beckett's sensibility has similarities with that of T.F. Powys.

In *Murphy* the targeted monolith is the concept of a socially-regulative normality. Concerning the mental patients at the Mercyseat we are told that

> [they] were described as "cut off" from reality [...] the function of treatment was to bridge the gulf, transfer the sufferer from his own pernicious little private dungheap to the glorious world of discrete particles, where it would be his inestimable prerogative once again to wonder, love, hate, desire, rejoice and howl in a reasonable balanced manner, and comfort himself with the society of others in the same predicament. (Chapter ix)

But for all its choice of a solipsistic remedy, the book operates within traditional comic conventions: it contains an ironic narrative and comical characters such as the hapless Cooper, who cannot (until the novel's end) sit down; or the smelly landlady Miss Carridge (Beckett's puns are too blatant to be sly); or the dwarfish medium, Rosie Dew.

> Miss Dew's control, a panpygoptotic Manichee of the fourth century, Lena by name, severe of deportment and pallid of feature, who had entertained Jerome on his way through Rome from Calchis to Bethlehem, had not, according to her own account, been raised so wholly a spiritual body as yet to sit down with much more comfort than she had in the natural. But she declared that every century brought a marked improvement and urged Miss Dew to be of good courage. In a thousand years she might look forward to having thighs like anyone else, and not merely thighs, but thighs celestial. (Chapter v)

Beckett's use of medical terminology and his fascination with physical malfunctioning are essential parts of his comic methodology.

Should we laugh or cry? As one character remarks, 'Humanity is a well with two buckets [...] one going down to be filled, the other coming up to be emptied'. (Chapter iv) Accordingly, *Murphy* is no solemn allegorical fable: it resists all forms of monolithic categorisation, much as Murphy's injunction that his ashes be flushed down the lavatory of the Abbey Theatre, Dublin, is frustrated during a pub brawl, so that the 'body, mind and soul of Murphy were freely distributed over the floor of the saloon; and before another dayspring greyened the earth had been swept away with the sand, the beer, the butts, the glass, the matches, the spits, the vomit'. (Chapter xii) And yet the overall tone of *Murphy* is not bitter.

Beckett's subsequent fiction grows out of this farcical disposal of traditional fictive modes into analogistic dust and ashes. *Watt* (1953) virtually eliminates any sense of rational continuity, through repeated farcical parodies of manipulative categorisation. Watt himself (like Beckett's other protagonists, he is without a forename) finds employment in the house of Mr Knott. He exists in a strictly regulated routine, in which the 'what' of all his speculations as to 'how' and 'why' is met by the 'not' which leaves him a consciousness of simple being from which all rationalising accountability has been eliminated. Through its very stylistics the book forbids exposition. It describes its mental predicaments so as virtually to enact them, and at such a length as to frustrate quotation, involving one in a process of exhaustive, and at times exhausting, coverage where the narrative's logistical problems are in question. *Watt* is a sustained satire on human attempts to evade contingency: contrivance and control are laughed out of court through the unrelenting recital of alternative possibilities.

> No fence was party, nor any part of any fence. But their adjacence was such, at certain places, that a broad-shouldered or broad-basined man, threading these narrow straits, would have done so with greater ease, and with less jeopardy to his coat, and perhaps to his trousers, sideways than frontways. For a big-bottomed man, on the contrary, or a big-bellied man, frontal notion would be an absolute necessity, if he did not wish his stomach to be perforated, or his arse, or perhaps both, by a rusty barb, or by rusty barbs. A big-bottomed, big-bosomed woman, an obese wet-nurse, for example, would be under a similar necessity.

We are then taken through an exhaustive list of anatomical combinations, none of whose owners would if they were in their right senses, commit themselves to this treacherous channel, but turn about and retrace their steps, unless they wished to be impaled, at various points at once, and perhaps bleed to death, or be eaten alive by the rats, or perish from exposure, long before their cries were heard, and still longer before the rescuers appeared, running, with the scissors, the brandy and the iodine. (Chapter iii)

The unruffled gruesomeness of that conclusion is entirely characteristic: if *Watt* is full of bravura comical set pieces, it is also haunted by a pessimism whose sardonic humour rules out any sense of heroic defiance. Indeed, the account of the multitudinously-afflicted Lynch family would seem positively to relish the miseries of the human lot.

There was Tom Lynch, widower, aged eighty-five years, confined to his bed with constant unidentified pains in the caecum, and his three surviving boys, Joe, aged sixty-five years, a rheumatic cripple, and Jim, aged sixty-four years, a hunchbacked inebriate, and Bill, widower, aged sixty-three years, greatly hampered in his movements by the loss of both legs as the result of a slip, followed by a fall, and his only surviving daughter May Sharpe, widow, aged sixty-two years, in full possession of all her faculties with the exception of that of vision. Then there was Joe's wife née Doyly-Byrne, aged sixty-five years, a sufferer from Parkinson's palsy but otherwise very fit and well, and Jim's wife Kate, née Sharpe, covered all over with running sores.... (Chapter ii)

And so the list goes on for two and half more pages, twenty-eight sufferers all told. Horror mounts until it turns to laughter by way of self-defence.

Beckett needs to be quoted at length if his terse, detached precision, his irony (Swiftian in its bite, but more good-humoured), are to be savoured. (The fact that in his later fiction he should drastically abstain from chapter divisions may be accepted as a joke at the expense of the would-be over-orderly, self-protectively referential explositor.) His good humour, indeed, deserves more emphasis than it receives. His nihilism is fleshed out by an unresentful appreciation of the absurd.

One evening I ran into him on Westminster Bridge. It was snowing heavily. I nodded, heavily. In vain. Securing me with one hand, he removed from the other with his mouth two pairs of leather gauntlets, unwound his heavy woollen muffler, unbuttoned successively and flung aside his great coat, jerkin, coat, two waistcoats, shirt, outer and inner vests, coaxed from a washleather fob hanging in company with a crucifix I imagine from his neck a gun metal half-hunter, sprang open its case, held it to his eyes (night was falling), recovered in a series of converse operations his original form, said, Seventeen minutes past five exactly, as God is my witness, remember me to your wife (I never had one), let go my arm, raised his hat and hastened away. A moment later Big Ben (is that the name?) struck six. (Chapter i)

The 'is that the name?' might have come from Firbank; but only Beckett would have added the comment, 'This in my opinion is the type of all information whatsoever, be it voluntary or solicited.'

There is a particularity about Beckett's writing that induces empathy, and his outlook is embodied in his command of prose rhythms, which renounce histrionics in favour of a more formidable calm. His humour is genuine gallows humour, his fantastic presentation of the human predicament being strangely glorified in a spirit of redoubtable placidity that avoids self-pity. The ultimate in solipsism, his fictive world constitutes a quest for simplicity of being, through a series of literary amputations influenced, perhaps, by the many real ones that he witnessed as a medical orderly in wartime France. The trilogy of *Molloy* (1950), *Malone Dies* (1951), and *The Unnameable* (1952) explores the process of seeking the self through the mask of successive fictions, a gradual stripping that leads to the anticipated silence when, if ever, the self can know its own being – or rather, be its own being. Beckett refutes the pretensions of selective, dramatised fiction to be a valid naturalistic record of human experience; and if the broad comedy of the earlier novels takes on a more corrosive quality in the later ones and in the plays, the basic attitude to its material remains that of a farcical process of demolition that performs the function of a purgative. In this instance, the medical metaphor is, despite appearances, consistent.

A light pastry hand: Sylvia Townsend Warner

Angus Wilson's 'A Little Companion' concerns a middle-aged spinster who is haunted by the spectre of a snivelling little boy. Characteristically, it is not the supernatural status of the event which interests the author: Miss Arkwright is placed in a literary context.

She accepted her position as an old maid with that cheerful good humour and occasional irony which are essential to English spinsters since the deification of Jane Austen, or more sacredly Miss Austen, by the upper middle classes, and she attempted to counteract the inadequacy of the unmarried state by quiet, sensible and tolerant work in the local community. (*Such Darling Dodos* (1950))

She is a familiar figure in the fiction of her time, in that of E.H. Young, for instance, or Barbara Pym. The haunting itself parodies the gentler kind of supernaturalist fables (such as Edith Olivier's *The Love Child* (1927)) which were popular in the early twentieth century; and Wilson is even prepared to parody the more whimsical aspects of Virginia Woolf and of her cult among readers who prided themselves upon superior sensitivity.[5] The matter-of-fact Miss Arkwright, however, suggests a typical admirer of Sylvia Townsend Warner.

Poet, musical scholar, political activist and countrywoman, Warner is a writer who stubbornly resists categorisation; and her fiction has a tendency to venture upon genres to which it then refuses to conform – witness *Lolly Willowes* (1926) and *Mr Fortune's Maggot* (1928), the one the story of a witch, the other of a missionary. In both cases a predictable Christian reading of the material is amiably debunked. Quiet upper-class Miss Willowes discovers in a commitment to Satan's 'profoundly indifferent ownership' a greater spiritual release than is afforded by dutiful conformity to her family's expectations of her as a spinster aunt; while the Reverend Timothy Fortune makes one solitary convert on his South Sea island, proceeds to fall in love with him, and then loses his own faith. But the irony is not bitter. Both novels repose on a serene imaginative self-assurance.

They could be called parodic by implication. While arising out of literary models, they do not imitate them; they simply rewrite them. And such a rewriting goes for Warner's approach to the past. As a Communist unrepentant even following the death of Stalin, in treating such subjects as seventeenth-century rural Spain, a fourteenth-century Fenland nunnery, or nineteenth-century Norfolk, her perspective is Marxist in its concentration on conditioning economic factors. In each case her people reflect their physical environment, while still being presented subjectively as individuals. Warner's art owes nothing to popular sentiment, and casts a somewhat cold eye on the family worlds of life, of death. Nowhere is this more evident than in her final novel, *The Flint Anchor* (1954). This opens with a fulsome mid nineteenth-century epitaph (the tablet is 'a brass one, large and showy') in tribute to John

Barnard, 'Deeply conscientious in the performance of every Christian and social duty [...] a devoted Husband and Father, an example of industry, enterprise and benevolence to his native town....' The ensuing novel amounts to an extended commentary on this text, ironically exploring the truth beneath the profession. It closes with Barnard's death-bed request for his epitaph to be 'Only my name, and after that, Lord, have mercy upon me a sinner.' This amounts to a comic – or is it a tragic? – reversal.

Warner's novels omit the customary organisation into carefully separated dramatic scenes (*The Flint Anchor* is not even divided into numbered chapters) – one keeps waiting for something to happen, only to realise that what happens is happening all the time. Nowhere outside the final novels of George Moore has such a sense of seamless continuity been achieved. The reader-as-spectator is slyly drawn into the narrative record: the method is to solicit and to obtain one's inconspicuous involvement.

> Meanwhile, he had to give Ellen lessons in arithmetic. The weather was close, and he could not rid himself of a conviction that the blemish on Ellen's face brought in bluebottles. Much as Thomas disliked Ellen, Ellen disliked Thomas infinitely more, and before long she was hating him with a virgin intensity. If he had been even a little kind to her—Ellen's fondest dream was to reward a momentary kindness by the devotion of a lifetime—she would have been a willing pupil. But finding her even more repulsive when she goggled and puffed at him, he wore his coldest manner as he hunted her through vulgar fractions, extorting from her every pennyworth of the bargain which he piqued himself on paying in full to the landlord of the Anchor House Inn.

This reads more like the work of an observer than of a novelist: indeed, Warner's novels and tales are alike in seeming to be recorded rather than composed. For all their stress on singularity and the unexpected, they are ironically plausible in the manner of their telling.

Characteristic of her method is the title story of *One Thing Leading To Another* (1984), concerning the Scottish housekeeper of two Catholic priests who accidentally serves up a curry made with snuff. Neither man notices the difference; and this causes her to speculate.

> Invention, not mere accident, could play a part in cookery, and that not just with the accepted anomalies – the pinch of salt that

seizes the flavour of a chocolate icing, the trickle of anchovy essence that gives life to stewed veal – but by more arresting innovations and bolder departures: caraway seeds in a fish pie, for instance; a lentil soup enriched with rhubarb; horse-radish in a tapioca pudding. It would be a way of getting oneself attended to, she thought.

Accordingly she experiments.

She bought nothing out of the usual, and except when she sauced a boiled suet pudding with cough linctus, she used no extraneous ingredients. All was wholesome and homemade, the same thrifty traditional home cooking she had been practising for years.

Still the men do not respond; a series of accidents and misunderstandings cause her to hand in her notice; and she ends up by running a small grocery business of her own. There is no plot, no contriving to impose a shaping theme. One simply watches, unconscious of authorial artistry. At times Warner's work would even seem to suggest that conscious literary fabrication may be fraudulent. The fact that her books should be so pleasurable only heightens the irony of that particular question.

For the irony resides in the fact that Warner's characters are inseparable from her distinctive narratorial voice: it is of the artistry of presentation, rather than of structure, that one becomes aware. Her tone is good-humoured, unresentful, and reductive. In particular she is a mistress of the exactly-rendered simile. 'Her voice was heavy with commiseration. It fell on Aston like a wet sponge.' 'The cake was stale and so dry that she could hardly swallow it. It seemed to be moving about her mouth like a sand-storm.' 'They rushed into the escape of love like winter-starved cattle rushing into a spring pasture.'[6] Along with this grasp of what is relevant and appropriate and physically immediate, Warner displays an unruffled curiosity concerning people's fermenting inner lives, their capacity to be individual and odd. Here is her account of a fourteenth-century nun at work on the illumination of a psalter.

The first psalm was behind her, and already the distaste for David which became so marked in her later years had begun to form itself. The man talked like Dame Helen: he said what he had to say, often silly enough, and then immediately said it all over again in rather different words. As something to sing it might be well enough, but as a statement from one rational being to another—and God is the sum of rational being—it was poor. The sunlight fell on the page and lit her scarred face and the few light eyelashes stuck in her swollen eyelids. Her hand, moving in the sunlight, displayed all its defects, the toad-skin, the misshapen nails, the look of being ingrained with dirt which overlies unwholesome blood. Her attitude and expression showed a slow-burning thrifty happiness, and she resembled a virtuous wolf. Wolfishly, she had got her teeth into the psalter, she was at last doing something positive and profitable.

(*The Corner That Held Them* (1948), Chapter x)

Any idea that a mediæval convent resembled the dewy religiosity of some pre-Raphaelite painting is unsparingly dispelled; yet the picture is full of a pre-Raphaelite nicety of detail. Warner would seem to have been incapable of writing a dull sentence, so close and attentive is she to the sounds and textures of the physical world. Her novels may be materialistic parodies of sentimentally-exploited fictive categories, but the parody rebounds upon itself. Alert to the incongruities that beset the peregrine spirit caged in daily expectations and routine, her short stories are filled with the same fascinated pleasure in the 'comfortable amble of day to day' that informs her supremely entertaining letters.

Warner's parodic consciousness reaches its term in *Kingdoms of Elfin* (1977). This collection of fairy stories amounts to a complete revision of the genre. It resembles the work of Tolkien in its creation of an entire other-worldly cosmos, but differs from it in its materialistic anthropology, and in the sociological nature of its emphasis: these elfin societies bear no resemblance to the majestic beings that inhabit Middle Earth. Their world is contemporary with our own, and one which their creator analyses with dry, wry, witty observation.

Elfhame is in Heathendom. It has no christenings. But when a human child is brought into it there is a week of ceremonies. Every day a fasting weasel bites the child's neck and drinks its blood for three minutes. The amount of blood drunk by each successive weasel (who is weighed before and after the drinking) is replaced by the same weight of a distillation of dew, soot, and aconite. Though the blood-to-ichor transfer does not cancel human nature (the distillation is only approximate: elfin blood contains several unanalyzable components, one of which is believed to be magnetic air), it gives considerable longevity; up to a hundred and fifty years is the usual span. During the seven days, the child may suffer some sharpish colics, but few die. On the eighth day it is judged sufficiently inhumanized to be given its new name.

('The One and the Other')

The matter-of-fact precision of tone, with its implicit mockery of human institutions and beliefs, resembles that of Butler's *Erewhon* (1872) as much as it does that of Warner's acknowledged inspiration, Richard Garnett's *The Twilight of the Gods* (1888). The opening story, from which this passage comes, charts the fortunes of a human and an elfin child who have been exchanged at birth. The whole enterprise would seem to parody not only Tolkien's far less detailed and systematic account of his imaginary universe, but also the seventeenth-century speculations and records of Robert Burton, John Aubrey or Sir Thomas Browne: had Aubrey's account of the apparition near Cirencester, which disappeared with 'a faint perfume and a most melodious twang'[7] been the product of Sylvia Townsend Warner's pen, both twang and perfume would have been scientifically accounted for. Originating not in the region of myth but in post-Shakespearean folklore, her elfin world is deliberately heartless.

Warner engages the would-be systematic critic in an unending game of hide-and-seek: despite its variety of genre and subject-matter, her work shows little development beyond outgrowing that of her friend T.F. Powys. The calm decisiveness of her later manner, so crisp and pungent, belongs to one whose stylistic aim was to achieve, in her own words, 'what in cookery is called "a light pastry hand".'[8] There is an immediacy and a precision about it, a tactile quality, which differentiates it from the more gentle, knowing ironic writing of such contemporary women novelists as E.M. Delafield or Elizabeth Taylor (with either of whom Angus Wilson's Miss Arkwright would presumably have been familiar also). Warner is anything but a reassuring novelist; for all her elegant wit and her preoccupation with subjects dear to the readership her fictions apparently set out to attract, her work is quite unsparing in its allowance for life's brutality, discomforts, and ignominious reversals. In this author's world the maypole and the gallows are within each other's view.

Propitiating magnates: John Cowper Powys

Sylvia Townsend Warner was a niece by marriage of Arthur Machen, a writer scarcely less an individualist than she was herself. In an impassioned literary polemic entitled *Hieroglyphics* (1902) he sets out to define the difference between an artist and an artificer, as one means of answering the age-old question, What is True Art? Machen voices the high romantic view that 'the artist continually mirrors nature in its eternal, essential forms', arguing that the mark of genuine *literature* is that it should induce a sense of ecstasy – meaning by that, not so much rapture as a standing outside purely physical experience – and that it should witness to an esoteric dimension. Accordingly he praises Dickens at the expense of Thackeray (not to mention Jane Austen, Anthony Trollope, and 'poor, dreary, draggle-tailed George Eliot' – a declaration to send a shiver down the academic spine). But for all his one-sided exaggeration, Machen does make a valuable distinction between emotion and feeling, between two levels of response, the first drawing one out of oneself, the second self-reflexive and essentially passive. In terms of comedy, the former might be connected with wit and celebration, and at the other end of the scale with parody and farce; but the three remaining categories of irony, satire and burlesque tend to refer one back to the subject of comedy rather than to arise out of it. Machen was unresponsive to literary satire, as was a more formidable post-romantic writer, John Cowper Powys, who once declared that it was about as abhorrent as anything that he could think of.[9]

And yet, ironically, Powys's own career as a novelist might be read as itself a satire on established fictive naturalism. His early novels are much concerned with 'feelings' set against elaborately-rendered landscape backgrounds, drawing on literary models that conveyed an encoded fatalism and frustrated sexuality: there is little comedy in these books. But with *Wolf Solent* (1929) emotion breaks forth: fictive conventions are burlesqued in a plot that reads like a parody of rural melodrama fit to stand alongside *Cold Comfort Farm*, but which ends on a note of stoical endurance and a sober but not unecstatic accommodation to reality. And much of it is in the process very funny, as the protagonist's private manias and obsessions are reflected back to him through the exasperated reactions of the other characters.

Powys's subsequent novels are for the most part sustained on a comic undertow. His aim is to be as inclusive as possible: in him the artist (Machen would say the artificer) works instinctively, instead of imposing order from without – in this, if in nothing else, he resembles Townsend Warner. *A Glastonbury Romance* (1932) and *Weymouth Sands* (1934) regularly frustrate one's expectation that some story or pattern will give shape to the whole: events are always in the hands of chance. What Hardy views as tragedy, Powys treats comedically. Moreover, by including 'everything' in his fiction, he includes the hypothetical and the 'impossible' as well. For him, mental reality is as valid as physical reality, and is neither to be divorced from the latter nor contrasted with it. The comic scandal of Powys's fiction is that he is prepared to treat of the spiritual on the same terms as the physical, to include what on a materialistic reading is the impermissible. Thus in *A Glastonbury Romance*, following the description of a funeral and the subsequent reading of a will, the corpse in his coffin is also allowed his say; hypothesis becomes actuality in the dialogue between two very substantial disembodied spirits.

Powys's comedy also dismantles one's sense of scale. He will treat the distress of an insect in a bubble of saliva in as much loving detail as he will the progress of a public meeting or a vision of the Holy Grail. *A Glastonbury Romance*, with its super-abundance of physically felt life, its queer lonely eccentrics, gangs of small children, and meticulous contemplation of the colours and textures of the visible world, rebukes that careful sectioning and distinguishing, and anxiety to control and shape events, which Beckett treats so farcically in *Watt*. Indeed, Beckett and Powys have more in common than might be supposed. Powys's *The Inmates* (1952) portrays a mental home in a mood not so far removed from that of *Murphy*, the supposedly mad being a good deal more sane than are their keepers; while the following vignette reveals a sensibility akin to that of Beckett's plays.

> The old clerk was so used to having that lack-lustre, bored look fixed upon him that he had come to assume that this look was the natural look of the human race [...] Herb had only to turn his face towards any living thing and the eyes of that thing grew as glazed as the eyes of old Gideon. When he went to the privy these autumn mornings and just glanced through the wet mist over the nettles and burdocks of Mr Cole's hedge to catch the yellow eye of Mr Cole's great sow, the creature, in plain pig-language, told him he was a nuisance.
>
> (*Weymouth Sands*, Chapter xiii)

At other times Powys's humour can be indirect and subtle.

> He continued to catch snatches of the conversation round him. Somebody [...] had started them off on the subject of prayer; and

216 Alchemy of Laughter

> [he] noticed, as a touching human trait, that the waiter showed an interest in this that he hadn't displayed before, and as for the old ladies, they listened in spell-bound fascination.
> "Certainly I do," he heard Mr Cumber reply. "Not *long*, you know; but I do. I wouldn't feel comfortable; I wouldn't have the proper grip of my day's work; I wouldn't—"
> (*Maiden Castle* (1936), Chapter v)

The nature of materialistic spirituality could not be more precisely caught in all its staid embarrassment. It adds to the sly humour of the passage that the old ladies should be hotel residents at another table: Powys's comedy is always homely, when in the satirical vein, gentle but observant.

Elsewhere, especially in his later novels, he appears to be satirising, through the use of surrealistic burlesque, the pretensions of any kind of rationalistic interpretation of the universe.

> In fact those cracks in the wall gave the impression that, were they enlarged so that a small person could worm himself into them, they might be found to lead, if the explorer had the courage to persevere and follow one of them to the bitter end, right to the very centre of the whole planet, where such an explorer would be liable to be devoured by that fabulous creature called the Horm, the legends about whom were evidently so appalling, and so likely to be disclosing a horrible reality, that, long before any written chronicle existed, they must have been deliberately suppressed by the self-preservative consciousness of the human race.
> (*The Brazen Head* (1956), Chapter x)

Such a wayward piece of epistemological jesting indicates Powys's indebtedness to Rabelais. What he writes of the latter's humour is no less applicable to his own, that it is 'so zanyishly fantastical and artlessly Simple-Simonish that I can quite understand a "responsible modern thinker", or a religious or scientific "leader" turning from it in distaste.'[10] Those inverted commas say a lot, and in *Autobiography* (1934), which chronicles the evolution of his humorous philosophy of life, he recalls with approval the injunction given to him by an elderly poet, 'Powys, we must propitate Magnates'.[11] Few writers can demolish worldly pretensions with such affable aplomb, just as he is one of the few novelists to inject a theological joke into passages of social satire.

"It's all so confusing to most of us, Mattie dear," murmured Mrs Otter. "We can only hope and pray that the Judge of all the earth will do right."

(Wolf Solent, Chapter xix)

Powys's insistence upon a naturalistic technique in order to portray experience for which the materialist philosophy underlying naturalism can find no room, reaches its climax in the account of the death of the two giants in *Porius: A Romance of the Dark Ages* (1951), of which Jerome McGann has remarked that so outrageously material an embodiment of the mythical and marvellous in a naturalistic narrative is 'an allegory of the threat that writing and imagination bring to the reality of the marvellous'.[12] Powys's attempt to 'incorporate the novel back into its romantic origins' satirises traditional fictive methodologies, while risking annihilation in the quagmire of the absurd. His comedic intention is to subvert the solemnities of Arthurian epic and to replace the powerful Merlin of tradition with a being who is at once helplessly indecisive and yet also a medium for the self-renewing forces of the earth itself. The whole enormous comedic romance constitutes a refusal to bow to monolithic ideologies and to their accompanying oppressiveness; it specifically declines to propitiate magnates, literary or otherwise.

But if *Porius* programmatically voices Powys's rejection of the constraints of literary theory and materialistic sanctions, *A Glastonbury Romance* remains the finest presentation of his comic vision. His delight in homeliness and his sense of the sublime are combined in the account of the religious revivalist, 'Bloody Johnny' Geard, holding his own private Easter communion service in his front garden:

> he sank down on his knees in the presence of a little square patch of grass, a few privet hedges, and a tiny round bed with three dead hyacinths in it, and in this position began, with a sort of ravenous greed, tearing open the loaf and gobbling great lumps of crumb from the centre of it. These mouthfuls he washed down with repeated gulps of port wine.

This burlesque of customary religious devotion is disconcerting enough – observe that phrase 'in the presence of' – the natural is implicitly accorded supernatural status – but Powys also incorporates the reader's response in a manner peculiarly his own.

So queer a figure must he have presented, and with so formidable a stare must he have racked that small enclosure, that a couple of wagtails who were looking for worms in the grass instead of flying off hopped towards him in hypnotised amazement, while a feeble chaffinch that had alighted for a second on one of the privet bushes left the bush and joined the two wagtails upon the patch of grass.

And then the author transcends the immediate scene in a speculation that seems to discard the pages of the novel altogether.

The more greedily Mr Geard ate the flesh of his Master and drank His Blood, the nearer and nearer hopped these three birds. What other smaller dwellers upon this clouded earth, such as worms and snails and slugs and beetles and wood lice and shrew mice joined with these feathered creatures to make up the congregation at this heretical Easter Mass, neither the celebrant himself nor anyone else will ever know. (Chapter xv)

Such a passage is quite without the sophistication of style that one would find in a self-conscious Modernist writer, though Powys himself was interested in, and in his own way shared in, the Modernist movement. What is peculiar to him is the directness, almost the naivety, of presentation. It is this quality which perhaps most scandalises and repels those magnates of the literary world whose metropolitan parochialism Powys's self-imposed exile and eremitical way of life subordinated to his own comedic outlook.

A talent for abuse: Wyndham Lewis

Whereas John Cowper Powys operated in isolation from the trend-setting literary self-consciousness of the metropolis, and could boast that 'of all writers I am the least artistic', Percy Wyndham Lewis was a painter, poet and historical philosopher whose fiction derived not so much from nature, inanimate or human, as from art. In describing his early novel *Tarr* (1918) as being 'in a sense, the first book of an epoch in England',[13] he exhibits what might seem excessive self-confidence as to his membership of an *avant-garde*; but as *Tarr* was written in 1914, the claim is not unwarranted, since the book preceded the experimental Modernist novels of Virginia Woolf, James Joyce and Ford Madox Ford, and bears the hallmarks of an innovative project.

Tarr is a comic novel that both parodies and rejects the psychological legacy of Romanticism, its author insisting that 'everything we *see* [...] must be reinterpreted to tally with all the senses and beyond that with our minds'. (VII:ii) Its group of Left Bank expatriate artists and their hangers-on (English, German, American, Polish) are observed as mechanisms, as body–soul complexes whose motivations are confused by inherited pre-emptive sentimentality: what they want and need is disguised from them in clouds of self-deception. They are very different from their predecessors in the widely-read pages of George du Maurier's *Trilby* (1894): it is their sexuality, their physicality rather than their artistic ideals which interests their creator. Tarr's own need to choose between his bourgeois mistress, Bertha, and the more aggressively emancipated Anastasya is resolved on a 'both-and' rather than on an 'either-or' basis. The two women have powerful egos of their own and are motivated by life-illusions which are socially and sentimentally conditioned; *Tarr* is comedic in demonstrating the discrepancy between human beings as idealistically motivated subjectivities and as physically operative psychic organisms. The very syntax and texture of Lewis's prose insists on the primacy of physicality. In Bertha's emotional appeal to Tarr not to desert her, the two levels of encoded sentiment (false art) and of real emotion are unblinkingly objectified.

> Then with the woman's bustling, desperate, possessive fury, she suddenly woke up. She disengaged her arms wildly and threw them round his neck, tears becoming torrential. Underneath the poor comedian that played such antics with such phlegmatic and exasperating persistence, this distressed being thrust up its trembling mask, like a drowning rat. Its finer head pierced her blunter wedge. (I:iv)

The word 'comedian' refers us back to an indictment of what Tarr has already denounced as the English 'university of Humour'.

> All english training is a system of *deadening feeling*, a stoic prescription – a humorous stoicism is the anglo-saxon philosophy. Many of the results are excellent: it saves from gush in many cases; in times of crisis or misfortune it is an excellent armour [...] once this armature breaks down the man underneath is found in many cases to have become softened by it; he is subject to shock, *over*-sensitiveness, and indeed many ailments not met with in the more direct races. (I:ii)

This analysis relates instructively to Lawrence's attack on personalised sexuality in *Women in Love* (1920); but more to the present purpose, it proffers an understanding of humour that ignores, rather than denies, its comedic function.

But *Tarr* can be extremely funny. With linguistic resourcefulness Lewis depicts a physicality that seems to bulge out of the page.

> She crossed her legs. The cold grape-bloom mauve silk stockings ended in a dark slash each against her two snowy stallion thighs which they bisected, visible, one above the other, in naked expanses of tempting undercut, issuing from a dead-white foam of central lace worthy of the Can-Can exhibitionists of the tourist resorts of Paris-by-night.

The sophisticated knowingness only serves to emphasise the animality of the perception ('undercut' suggests butcher's meat), an animality that is expanded in the succeeding paragraph.

> Tarr grinned with brisk appreciation of the big full-fledged baby's coquetry pointing to the swinish moral under the rose and mock-modesty belowstairs, and he blinked and blinked as if partly dazzled, his mohammedan eyes did not refuse the conventional bait; his butcher sensibility pressed his fancy into professional details, appraising this milky ox soon to be shambled in his slaughter-box, or upon his high divan. (VII:ii)

'Stallion', 'swinish', 'ox' – both consistency and continuity of association are abandoned in this evocation of overwhelming sensual-psychic response. It satirises, yet endorses, the conventionalised titillations of sexual innuendo in what amounts to a burlesqued salacity.

Lewis's manipulation of audio-visual effects is frequently employed for analytic purposes.

> The dancers were circling rapidly past with athletic elation, talking in the way people do when they are working. Their intelligences floated and flew above the waves of these graceful exercises, but with frequent drenchings, as it were. Each new pair of dancers seemed coming straight for him: their voices were loud, a hole was cut out of the general noise, as it were opening a passage into it. The two or three instruments behind the screen of palms produced the necessary measure to keep this throng of people careering, like

the spoon stirring in a saucepan: it stirred and stirred and they jerked and huddled insipidly round and round, in sluggish currents with small eddies here and there. (III:ii)

The failed artist Otto Kreisler's hysterical attitudinising at the dance is a masterpiece of comic writing. His tragi-comical collapse forms the comedic heart of the book, epitomised in the duel he fights with the Pole, Soltyk: at this point Lewis's novel attains an hysterical extravagance such as one finds in those of Dickens, Dostoevsky and John Cowper Powys. It amounts to a systematised deconstruction of all accepted codes of honour, dignity, and even decency, an instance of farce stripped of all its whimsicality and sense of fun.

Tarr is indeed a critique of, and an attack upon, conventional codes and modes of sentiment. It insists on the divergence between life and art.

> *Death* is the thing that differentiates art and life. Art is identical with the idea of permanence. Art is a continuity and not an individual spasm: but life is the idea of the person.

Developing this notion, Tarr declares,

> Deadness is the first condition for art: the second is absence of soul, in the human and sentimental sense. With the statue its lines and masses are its soul, no restless inflammable ego is imagined for its interior: it has *no inside*.... (VII:ii)

Lewis portrays his characters as objects obedient to their own laws, rather than as embodiments of ideas or states of mind. *Tarr* is the least idealistic of novels, and returns the monolith to itself, confirmed as being exactly that, entrapped in its own pretensions.

Such an entrapment is at the core of *The Apes of God* (1930), Lewis's lengthy and unsparing indictment of what he dubs 'the societification' of art at the hands of his contemporaries, described by one of his critics as 'the prosperous amateurs who have monopolised the artistic world and frozen out those with real talent, making the creation and survival of true art virtually impossible'.[14] The scene is London, and such (by now) well-known figures as the three Sitwells, T.S. Eliot and Lytton Strachey are savagely pilloried, treated more like dolls than human beings. But Lewis also wrestles with his own involvement in this world of self-conscious 'art'. He is too much a part of it to be an effective satirist: purely personal rancour gets in the way. But if his comic portrayals run to burlesque, he also shows that the ideal of impersonality can itself become a monolith and, as such, potentially tyrannical.

> The 'impersonality' of science and 'objective' observation is a wonderful patent behind which the individual can indulge in a riot of personal egotism, impossible to earlier writers, not provided with such a disguise [...] Instinctively he uses the 'impersonality' presented him by natural science, or by popular superstition, rather (as he uses everything else,) to be *personal* and *partial* with. (IX)

Although *The Apes of God* can in places read like a sustained outbreak of bad temper, it is often brutally amusing. Not so much in its sadistic account of the misfortunes of the naïve young Dan Boleyn, protégé of the officious, prophetic man-about-art Horace Zagreus, but in the gusto with which the various 'apes' are conjured up, and above all in the author's gift for describing physical movement. Here is a chauffeur arriving to collect some picture-frames from a fashionable art-gallery.

> Dreamy little pack-animal, he received a pleasurable shamefaced sensation. It was the chief show-girl of the shop-staff of the Maltster Galleries that gave it him, who hovered in lanky elegance near the entrance, in wait for Kensington customers, to float before them, with mesmeric hip, towards a parchment lampshade or a jacket-cover wall-paper—and he looked pleasant in response to the sensation, looking politely his best, as he removed his certified-driver's car-cap with the same civil wobble of the body that served for the foot-scrape upon the mat. (VI)

Lewis's wit is likewise illustrated in his account of Dick Whittingdon's entry into his aunt's drawing-room.

> This huge ray of sunshine hung fulgurously in the doorway. All towering bright-eyed juvenility, Dick was respectfully backward in coming too rapidly forward. But at last [...] he started himself off. Flinging forward tremendous feet to left and to right, he got well into the place, piecemeal, in jolly sprawling fragments, and looked round with the near-sighted surprise of a rogue elephant who had perhaps burst into a parish church. (I)

Another of Lewis's stylistic tricks is to invert customary perspectives. 'The conversation languished in the studio as the tea, the *friandises*, and the tiny sandwiches found their way into the assembled stomachs'. (VI) What is normally the object becomes the subject of the sentence. Elsewhere one finds intellectual verbal play, as when 'she faced him in the manner that is indicated by the word *roundly* and by the word *squarely*'. (VIII)

Here the draughtsman is heard speaking: in these early novels at any rate, the visual and tactile qualities of Lewis's prose, and its surface texture, tend to confuse the insights into early twentieth-century consciousness which are more deliberately set down in such historical polemic works as *Time and Western Man* (1927). If Lewis's fiction distracts one by its very forcefulness and brilliance, so that, as G.S. Fraser observes, the reader 'feels like a punch-ball, receiving thud after thud, rocking upon his foundations [...] never allowed to rest',[15] this goes to show how ethically opaque a too single-minded deployment of burlesque can be; and how by itself it can induce a sense of moral bankruptcy.

A manner of speaking: Elizabeth Bowen and Henry Green

The early works of Wyndham Lewis pinpoint the danger inherent in all forms of satirical burlesque – the danger that, in so far as its energy is in excess of its occasion, it diminishes the status of its victims at the cost of its own credibility. All forms of verbal humour can be self-defeating (too clever by half, as people say), a liability to which satire in particular is prone. For since its objects are distanced and reified according to the requirements of the satirist, from being formidable enemies they can shrink into victims calling out for sympathy. In English fiction this tendency is compounded by the dictates of class. With a few honourable exceptions (Gissing, Bennett, Lawrence, Moore most notably), up to the end of the Second World War the majority of novelists tended to marginalise the working class as objects of pity or as comical 'characters'. And being funny did not include participation in the comedic process.

The more intellectual, or to use a short-cut term, the more highbrow, a novel is, the more divorced from the lives of working people its readership appears to be – one says 'appears', because what is at issue is authorial manipulation: some novels seem to be deliberately tilted towards certain levels of the social structure. Those of Elizabeth Bowen are a good case in point. Their tone is both confident and confidential, since this is fiction written at its utmost stretch for the well-to-do upper-middle-class world which it none the less submits to serious and occasionally comic scrutiny. Comparison with the later work of Henry James is inescapable. Yet Bowen's tone can be caustic and robust, with surreally effective turns of phrase that counteract the preciosity. 'A zip fastener all the way down one back made one woman seem to have a tin spine.' Or she can write of an adolescent girl that 'her personality was too much for her, like a punt-pole' – a simile that Sylvia Townsend Warner might have used. But what makes Bowen unusual among satirical writers is the way she handles problems of linguistic communication that arise from contrasting social usages determined by the fact of class.

Her own controlling language is mannered and distinctive: all her novels are patently works of authorial contrivance and of authorial style. She was well aware how tendentious literary conventions could be, remarking of one of her own characters that 'By the rules of fiction, with which life to be credible must comply, he was as a character "impossible" – each time they met, for instance, he showed no shred or trace of having been continuous since they last met'. (*The Heat of the Day* (1949), Chapter vii) But, by those very laws, fictive personages, to be integrated into a novel have to become citizens of that novel and be subordinate to its view of life. Bowen's world being so articulate, the semi-articulate – still more the inarticulate – are difficult to incorporate within it; but in *The Heat of the Day*, through manipulative mimicry, she attempts to achieve just that, resorting to a burlesque of the mannered idiom employed by the transmitting authorial consciousness.

> We left it I was to give him a ring again first thing next morning when he'd got back to London. When I did ring, the fat was in the fire. The hotel had just been notified he'd popped off. And more, his lawyers had taken over, and on their instructions they'd locked his room up; which was the devil, he having some stuff of mine. Of course I went round, but the management were not playing. So I then thought, well, the remaining thing one can do is to stand by the poor old boy through the final round. (Chapter ix)

The sheer ugliness of this, its illiterate use of metaphor, its awkwardness and insensitivity, is yet syntactically and rhythmically constructed so as not to clash with the overall elegance of the book's linguistic texture. Elsewhere Bowen is prepared to comment more directly on the nature of verbal insufficiency, through the character of the inarticulate, forlorn young drifter, Louie.

> It isn't you only. It's the taking and taking up of me on the part of everyone when I have no words. Often you say the advantage I should be at if I could speak grammar; but it's not only that. Look the trouble there is when I have to only say what I *can* say, and so cannot ever say what it is really. Inside me it's like being crowded to death – more and more of it all getting into me. I could more bear it if I could only say. (Chapter xiii)

Working-class girls do not speak like this. Their kind of language is being reworked analytically so as to harmonise with the linguistic and imaginative subtleties of the novel as a whole.

But the majority of novelists have preferred to treat the working classes *en masse*, as objects of explication or of charity; for whatever the change in social fortunes, the social structure continued to be hierarchical, and with it the problem of literary presentation continued well into the twentieth century. The late nineteenth-century novels of George Gissing do their best to resolve the dilemma; but even here the dialogue is necessarily refined to suit the canons of the circulating libraries and the conventions of the day; while the descriptive material is presented in an informative, and thus detached, prose more appropriate to the educated middle-class reader. The language which working-class people used among themselves could be imitated picturesquely when in a rural setting (as by Hardy or the Powys brothers) or by a music-hall style of imitation (embarrassingly attempted by T.S. Eliot in Part Two of *The Waste Land*); but the narratorial language continued to be that of the employer class, for whom the 'cultural' limitations of the workers existed to provide subjects for patronising compassion or for laughter.

Arguably the most successful attempt to escape from this stylistic impasse was made by Henry Green in his second novel, *Living* (1929). An account of life in a Birmingham engineering works, the book's immediacy excludes any impression that this is a story told *about* the workers there. Green achieves this result through a stylistic experiment. He quite simply reduces to a minimum both punctuation and the number of definite and indefinite articles.

> Mr Craigan smoked pipe, already room was blurred by smoke from it and by steam from hot water in the sink. She swilled water over the plates and electric light caught in shining waves of water which

> rushed off plates as she held them, and then light caught on wet plates in moons. She dried these. One by one then she put them up into the rack on wall above her, and as she stretched up so her movements pulled all ways at his heart, so beautiful she seemed to him. Mr Craigan would never have windows open at evening so was a haze in that room, like to Dale's feeling. (Chapter xii)

The effect here is to create a distinctive linguistic ambience which dignifies the working-class way of life from within; the result is, as the author intended, to make the book 'as taut and spare as possible, to fit the proletarian life'.[16] The omission of definite articles serves also to bring the reader closer to the objects described, so that one becomes a participatory rather than an evaluative presence. There is complete linguistic equalisation; speech and narrative are fused, often to comedic purpose.

> Just then Mr Gates came out of public house. He was drunk and in state of righteous indignation. Mr Tupe came out after him. He was in same state as Mr Gates. He said to find her out, to go and give her a good thraipin', ah, to make her give up all these mad thoughts and to marry decent and regular, to a respectable man, to Mr Dale, he said, that everyone in factory respected along with Mr Craigan. This he meant and he was sincere in this for he saw many free drinks in money Joe would get from that old man. But misfortune was following him like a dog for Mr Gates at that moment suddenly became aware to full extent of his own misfortunes come upon him this day. He broke loudly into long recitation of all the oaths known to him. This was more than what policeman on the corner would stand for and this one ran him in, took him to police station, locked Joe up. (Chapter xvii)

This combines narrative, mental states, corporate tone of voice, to produce an effect that is genuinely funny. The finality of those last words have a fatalistic ring that borders upon gallows humour.

Green can achieve more specific forms of satire while using the same linguistic methodology.

> "Mr Dupret, sir," he said, "the office have asked me to come on behalf of them all to convey their condolences in your bereavement, which is also ours, sir, but to a smaller degree of course. It is an honour I very much appreciate, if I may say so, in that I did not

have the – the honour to work under him so long as some who have been in this office all their lives [...] I remember once as I happened to be sharpening a pencil he came up behind me without I heard him. He put his hand on my shoulder and said, 'Archer, go on as you are going on now and you will be all right!' I don't think I shall ever forget that, Mr Dupret, as long as it pleases our common father to spare me. The Lord giveth and the Lord taketh away, sir."
Mr Dupret, embarrassed, said the wreath they had sent looked very beautiful on the coffin. Archer went away delighted. (Chapter ix)

There are echoes of Mr Pooter here; but one notes the subtlety with which Green suggests the self-promotion behind Archer's speech, the unctuous yet faintly defiant piety, and the verbal clumsiness. But there is no abrupt switch from his mode of discourse to that of his employer; and Green is at pains in his scenes of Dupret's social life to adopt the terse and offhand tone that he employs for his numerous scenes of factory gossip and manœuvring. The two strata of society comment on each other; the satire is reciprocal.

Green is no less inventive when it comes to writing about those members of the working class with whom most novel-readers of his time would have been familiar – domestic servants. To a readership that belonged to their employers, these were potentially subversive figures – as Thackeray had realised early on in his career when he wrote his satirical memoirs of a footman, *The Yellowplush Papers* (1841), even if their comical vocabulary and misspellings tended to neutralise any damaging satirical force they could have had. This is what might be called defensive comedy, in which the cultural limitations of the servant class were exhibited through quaint sayings as well as emphatic loyalties and prejudices. By the time in which Green is writing (1925–50) domestic servants were gradually becoming the exclusive perquisites of the very rich – this is certainly true after 1945, by which time they had become marginal figures in the world of fiction. A more serious and analytic treatment of their situation can be seen in a novel like Elizabeth Bowen's *The Death of the Heart* (1938), where the elderly servant Matchett provides a moral centre for the story, through her awareness of her own precise place in its hierarchy of social values. Her comments on her former employer put the entire servant-mistress relationship in sober comedic perspective.

She liked me to feel that she thought the world of me. "I leave everything in safe charge with you, Matchett," she'd say to me on the doorstep, times when she went away. I thought of that as I saw her coffin go out [...] She liked what I did, but she never liked how I did it. I couldn't count how often I've heard her say to her friends, "Treat servants nicely, take an interest in them, and they'll do anything for you." That was the way she saw it. Well, I liked the work in that house from the first: what she couldn't forgive me was that I liked the work for its own sake. (I:vi)

Green's *Loving* (1945), the account of a group of English servants employed on an Irish estate during the early days of the Second World War, substitutes empathy for the implicit analysis found in *Living*. This novel is the portrait of a civilisation in decline, its characters comedically depicted as part of a reality they cannot comprehend. Kinalty Castle is largely shuttered up, as a result of the earlier troubles, and is inhabited by its owner, Mrs Tennant, and her daughter-in-law, plus no less than ten servants – butler, lady's maid, nanny, two housemaids, two kitchen maids, gardener, pantry boy and cook. Employers and employees lead separate lives, but the degrees of control exercised by each over the other are complementary and reciprocal: there is comedy implicit in the very situation, and there is a wealth of comic observation, both of the wrangling among the servants about status and position, and of the careless arrogance of their employer. This is a world on the brink of disintegration.

The narratorial voice scarcely intrudes. While Green no longer omits the definite article, in many cases he employs the denotative one to replace it, 'that' and 'those' having a distancing effect – but keeping the reader at a distance from the characters rather than the other way round. The latter are thus granted total fictive autonomy. At the same time the relationship between employer and employees is captured purely by the use of dialogue. Here is Mrs Tennant discussing with the butler the disappearance of a valuable sapphire ring.

"Well this was not exactly a pleasant experience madam. More like the third degree Madam. And it seemed to throw my boy Albert right off his balance, Madam."
"Raunce may I say something?"
"Yes Madam."
"Don't Madam me quite as much as you do. Put in one now and again for politeness but repeating a thing over and over rather seems to take away from the value,' and she gave him a sweet smile really.
"Very good Madam."[17]

That 'really' conflates the attitudes not only of the two participants but also of the author; it renders the scene intimate rather than dramatic.

The close involvement of narrative with consciousness which Green establishes in all his mature novels is achieved in *Loving* through his skilful use of dialogue. On the stage everyone has to speak in turn: in real life they overlap. Accordingly he provides some amusing moments when two servants, preoccupied with their own concerns, converse through alternating monologues. At other times speech is drawn out of people by the effect upon them of their interlocutor. Here is Raunce taking it out of the pantry boy.

> "I don't say I blame you," [he] went on after pondering a moment. He was picking his teeth with a needle he had taken from underneath the lapel of his coat. "But one thing we will get straight here and now," he said. "Keep all of it to yourself if you wish. And clean your teeth of course before you have anything to do with a woman. Yet if I 'ave any more of that side from you there's one thing you can bet your life. A word to Mrs T. from me, just one little word and it's the Army for you my lad, old king and country and all the rest d'you understand?"

Raunce seems not so much to be speaking as to be spoken, (his words being the product of the novel's tone in its entirety,) much as those of Harrison and Louie were in Bowen's *The Heat of the Day*. The point is furthered towards the conclusion as he and the housemaid Edith discuss whether to leave their present employment and return to England.

> "Go on with you," she replied. "Why if Mrs Tennant loses all her dough there'll always be those that took it. Don't you tell me there isn't good pickings to be had in service long after our children have said thank you madam for the first bawlin' out over nothing at all that they'll receive." She was beginning to speak like him.

That terse authorial comment encapsulates Green's particular species of linguistic comedy, and emphasises his crafty deployment of vernacular locutions in what amounts to a comedic parody of verbal wit.

The ineluctable modality of the oral: James Joyce

It took a writer as steeped in the comic sense as James Joyce to provide one of the masterworks of Modernist fiction with the sentence which opens *A Portrait of the Artist as a Young Man* (1916).

Once upon a time and a very good time it was there was a moocow coming down along the road and this moocow that was coming down along the road met a nicens little boy named baby Tuckoo....

Even Beatrix Potter could manage a more impressive opening than that. 'It is said that the effect of eating too much lettuce is "soporific".'[18] That effect is quite Austenian; and it might be argued that its author had a better idea of how to speak to small children than had Simon Dedalus. But Joyce is being characteristically faithful to observed reality: this is how most adults choose to address the very young.

Joyce was also being consistent: *Dubliners* (1914) had been written with a 'scrupulous meanness', following the precepts of French naturalism as championed by his fellow Irishman, George Moore.[19] In affronting contemporary popular taste, however, *Dubliners* goes well beyond the stories in Moore's *The Untilled Field* (1903): Joyce's drabness is urban, not rural; is sardonic, not pathetic. But this overriding shabbiness is turned upon itself in the final story, 'The Dead', in which a stylistic change appears to comment upon the low-key mode in which the preceding pages have been written. The final three paragraphs describing a husband's response to his wife's account of her dead suitor are written with a grave sonority that appears to rebuke the systematically reductive nature of what has gone before.

But Joyce's comprehensive artistry forbids him to endorse, or rest in, any such stylistic or emotional dichotomy. In *A Portrait* the five stages of Stephen Dedalus's experience are conveyed in a prose appropriate to each in turn: through a species of mimetic free association of images and ideas, naturalism is extended from what is perceived to the mode of the perception. The text evolves from the opening baby Tuckoo passage, through Stephen's fragmented memories congesting in the recollections of schooldays at Clongowes, and a verifiable transcript (the horrific sermon about Hell), to the more conventionally coherent style that recounts his refusal of the suggestion that he has a vocation to the priesthood.

Towards Findlater's church a quartet of young men were striding along with linked arms, swaying their heads and stepping to the agile melody of their leader's concertina. The music passed in an instant, as the first bars of sudden music always did, over the fantastic fabrics of his mind, dissolving them painlessly and noiselessly as a sudden wave dissolves the sandbuilt turrets of children. Smiling at the trivial air he raised his eyes to the priest's face and,

seeing in it a mirthless reflection of the sunken day, detached his
hand slowly which had acquiesced faintly in that companionship.

The wiry beauty of this passage is immediately modified, however, in terms appropriate not to Stephen's youthful spirit but to the ecclesiastical world that would draw him back into itself.

As he descended the steps the impression which effaced his troubled self-communion was that of a mirthless mask reflecting a sunken day from the threshold of the college. The shadow, then, of the life of the college passed gravely over his consciousness. It was a grave and ordered and passionless life that awaited him, a life without material cares. He wondered how he would pass the first night in the novitiate and with what dismay he would wake the first morning in the dormitory. (IV)

The verbal repetitions, the graceless abstractions, the sense of systematic argument, appear to be subverting the apparent 'rightness' of the preceding passage: one is not to equate the account of a moment's insight with the spiritual condition which may or may not be prompting it. The stylistics of *A Portrait* are geared to a comedic refusal to mistake any one moment of Stephen's progress for the defining one. And the book's fifth section, with its hurly-burly of discussion, of student banter, together with the adolescent pomposity of the diary entries at the end, persistently modifies the rhapsodic emotional epiphany that concludes Part Four.

The epiphany of the girl on the shore turns up again, parodically, in *Ulysses* (1922), when Leopold Bloom is transfixed in a far more explicitly sexual manner by the sight of Gertie McDowell as she provokes him to look up her skirt. Here the use of the language of cheap romantic novelettes such as Gertie reads describes her feelings in a way that transforms parody into a means of emotional expression.

Here was that of which she had so often dreamed. It was he who mattered and there was joy on her face because she wanted him because she felt instinctively that he was like no-one else. The very heart of the girl-woman went out to him, her dreamhusband, because she knew on the instant it was him. If he had suffered, more sinned against than sinning, or even, even, if he had been himself a sinner, a wicked man, she cared not. Even if he was a protestant or methodist she could convert him easily if he truly loved her. There were wounds that wanted healing with heart-balm. (XIII)

The vocabulary, the phrasing, and the pacing of the prose indicate the sub-cultural ambience which has formed Gertie's sensibilities, and evaluate them in relation to it. Any element of patronage is subsumed into the overall pattern of parodic methodology which constitutes this novel's style: Gertie is but one motif in a veritable symphony of linguistic relativities. Parody in *Ulysses* is a matter of celebration rather than of satiric scrutiny. The book's various linguistic procedures comically show each other up, being united by the events of Bloomsday which they reflect, and by the consciousness of its various participants. Whereas the language of *A Portrait* is chronologically aligned with the evolving consciousness of its protagonist, that of *Ulysses* is contemporaneous in space as well as time, involving the reader as much as the characters in its shaping of the complex of physical and mental imagery that it reflects.

Language is indeed the name of the game in *Ulysses*: Joyce's gifts for parody and pastiche allow him to distil his sense of time through verbal and stylistic mimicry. The book is to that extent an historical novel, a realisation of Dublin on a particular June day of 1904, with all its religious, social and political concerns as active in the minds of the characters as are the sense of touch and smell to that of the reader; but it differs from other historical novels in its freedom from portentousness and its refusal to detach its people from their environment. The systematic deployment of mythological imagery and the use of the Odyssey to provide a narrative framework, while they align *Ulysses* with such Modernist poems as *The Waste Land* or the *In Parenthesis* (1937) of David Jones, do not obviate the justice of Wyndham Lewis's comment that

> Joyce is steeped in the sadness and the shabbiness of the pathetic gentility of the upper shopkeeping class, slumbering at the bottom of a neglected province, never far from its snobbishly circumscribed despair, from the pawn-shop and the 'pub'.[20]

But the mythological overtones of *Ulysses* are not there exclusively to raise the life of Dublin to some supposititious higher level, or to subject it to a comical reductiveness; rather, both effects are achieved in a comedic two-way traffic. The monoliths of idealism and materialistic theory are alike undermined. As Harry Blamires observes of Bloom's encounter with the dogmatic 'Citizen' in Barney Kiernan's bar,

Rebel and conservative alike are here cut down to size. The machinery of state officialdom and the effervescence of mass-taste which together express the futility of our century are here held before a mature and human comic gaze.[21]

Ulysses is a wryly compassionate description that amounts to a celebration of the life that it portrays: in doing so it incorporates all six of the other aspects of comedy. Parody is of the very essence of its literary methodology, ranging from the masterly (if self-indulgent) succession of pastiches in 'The Oxen of the Sun' to what is arguably the funniest passage in the book, the take-off of journalistic rhetoric in the account of Rumbold's execution, which interrupts the Cyclops episode. Elsewhere farce combines with burlesque in the exhausting Nighttown sequence, and again, more mildly, in the innumerable small indignities to which Bloom is subjected throughout the day. His own observations are full of black comedy, as on the way to Paddy Dignam's funeral.

He passed an arm through the armstrap and looked seriously from the open carriage window at the lowered blinds of the avenue. One dragged aside; an old woman peeping. Nose whiteflattened against the pane. Thanking her stars she was passed over. Extraordinary the interest they take in a corpse. Glad to see us go we give them such trouble coming. (VI)

Irony in *Ulysses* is bound up with the very mythological parallels themselves, and with the coincidences and narrative concurrences; while wit erupts in the constant play of puns and verbal coinages.

She's not exactly witty. Can be rude, too. Blurt out what I was thinking. Still I don't know. She used to say Ben Dollard had a base barreltone voice. He has legs like barrels and you'd think he was singing into a barrel. Now, isn't that wit? They used to call him big Ben. Not half as witty as calling him base barreltone. Appetite like an albatross. Get outside of a baron of beef. Powerful man he was at storing away number one Bass. Barrel of Bass. See? it all works out. (VIII)

But satire? Here one receives a check: the atmosphere of *Ulysses* is so fundamentally benign that it is hard to detect an authorial standpoint. But satire there is, not only at the expense of sanctimoniousness, the human eye to the main chance, and the coalescing of lechery with sentiment, but also at the expense of the detached reader whose own measured evaluations and 'informed literary judgements' are affronted by a book which allows no power of leverage to such responses. Indeed there is, as John Cowper Powys points out, 'a fine moral purgative against testy priggishness in a work that compels us to catch the Pythagorean music in the grossest human speech'.[22] Elsewhere Powys, one of *Ulysses*'s earliest champions, defines Joyce's main object of satirical attack as 'that particular brand of romantic idealism [...] that whips up the sweets of sex with the egg-flip of mysticism, thickens it with the brown sugar of unctuous sentiment, and finally sprinkles it with the grated nutmeg of moral superiority'.[23]

Gross, disenchanted, unsentimental, *Ulysses* floats on a tide of verbal exuberance that goes well beyond any mere comic celebration of an exhortatory (say, of a Chestertonian) kind. Stephen Dedalus's 'agenbite of inwit', Bloom's melancholy, Marion's acquiescence in the female lot, all insure it against any superficial jollity. Yet few novels are so profoundly funny. The comical Rabelaisian lists of names and the delighted observation of the absurdities of the second-rate evince a pleasure in life that positively erupts in the description of two barmaids in a fit of giggles.

> Shrill, with deep laughter, after bronze in gold, they urged each other to peal after peal, ringing in changes, bronzegold goldbronze, shrilldeep, to laughter after laughter. And then laughed more. Greasy I knows. Exhausted, breathless their shaken heads they laid, braided and pinnacled by glossycombed, against the counterledge. All flushed (O!), panting, sweating (O!), all breathless. (XI)

This comes from the Sirens episode, with its imitations of musical notation: Joyce's allotment of various arts, colours and physical organs to each section of his novel is a further instance of its celebratory quality.

But the comedy of *Ulysses* has its intellectual formulation within the text itself. In the penultimate stone-cool sober Ithaca episode a precise refutation of all monolithic pretensions is adumbrated in question-and-answer form as Bloom slides into bed.

> If he had smiled why would he have smiled?
> To reflect that each one who enters imagines himself to be the first to enter whereas he is always the last term of a preceding series even if the first term of a succeeding one, each imagining himself

to be first, last, only and alone, whereas he is neither first nor last nor only nor alone in a series originating in and repeated to infinity. (XVII)

This defines the underlying comic vision that unifies the book's complex ingredients. Not only Gertie McDowell's novelettish reverie, but also Molly Bloom's unending flow of free-associative rumination, Bloom's staccato observations and assessments of all that he encounters, the bully-boy dogmatism of the Citizen, the hoity-toity gentility of the Misses Kennedy and Douce, even the tortuous academic sentences uttered by Stephen to himself, all go to make up the symphonic variety and interrelatedness of Joyce's linguistic virtuosity.

And yet his delight and belief in language is such that, just as the comedic element in the development of his art can be detected in the growth of its stylistics, so one might discern in *Finnegans Wake* (1939) the ultimate, non-monolithic verbal monolith. The work is *sui generis*, inimitable and unrepeatable, demanding (and from some readers obtaining) a lifetime's study and allegiance, even though for the majority it probably remains unreadable as a systematic narrative. But it may also be viewed as Joyce's own logical jest at the expense of the fictive naturalism that his previous literary undertakings had been refining and expanding. In *Finnegans Wake* naturalism implodes. Is it, in G.S. Fraser's words, 'pure musical soup'[24] or is it the most extended sub-text and elaborate palimpsest that the English language has to offer? Or all three? Whatever else, open it anywhere and the monolith of restrictive signification is dissolved. And so

> Good marrams and good merrymills, sayd good mothers gossip, bobbing his bowing both ways with the bents and skerries, when they were all in the old walled of Kinkincaraborg (and that they did overlive the hot air of Montybunkum upon the coal blasts of Mitropolitos let there meeds be the hourihorn), hibernating after seven oak ages, fearsome where they were he had gone dump in the doomering this tide where the peixies would pickle him down to the button of his seat and his sess old soss Erinly into the boelgein with the help of Divy and Jorum's locquor and shut the door after him to make a rarely fine Ran's cattle of fish. (Chapter xi)

Here is Joyce's fictive art in its true and glorious colours. It provides one not simply with books to read but, in *Finnegans Wake*, with a game to play as well.

However seriously individual novelists may take their craft, there is indeed something of a game about the art of fiction – a bit of a lark, as people say. The element of 'let's pretend' can be so persuasive that from the very inception of the European novel writers have been prepared to satirise their readers for taking their productions overseriously. *Don Quixote* itself grows out of such a situation, and the first two major English novelists between them, in *Pamela* and *Joseph Andrews*, provide the occasion for, and the correction of, such confused participation. And if the danger of over-persuasiveness can be detected no less in the oven-sealed selectiveness of Henry James's late manner than in the blatant flouting of formal organisation that one finds in Sterne, the fact that novelists are all potential archdeceivers is implicit in their craft. Comedy inheres in the very practice of novel-writing as such.

All the novelists discussed in this book to some extent or other comedically question their own nature by employing various comedic strategies. Parody examines the basic elements of fictive processes by seizing on clichés and mannerisms as evidence for the bogus and the second-rate: fictive credentials, if not discussed, are closely questioned. Farce carries this process to a further extreme: plausibility itself is no longer a requirement. Ironic writing, on the other hand, pretends that it is one, and in the process lays traps for the unwary reader. Satire, on the other hand, acts as a governess, pointing out the moral of the tale and that a story is not an end in itself. Burlesque, however, noisily insists that this is wrong: if a tale is like life, only more so, then that 'more' means more, not less. With which the witty writer would agree: life is what you make it, and is best recorded in keeping with that sentiment. Here indeed is the philosopher's stone through which 'fact' and 'fiction' are known as aspects of a reality encompassing them both. Life itself becomes the game. Yet even a comprehensive vision such as this remains one too.

This knowledge pervades the most applauded fiction of the present time and the critical approaches that both elicit and approve it. In late twentieth-century writing parody, pastiche and intertextuality have become familiar items in the novelist's equipment. Postmodernism, with its insistence upon linguistic relativities and its delight in dialogic relations with its readers, is a far cry from the spinning of engrossing and convincing yarns: the tribal magician has been replaced by the conjuror at the children's party. The contemporary status of the novel assumes a literate, intellectually supple, readership, one well-accustomed to the idea that fiction is anything but a naturalistically rendered record of encounters and dramatised events: the shape-shifting capabilities of the imagination are a staple of contemporary writers' understanding of humanity, together with the self-propagating nature of linguistic inheritance and verbal association. This topic has become the occasion for a good deal of critical solemnity (the word 'ludic' does after all have a more responsible ring to it than does the word 'playful') and the rationalisation of what might seem to be irresponsible readings of the quotidian norm is a necessary step in the critic's bid for explicatory authority over a wayward text. But that particular effort is not a matter of merely literary concern; and the dangerous yet beguiling rôle that fantasy can play in daily life is the actual subject-matter of a good deal of contemporary fiction, just as it was when Cervantes wrote *Don Quixote*, Jane Austen *Northanger Abbey* and Gustave Flaubert *Madame Bovary*. Literature is subordinate to life.

And yet.... In 1920 Max Beerbohm published a short essay called 'The Crime',[25] in which he tells how, marooned in bad weather in a country cottage, he was driven to take up a novel by a successful woman writer of the day, 'an habitual, professional author, with a passion for her art, and a fountain pen and an agent, and sums down in advance of royalties on sales in Canada and Australia, and a profound knowledge of human nature and an essentially sane outlook' – these last two attributes bestowed on her by reviewers. It is all too much.

I had an impulse which I obeyed almost before I was conscious of it [...] The book stood closed, upright, with its back to me, just as on a book-shelf, behind the bars of the grate.

The impulse would seem to be in the name of life itself; nor does Beerbohm apologise for what he's done. And one has every sympathy; the book has sounded predictable and dull; literature surely is secondary to life. And yet.... In the very process of its immolation the book puts out the fire.

11
Epilogue: the Alchemy of Laughter

> Who says, 'Youth's a stuff will not endure?' It lasts as long as we do, and is older than age.
>
> Anne Thackeray Ritchie, *Letters*

Nowhere is the triumphant alchemy of the comedic process more happily illustrated than in the opening chapter of Peacock's *Nightmare Abbey*. The mansion's atrabilious proprietor always chose his servants 'by one of two criterions – a long face, or a dismal name'.

> On one occasion, being in want of a footman, he received a letter from a person signing himself Diggory Deathshead, and lost no time in securing this acquisition; but on Diggory's arrival, Mr Glowry was horror-struck by the sight of a round ruddy face, and a pair of laughing eyes. Deathshead was always grinning, – not a ghastly smile, but the grin of a comic mask; and disturbed the echoes of the hall with so much unhallowed laughter, that Mr Glowry gave him his discharge. Diggory, however, had staid long enough to make conquests of all the old gentleman's maids, and left behind him a flourishing colony of young Deathsheads to join chorus with the owls, that had before been the exclusive choristers of Nightmare Abbey.

As a comic artist Peacock is always incorrigibly cheerful, but never oppressively so. An interplay of linguistic associations lend that concluding sentence a touch of astringent wit.

I

'The only end of writing is to enable readers better to enjoy life, or better to endure it:'[1] Samuel Johnson's definition of the uses of literature places them squarely in the context of human suffering and need. His outlook is remedial, the reiterated word 'better' asserting the possibility of change and growth. As to 'enjoyment' and 'endurance', they reflect that simultaneous awareness of pleasure and of pain from which the comedic spirit takes its rise. Johnson's definition recognises that the human imagination is potentially self-transforming, and that its function is alchemical.

The object of comedy is to promote endurance through the cultivation of enjoyment, and to promote enjoyment through the strengthening of endurance. The former purpose is achieved primarily through parody, farce, wit and celebration, all four exercises being concerned to induce a pleasurable participation in inconsistency and absurdity, as a key to unlock the stultifying self-enclosure of monolithic concepts and dictatorial points of view. The second and more ostensibly serious purpose is served by the close engagement with the painful aspects of the discrepancy that is found in irony, satire and burlesque. But if endurance and enjoyment complement each other in the totality of comedic vision, it must be admitted that in some human experience the necessity to endure is liable to be so overwhelming that it excludes enjoyment altogether. An abstract belief in the reconciliation of opposites remains the prerogative of the secure and fortunate.

II

Comedy is a vehicle of communication, a transportation of divisive monoliths into an acceptance of differing beliefs and attitudes, and into a recognition of the inevitable relativity of every human aspiration to finality and truth. It thus voices an attitude born of a particular experience of life, and comedic artists from Fielding to Joyce have always portrayed that experience as being most evidently reflected in the lives and reactions of unheroic people who rely for their survival on co-operation rather than on competition (itself the natural consequence of holding tenaciously monolithic points of view).

One sees this preference for moral and social accommodation illustrated in the evolution of naturalistic prose fiction during the course of the eighteenth century. The ideals and standards of the increasingly prosperous middle classes, and their collision with vestigial rigid hierarchies, are by the time of Jane Austen reflected in a fiction which presents a modification of monolithic attitudes and social structures. In place of these one finds a concern with civilised behaviour, since polish and refinement existed in order to promote communication.

A polite young man was someone polished, in the sense that he had no irregularities which limited his contacts with other people. [...] The polite man was essentially social, and as such distinguished from arrogant lords, illiterate squires and fanatical puritans. All in their own way were angular rather than polished.[2]

For 'angular' one may read 'monolithic', and monolithic humours were easy targets for the naturalistic novelist's witty satire. As the favoured reading-matter of polite society, novels were necessarily vehicles for a sense of comedic relativity.

In English fiction up to the end of the Second World War, the monolith could be located in personal morality, social conventions, political institutions, religious profession, and psychological behaviour-patterns: the rôle of comedy had been to sift, to demolish, to mock, to analyse, to deride and thus to expose its claims to infallibility. But, as has been said, the joke at comedy's own expense has always been that it needed the monolith to be a monolith in order to play its own particular game. But today, with the gradual dissolution of social barriers, inhibitions and taboos that gathered speed once the middle of the twentieth century was passed, the presence of the monolith becomes elusive. What is an idol in an age of indifferent iconoclasm? Targets for comic scrutiny certainly remain: parody, irony, burlesque all continue to be viable – but what of farce in an age of ever-increasing relativities? Or satire, where no accepted norm of moral or religious standards exists, except of the most general kind? Or wit, when the intellectual basis of society is called in question, when 'elitism' is a shibboleth, when social groupings are in a state of flux?

This is not so much to say that the present age is deficient in comic writing (it is not) as that its relation to the monolith changes. Or rather, the spirit which engages with the monolith has changed. An analogy might be drawn here with the evolution of the dance in Western society. At one time a formal, ritualised pattern of movements, in which each participant had a function within the whole, it then changed into the synchronised movement of couples at close quarters. Those who regarded the waltz as scandalous were perhaps more prescient than they knew, for it signalled a dissolution of community and an emphasis upon sexuality and individual characteristics. And now in the late twentieth-century, people dance as individuals, expressing their separate selves, marking the transfer from unselfconscious participation in a regularised measure to an itemised, instinctual, fragmentary world of continual improvisation. Perhaps it is with individual consciousness that the comedic process now has to reckon.

III

Both the eighteenth-century Enlightenment and nineteenth-century Romanticism in their different ways encouraged in people the sense of self-sufficiency that issued in twentieth-century convictions as to the human right to spiritual autonomy and the importance of achieving personal fulfilment. Implicit in these different channels for the exercise of mental, spiritual and emotional exploration was a belief in self-perfectibility. Novel after novel centres on a protagonist beset by potentially restrictive social pressures, occasionally (as in Hardy's *Jude the Obscure*) with a tragic outcome. But since novels do not lend themselves readily to the selective, concentrated treatment of their material that tragedy requires, they more frequently handle this particular tension in terms of comedy. A balance is struck between the contending forces of private need and public pressure, whose divergent claims provide the novel's comic tension. But comedy is above all concerned with *pre*-tension, the pretension within the self which results in the competitive, distrustful outlook that is opposed to social harmony. In English fiction we can see this process at work as the seven aspects of the comedic transmutation confront the monolithic pretensions of the hubristic individual self.

Parody, which assaults the monolith of literary stereotypes, also has its human application. By imitating pretentiousness, it affirms it, though only to ridicule it through exaggeration: the very idea of the monolith becomes ridiculous – to far-reaching effect. One can see this process at work in the nasty way that certain two-dimensional fictional characters can become three-dimensional in the persons of their readers, who in their turn become the objects of the parody. Have we not all of us at one time or another heard ourselves talking like Pecksniff, Charlotte Bartlett or Mr Brooke in *Middlemarch*?

Farce, on the other hand, deals with human pretensions by disregarding them; in a reversion to private fantasy, it defies the social monitor, so that its target is helplessly and hopelessly embarrassed. The blatant nonsensicality of farcical situations and behaviour is a reminder of how constantly and teasingly unpredictable the circumstances that overthrow all human efforts at self-mastery can be. The misadventures of Nathaniel Winkle, Apthorpe and Jim Dixon are the products of an open-ended literary game that implicates its readers likewise in its debonair impertinence.

Ironic novels employ the literary tactic of constructing a verbal fortress, an ostensibly safe position from which to keep pain at bay, and to build up the shelter of a morally encoded discourse. But while irony needs to be straight-faced, it is in fact a witness to relativity. It would not be possible to interpret a novel as being ironic if one were not oneself to read it ironically. Irony is a state of mind that desires to have things both ways. In it, pretension is allowed for, being assumed into a scheme of values that can afford to overlook its spurious claims. But while that scheme may exercise a provisional underwriting of those claims, the assertive self is punished all the more by this pre-emptive submission. Thus Conrad's *The Secret Agent* (1907), with its terrible sustained allowance for the frailties of its third-rate fanatical participants, may well be the most bitterly controlled ironic comedy in the language. The grim humour with which its squalid tale is told is discomfiting rather than redemptive in effect.

But of the comic modes, satire, which marks the turning point in the comedic process from rejection to affirmation, is the trickiest where the reader's implication is concerned. In this case we are set over against the fictive subject. More openly moralistic than irony, satire is for that reason less inclined to be pharisaical. It operates through analysis; and in satirising others, both worthy and unworthy, it the more readily enables readers to satirise themselves. As in parody, one winces at uncomfortable resemblances, but in a less personally painful way: Oliver Goldsmith's Doctor Primrose satirises innocence in a manner more generalised than Fielding's account of Parson Adams (which is maybe one reason why *The Vicar of Wakefield* (1766) is a lesser achievement than *Joseph Andrews*) and the more such potentially monolithic simplifications are brought into play, the safer will the reader feel.

If satire takes monolithic personal pretensions seriously, burlesque, like farce, submits them to indignity. But this is an altogether more painful process, for savage anger takes the place of flippant irresponsibility. Irreconcilable elements are confronted with each other, detachment becomes impossible. The monolithic consciousness is compelled into the miry welter of a common physicality, becoming implicated in the abrasive unmannerliness of bad taste, as life's discordances appear to grow more risible, yet threatening. The only way to deal with them is to merge with them, much as Kipling's schoolboys and soldiery triumphantly succeed in doing. Burlesque subverts its object by colluding with it, and the reader's comfortable detachment is compromised in the resultant mêlée.

But discrepancy endured can also, in the climate of wit, be discrepancy enjoyed. And with enjoyment comes detachment from self, as well as detachment from the pressure of one's surroundings. In wit the experience of delight is paramount: if this is a question of perception, even unkindly so, it is perception of what is potential in the world perceived and in the mind of the perceiver. And where the reading process is in question, wit unites author and critic in a conspiracy against those monolithic decipherers who would appropriate the text for self-promotional ends. At their best, literary studies and elucidations open up their subject-matter as vehicles for corporate as well as personal appreciation, tracking down monoliths in order to refute their pretensions: Peacock's novels also do this, in terms of fictive narrative and discourse, but with a celebratory quality that accepts even the monolith as part of an encompassing feast of good-humoured wit and laughter.

For celebratory comedy draws out, and responds to, the realities encoded in the text and in the self of which the text is an analogy, the selfhood shared by the critic with his readers. Personal pretensions are now revealed as implicit aspirations, as the monolith itself enters into the paradisal liberty of realising that everything in life is in the last resort provisional and relative and that, in Jung's saving phrase, 'Every human truth is a last truth but one'.[3] The monolithic temperament finds this a frustrating truth with which to come to terms, since it challenges the essentially idolatrous nature of its own beliefs.

In identifying the monolith with idolatry, one is abstracting the essential nature of a diversity of idols – absolutist ideologies, absolute methodologies, intolerance of diversity, imaginative inertia, opposition to everything outside the socially-conditioned self. To use theological terminology, the monolithic idol abrogates to itself the divine I AM. That declaration is inclusive of the totality of being: but the monolith seeks the Divine self-sufficiency without the Divine afflatus of creation.

This monolithic idol is, as it were, the refractory matter on which artists, and not least comic artists, set to work; it provides the intractable material they have to overcome if they are to realise their vision, and the material on which they effect their alchemical transmutations. Castigated by Blake as the arch-enemy of imagination and of love, the monolithic nature is the subject of another poet who, himself a political opponent of the monolith that would repress free speech, also defined it imaginatively in theological terms. The august person of Milton's Satan is the supreme embodiment of the monolith, a defining and definitive assertion of self-containment and self-sufficiency, 'A mind not to be changed by Place or Time.'

> What matter where, if I be still the same,
> And what I should be, all but less then hee
> Whom Thunder hath made greater?

It is Satan's fundamental error to equate the Almighty with a power of the same kind as himself. To him, it is superior force alone which accounts for his exile from Heaven: believing this, he interprets his rebellion in heroic terms. His position, however, is theologically meaningless, and his faulty verbal logic betrays him: 'th' Almighty hath not built / Here for his envy'. The attribution of envy to omnipotence is a contradiction in terms; so too is Satan's culminating flourish, 'Better to reign in Hell, than serve in Heaven'.[4] The qualitative transference from metaphysical concepts (Hell, Heaven) to human activities ('reign', 'serve') is a categorical confusion that brands him as being, in Blake's uncompromising terminology, a dunce. He is not a heroic tragic figure; he is merely incapable of relating to anything other than himself. He is thus incapable of comedy. Personifying the hubristic consciousness of post-Renaissance man, he contrasts significantly with the Satan of Dante, who embodies a teleological condition. The mediæval poet is not so much concerned with spiritual analysis as with metaphysical status. In *La Divina Commedia* the figure of ultimate evil is therefore depicted as a frozen inactivity. From the perspective of Paradise, Satan is upside-down: the anatomical imagery, so characteristically precise, allows for a grossness which is one aspect of the comic vision.

The comic sense is the reverse of the satanic. It witnesses to a perennial source of youthfulness in human beings, of imaginative inventiveness, of tolerance and hope and an unsentimental delight in each other's separate identities; and it is in keeping with this spirit that alchemists, who treated their science as enacted poetry, should have aspired towards uncovering the true nature of the material world, not so much by transforming it into a previously non-existent gold, but through realising its inherently golden nature. To approximate to such a vision is likewise the object of the comedic process. If, as we have seen, that process can involve discomfort, on occasion even downright pain, it declines to rest in such provisional conditions. Rather, it works towards achieving that paradisal knowledge through which it is possible to recognise the totality of one's experience as 'a pain by truth, a bliss by love' – to employ those hard-won words of Julian of Norwich: acceptance of the human condition, considering its afflictions and continued possibilities, could not go any further. As to comedy's metaphysical source and goal, only Dante has succeeded in envisaging, both intellectually and imaginatively, the state of unconditional beatitude. In the *Paradiso* sin and evil have no other point or being than as occasions for God's mercy and grace: this is what is signified by the words, Divine Comedy. But there is nothing sentimental about Dante's view of things: there are the *Inferno* and the *Purgatorio* to indicate that such knowledge can only be acquired through participation. 'The divine dance of life is not there till it is danced.'[5]

Comedy is indeed no mere expression of a facile optimism. The intuition it embodies is based on the frequently intolerable anomalies of humanity's earthly existence, anomalies which novelists confront in their infinite variety, some comedically, but all of them with an implicit sense that each discrepancy demands to be enjoyed as thoroughly as it needs to be endured. 'When we are in a festive mood and laughing, we seem to go out of our normally anxious, reflective selves into a different phase of being, and the comic flow within us dissolves our sense of limitation.'[6] The art of the novelist is thus altogether inconsistent with a monolithic point of view; it involves a refusal of the narrowly simplistic and mechanical in favour, not just of the spontaneous and unpredictable, but also of what is superfluous and beautiful. It is a choice similar to that exercised by Dante at the opening of the thirteenth canto of the *Paradiso*, in which he aspires to communicate the joy of Heaven through the likeness of a rose.

Notes

1 The Matter of the Work
1. Morton Gurewitch, *Comedy: the Irrational Vision* (Ithaca, 1975) p. 48.
2. P.G. Wodehouse, *Something Fresh* (1915), Chapter ix.
3. L.J. Potts, *English Comedy* (1948), p. 59.

2 Aspects of the Comedic Process
1. Hans L. Martensen, trans. T. Rhys Evans, ed. Stephen Hobhouse, *Jacob Boehme* (1949), p. 23
2. Morine Krissdóttir, *John Cowper Powys and the Magical Quest* (1980), p. 132.
3. Allun Rodway, *English Comedy: Its Rôle and Nature from Chaucer to the Present Day* (1975), p. 12.
4. Richard Ellman, *Oscar Wilde* (1987), p. 400–1.
5. Hesketh Pearson, *The Life of Oscar Wilde* (1946), p. 278. In his *The Smith of Smiths* (1934), Pearson had already shown himself adept in the portrayal of a great humorist's verbal achievements. If Ellman presents us with 'Wilde' in his massive biography of 1987, Pearson presents us with 'Oscar'.
6. Robert Hichens, *The Green Carnation* (new edition, 1949), 'Introduction', p. vi.
7. John Batchelor, *The Edwardian Novelists* (1982), p. 138.
8. V.S. Pritchett, *The Tale Bearers* (1980), p. 23.
9. Charles Lamb, *Elia* (1823), 'The Artificial Comedy of the Last Century'.
10. I am indebted to Mrs Sally Bowden for bringing the first two books to my attention.
11. The anonymous author was Sir Henry Howarth Bashford, a distinguished medical officer and an undistinguished man of letters. See Anthony Burgess's Introduction to the Boydell Press reprint (Woodbridge, 1985).

3 Parodic Comedy: the Separation of Elements
1. George Gissing, *A Life's Morning* (1888), Chapter i.
2. Sylvia Townsend Warner, *Jane Austen* (1951), p. 10.
3. David Cecil, *Max* (1964), p. 313.
4. Lawrence Danson, *Max Beerbohm and the Act of Writing* (1989) p. 239.
5. Ibid., p. 253.
6. The authors and dates of these novels are as follows: Sir Edward Bulwer-Lytton, 1858; Anthony Trollope, 1864; Charlotte Riddell, 1897; Charles Reade, 1869; Grant Allen, 1895; Rosa Nouchette Carey, 1869; Rhoda Broughton, 1870; Violet Hunt, 1897; Winifred Crispe, 1904; Ford Madox Ford, 1924; David Garnett, 1927; Edith Olivier, 1928; Stevie Smith, 1936; William Gerhardie, 1938; Oswald Blakeston, 1970; Iris Murdoch, 1979; Jeanette Winterson, 1989; Roddy Doyle, 1993.

4 Ludic Comedy: the Dissolution of Elements

1. F.R. Leavis, *The Great Tradition* (1948), p. 2.
2. Letter to John Hall Stevenson, August 1761.
3. William Hazlitt, *Lectures on the English Comic Writers* (1819), 'On the English Novelists'.
4. Q.D. Leavis, 'Mr E.M. Forster', *A Selection from Scrutiny* (1968) volume I p. 135.
5. E.M. Forster, 'Ronald Firbank', *Abinger Harvest* (1936).
6. Ellis Waterhouse, 'Ronald Firbank', *Ronald Firbank: Memoirs and Critiques*, ed. Mervyn Horder (1977), p. 219.
7. A similar discordancy of collocations occurs in Edith Sitwell's poem 'Hornpipe' in *Façade* (1922), a work that anticipated *Cardinal Pirelli* by four years.
8. Firbank's biographer, however, wildly overstates the case in claiming, 'The ideal in his novels is his concept of the spirit of Christ; the struggle in them is one between the world and the spirit.' Miriam J. Benkovitz, *Ronald Firbank: a Biography* (1969), p. 280.
9. *Letters of Max Beerbohm 1892–1956*, ed. Rupert Hart-Davis (1988), p. xii.
10. Letter to Sir William Elford, May 13, 1815 (*The Letters of Mary Russell Mitford*, ed. R. Brimley Johnson (1925), p. 129).
11. David Cecil, *Poets and Storytellers* (1949), p. 99.

5 Ironic Comedy: the Conjunction of Opposites

1. The deliberations between Sir Thomas and Mrs Norris concerning Fanny's status within the family are, in tone and content, reminiscent of Mr and Mrs John Dashwood's attitude to his sisters in *Sense and Sensibility* – a novel of which *Mansfield Park* is in some respects a reworking.
2. D.W. Harding, 'Regulated Hatred: An Aspect of the work of Jane Austen'. *Scrutiny*, volume VIII (1930).

6 Satirical Comedy: the Disjunction of Opposites

1. George Eliot, *Scenes from Clerical Life*, 'Janet's Repentance', Chapter iii.
2. Ibid., 'The Sad Fortunes of the Reverend Amos Barton', Chapter v.
3. Hazlitt, op. cit., 'On the English Novelists'.
4. Rodway, op. cit., p. 55.
5. Christopher Gillie, *A Preface to Forster* (1983), p. 116.
6. This novel consists of two parts, the earlier first published in *Phoenix III* in 1968, and the much longer and unfinished second portion in the Cambridge edition of Lawrence's works in 1984.

7 Subversive Comedy: the Infernal Marriage

1. T.H. White cites a contemporary Frenchman who likened the Duke to 'a dead body, hanged in chains, which was always fidgeting to be hanged somewhere else' (*The Age of Scandal* (1950), p. 171).
2. G.K. Chesterton, introduction to *Martin Chuzzlewit* (Everyman's Library edition), p. xiv.
3. Angus Wilson, *The World of Charles Dickens* (1971), p. 177.

4   T.R. Henn, *Kipling* (1967), p. 22.
5   Ethel M. Munro, 'Biography of Saki', *The Short Stories of Saki* (1930) p. 712.

8 Intellectual Comedy: the Distillation of Elements

1   Beatrix Potter, *The Pie and the Patty Pan* (1905), p. 21; *The Tale of Pigling Bland* (1913), p. 23; *Ginger and Pickles* (1909), p. 68.
2   James Austen-Leigh, *Memoir of Jane Austen* (1871), Chapter x.
3   Laurence Lerner, *The Truth Tellers* (1967), p. 102.
4   *The Novels of Thomas Love Peacock*, ed. David Garnett (1948), p. 70.
5   J.B. Priestley, *Thomas Love Peacock* (1927), p. 70.
6   George Eliot, *Selected Critical Writings*, ed. Rosemary Ashton (1992), p. 113.
7   In a note on 'Wild Animals and One's Relations' Butler writes, 'If one would watch them and know what they are driving at, one must keep perfectly still.' (*Further Extracts from the Notebooks of Samuel Butler* (1934), p. 112). And see Hilary Spurling, *Ivy When Young* (1974), pp. 263–7.
8   Charles Burkhart, *I. Compton-Burnett* (1965), p. 37.
9   George Meredith, *An Essay on Comedy*.

9 Celebratory Comedy: the Accomplished Work

1   Cibber was the one professional comedian to be appointed Poet Laureate and was a man whose powers of self-mockery enabled him on one occasion to get the better even of Alexander Pope (see Kenneth Hopkins, *The Poets Laureate* (1954), pp. 76–8).
2   C.E. Vulliamy, *Byron* (1948), p. 13.
3   G.K. Chesterton, introduction to *The Pickwick Papers* (Everyman's Library edition), p. xiii.
4   Henry James, *Partial Portraits* (1888), 'Anthony Trollope'.
5   *Barchester Towers* does not hold a monopoly of Trollope's irreverent clerical portraits. There are memorable comic depictions of the clergy in, to name but three instances, *Rachel Ray* (1863), *Miss Mackenzie* (1865) and *Is He Popenjoy?* (1878) as well.
6   Ian Littlewood, *The Writings of Evelyn Waugh* (1983), p. 38.

10 Comedic Stylistics

1   See Geoffrey Day, *From Fiction to the Novel* (1987).
2   *A Christmas Garland Woven by Max Beerbohm* (1912).
3   Neville Braybrooke, *Theodore: Essays on T.F. Powys* (1964), p. 53.
4   Isaiah xlv:7.
5   Angus Wilson, *Diversity and Depth in Fiction* (1983), pp. 120–1.
6   'But at the Stroke of Midnight', *The Innocent and the Guilty* (1971), p. 64; 'Under New Management', *Winter in the Air* (1955), p. 101; 'A Love Match', *A Stranger with a Bag* (1966), p. 105.
7   John Aubrey, *Miscellanies* (1696), Chapter vi, 'Apparitions'.
8   Sylvia Townsend Warner, in a letter to the author, 4 February 1972.
9   John Cowper Powys, *Autobiography* (1934), p. 268.
10 John Cowper Powys, *Rabelais* (1948), p. 304
11 *Autobiography*, p. 233.
12 Jerome McGann, 'Marvels and Wonders', *The Times Literary Supplement*,

    1 December 1995.
13 Preface to the second edition, 1928.
14 Paul Edwards, 'The Apes of God: Form and Meaning', *Wyndham Lewis. A Revaluation. New Essays*, ed. Jeffrey Meyers (1980), p. 145.
15 G.S. Fraser, *The Modern Writer and His World* (1953), Chapter vii.
16 Henry Green, *Surviving* (1992), p. 246.
17 *Loving* contains no numbered chapter divisions.
18 *The Tale of the Flopsy Bunnies* (1909), p. 9.
19 James Joyce, *Letters*, ed. Stuart Gilbert (1957), p. 64.
20 Wyndham Lewis, *Time and Western Man* (1927), Chapter xvi.
21 Harry Blamires, *The Bloomsday Book* (1966), p. 127.
22 John Cowper Powys, *James Joyce's Ulysses* (1975), pp. 10–11.
23 John Cowper Powys, *Obstinate Cymric* (1947), p. 25.
24 G.S. Fraser, op. cit., Chapter vii.
25 Max Beerbohm, *And Even Now* (1920).

11 Epilogue: the Alchemy of Laughter

1 Samuel Johnson, 'A Review of *A Free Enquiry into the Nature and Origin of Evil*' (1757).
2 Mark Girouard, *The English Town* (1990), p. 76.
3 C.G. Jung, *Introduction to the Religious and Psychological Problems of Alchemy*, §31 (*Collected Works* Vol.XII, 1981).
4 John Milton, *Paradise Lost* I:252–63.
5 Alec King, *Wordsworth and the Artist's Vision* (1966), p. 76.
6 Robert M. Polhemus, *Comic Faith: the Great Tradition from Austen to Joyce* (1980), p. 8.

Index

Addison, Joseph, 63, 114
Ainsworth, Harrison, 92
Amis, Kingsley, 3, 19, 20
  Lucky Jim, 19–20
Arnim von, Elizabeth, *see* 'Elizabeth'
Ashford, Daisy, 22
  The Young Visiters, 22–3
Aubrey, John, 213
Austen, Jane, 3, 9, 15, 28, 35, 43, 48, 54, 55, 56, 60, 83, 87, 88, 91, 92, 102, 114, 150, 151, 165, 185, 190, 214, 237, 239
  Emma, 6, 35, 150–5, 171
  'Evelyn', 43
  'Lesley Castle', 43
  'Love and Friendship', 43, 44
  Mansfield Park, 41, 45, 88–92, 151
  Northanger Abbey, 43–4, 237
  Pride and Prejudice, 45–8, 181
  Sense and Sensibility, 44–5, 89

Bashford, Sir Henry Howarth, 246 (n.11)
  Augustus Carp Esq, 38
Batchelor, John, 27
Beckett, Samuel, 5, 11, 71, 85, 102, 204–8, 215
  Malone Dies, 208
  Molloy, 208
  Murphy, 204–6, 215
  The Unnameable, 208
  Waiting for Godot, 205
  Watt, 138, 206–8, 215
Beerbohm, Sir Max, 49–54, 56, 76, 131, 200–1
  A Christmas Garland, 50
  'The Crime', 237
  Seven Men, 50–2
  A Variety of Things, 50
  The Works of Max Beerbohm, 53–4
  Zuleika Dobson, 52–3
Behn, Aphra, 198
Belloc, Hilaire, 50, 200, 201

  The Bad Child's Book of Beasts, 50
  The Green Overcoat, 200
Bennett, Arnold, 223
Benson, A.C., 50
Benson, E.F., 14, 24, 33–5
  Dodo, 24
  Lucia in London, 34
  Mapp and Lucia, 33
  Queen Lucia, 34
Beresford, James, 38
Besant, Sir Walter, 24
Blake, William, 143, 144, 243, 244
Blamires, Harry, 232
Boswell, James, 131
Bowen, Elizabeth, 102, 223–4, 227, 229
  The Death of the Heart, 6, 227–8
  The Heat of the Day, 224–5, 229
Braybrooke, Neville, 203
Brontë, Charlotte, 110, 114
Browne, Sir Thomas, 63, 213
Bulwer-Lytton, Sir Edward, 16, 48, 70, 92
  The Caxtons, 70
  Eugene Aram, 16, 92
Burnand, F.C., 38
Burney, Fanny, 44
Burton, Robert, 63, 213
Butler, Samuel, 115, 116, 117, 118, 168, 213
  Erewhon, 213
  Notebooks, 168
  The Way of All Flesh, 115–18, 168
Byron, Lord, 159, 160

Cardigan, Countess of, 39, 40
Carroll, Lewis, 149–50
Cary, Joyce, 142, 143, 145
  Herself Surprised, 142
  The Horse's Mouth, 142–5
  To Be a Pilgrim, 142
Cecil, Lord David, 83, 84
Cervantes, Miguel de, 180, 237

Index   251

Don Quixote, 9, 179, 236, 237
Chesterton, G.K., 36, 134, 187, 234
  The Man who was Thursday, 36
  The Napoleon of Notting Hill, 36–7
Cibber, Colley, 173
Coleridge, Samuel Taylor, 158, 159, 160
Collins, Wilkie, 16, 153
  The Moonstone, 16
  The Woman in White, 16, 153
Compton-Burnett, Ivy, 166–8, 170, 171
  Darkness and Day, 118
  Daughters and Sons, 167–8
  A God and His Gifts, 170–1
  Men and Wives, 168
  The Present and the Past, 168–70
  Two Worlds and Their Ways, 168
Conrad, Joseph, 6, 242
  The Secret Agent, 242
Cooper, William, 19
Cornhill Magazine, 30, 31

Dante Alighieri, 244, 245
Defoe, Daniel, 198
  Moll Flanders, 199
  Robinson Crusoe, 146
Delafield, E.M., 38, 213
  The Diary of a Provincial Lady, 38
Deloney, Thomas, 198
Dickens, Charles, 4, 5, 10, 16, 17, 25, 26, 33, 43, 74, 132, 134, 135, 136, 144, 177, 179, 180, 182, 183, 184, 185, 214, 221
  Barnaby Rudge, 132
  Bleak House, 113, 185
  David Copperfield, 179
  Great Expectations, 5, 6
  Little Dorrit, 17
  Martin Chuzzlewit, 132–6, 148
  The Mystery of Edwin Drood, 70
  The Old Curiosity Shop, 33, 132
  Our Mutual Friend, 33, 133
  The Pickwick Papers, 70, 179–87
Disraeli, Benjamin, 48, 188
  Coningsby, 188
Donleavy, J.P., 19
Dostoevsky, Fyodor, 221
Douglas, Lord Alfred, 24

Douglas, Norman, 199
'Douglas, O' (Anna Buchan), 84
Du Maurier, George, 219
Dunn, Mary, 40

Edgeworth, Maria, 136
Eliot, George, 17, 18, 103, 114, 115, 163, 164, 214
  Daniel Deronda, 113
  Middlemarch, 241
  The Mill on the Floss, 6, 115
  Romola, 195
  Scenes of Clerical Life, 103–4
Eliot, T.S., 127, 221, 225
  The Waste Land, 127, 225, 232
'Elizabeth' (Mary Annette Beauchamp), 76–80, 83, 116, 164
  The Caravaners, 77
  The Enchanted April, 120
  Elizabeth and Her German Garden, 80
  Father, 79
  The Jasmine Farm, 77
  Mr Skeffington, 79–80
  The Pastor's Wife, 77–8
  Vera, 77, 78–9, 164

Ferguson, Rachel, 55
  The Brontës Went to Woolworths, 55–6
Ferrier, Susan, 15
Fielding, Henry, 3, 15, 23, 33, 60, 85, 87, 102, 104, 108, 173, 174, 175, 180, 183, 195, 199, 239
  Amelia, 110
  Jonathan Wild, 85–8, 93
  Joseph Andrews, 174–9, 183, 187, 199, 236, 242
  Shamela, 23, 173–4, 175
  Tom Jones, 15, 20, 104–10, 113, 129, 199
Firbank, Ronald, 24, 71–6, 80, 83, 131, 208
  The Artificial Princess, 71
  Caprice, 71
  Concerning the Indiscretions of Cardinal Pirelli, 71, 74
  The Flower Beneath the Foot, 71, 76, 83

Inclinations, 71
The New Rythum, 72
Prancing Nigger, 71, 72–3
The Princess Zoubaroff, 76
Vainglory, 71
Valmouth, 71, 73–4, 74–5
Fitzgerald, F. Scott, 72
Flaubert, Gustave, 237
Ford, Ford Madox, 218
The Good Soldier, 6
Forster, E.M., 18, 45, 71, 116, 119, 120, 127, 201
Howards End, 6, 45
A Room with a View, 119–23
Where Angels Fear to Tread, 119
Fraser, G.S., 123, 235

Galsworthy, John, 18, 57
Garnett, David, 158
Garnett, Richard, 213
Gaskell, Elizabeth, 17, 29
Cranford, 29, 113–14
Wives and Daughters, 114–15
Gerhardie, William, 80–2, 83
The Polyglots, 80–2
Gibbons, Stella, 56
Cold Comfort Farm, 25, 56, 214
Gil Blas, 179
Gillie, Christopher, 120
Gissing, George, 42, 223, 225
Goldsmith, Oliver, 242
Gosse, Edmund, 50
Green, Henry, 225, 227
Living, 225–7
Loving, 228–9
Greene, Graham, 198
Grossmith, George and Weedon, 38
The Diary of a Nobody, 38–41

Hardy, Thomas, 6, 17–18, 56, 190, 225
Far from the Madding Crowd, 6
Jude the Obscure, 18, 241
Tess of the D'Urbervilles, 6, 18
Under the Greenwood Tree, 17–18
Harland, Henry, 166
Hazlitt, William, 64, 109
Henn, T.R., 138
Hewlett, Maurice, 50, 166

Hichens, Robert, 23, 24
The Green Carnation, 23–5
Hope Anthony, 24, 70, 71
The Dolly Dialogues, 24
Huxley, Aldous, 116, 127, 128, 192
Antic Hay, 127
These Barren Leaves, 127–8

Jacobs, W.W., 14
James, Henry, 42, 50, 95–6, 97, 98, 100–1, 102, 189, 190, 224
The Ambassadors, 97, 98–101
The Europeans, 97–8
The Portrait of a Lady, 6, 8
The Sacred Fount, 96–7
Jerome, Jerome K., 11, 38
Three Men in a Boat, 11, 38
Jerrold, Douglas, 38
Johnson, Samuel, 62, 131, 238–9
Jones, David, 232
Joyce, James, 58, 61, 218, 229, 234, 235, 239
'The Dead', 230
Dubliners, 230
Finnegans Wake, 235
The Portrait of the Artist as a Young Man, 229, 230–1, 232
Ulysses, 6, 58, 231–5
Julian of Norwich, 245

Kingsley, Henry, 172
Kipling, Rudyard, 50, 138, 139, 140, 148, 242
Stalky & Co., 135–40
Krissdóttir, Morine, 22

Lamb, Charles, 35
Larkin, Philip, 84
Lawrence, D.H., 18, 102, 123, 125, 127, 220, 223
Lady Chatterley's Lover, 123
The Lost Girl, 123–5
Mr Noon, 123
St Mawr, 123
'Tickets, Please', 123
The Virgin and the Gipsy, 123
Women in Love, 220
Leavis, F.R., 62
Leavis, Q.D., 71

Lennox, Charlotte, 43
Lever, Charles, 48
Leverson, Ada, 12, 70
Lewis, Wyndham, 49, 218
 The Apes of God, 221–3
 Tarr, 218–21
 Time and Western Man, 223
London, Jack, 198
 White Fang, 197, 198
Loos, Anita, 61
Lyall, Edna, 24

Macaulay, Rose, 34, 118, 201
 Potterism, 30, 118–19
Machen, Arthur, 213–14
 Hieroglyphics, 214
Mackenzie, Compton, 14, 71
 Vestal Fire, 71, 120
Measure for Measure, 138
Meredith, George, 17, 24, 163, 171
 The Egoist, 6, 163, 164–6
 An Essay on Comedy, 163–4
 Evan Harrington, 17
 Harry Richmond, 17
 The Ordeal of Richard Feverel, 6
Milton, John, 244
Mitford, Mary Russell, 83
Mitford, Nancy, 33, 190, 197
 The Pursuit of Love, 197
Moore, George, 24, 210, 223, 230
 The Untilled Field, 230
Munro, Hector Hugh, *see* 'Saki'
Murdoch, Iris, 19, 25

Nabokov, Vladimir, 51
Nesbit, E., 31, 137
 The Story of the Treasure Seekers, 31

Oliphant, Margaret, 17, 28
 Chronicles of Carlingford, 113
 Miss Marjoribanks, 28–30
 Phoebe Junior, 28
Olivier, Edith, 209
Osborne, John, 19
'Ouida' (Louise de la Ramée), 52

Pater, Walter, 201
Paul, Leslie, 19

Peacock, Thomas Love, 30, 155–8, 238, 243
 Crotchet Castle, 160–2
 Gryll Grange, 163
 Headlong Hall, 157–8
 Maid Marian, 156
 Melincourt, 158
 The Misfortunes of Elphin, 156
 Nightmare Abbey, 159–60, 238
Pearson, Hesketh, 24
Potter, Beatrix, 75, 149–50, 201, 229
 Ginger and Pickles, 150
Powell, Anthony, 19, 28, 190
Powys, John Cowper, 3, 214, 215, 216, 217, 221, 225, 234
 Autobiography, 216
 A Glastonbury Romance, 214–15, 217
 The Inmates, 215
 Porius, 217
 Weymouth Sands, 214
 Wolf Solent, 214, 217
Powys, T.F., 201–4, 205, 202, 203, 204, 205, 213, 225
 Mr Weston's Good Wine, 201–4
Priestley, J.B., 173
Pritchett, V.S., 34
Proust, Marcel, 31, 51
Punch, 38, 39, 48
Pym, Barbara, 84–5, 102, 209

Rabelais, François, 62, 216
Ransome, Arthur, 138
Richardson, Samuel, 7, 9, 109, 173, 175, 199
 Clarissa, 7–9, 129, 198, 199
 Pamela, 173–4, 198, 236
 Sir Charles Grandison, 109
Rolfe, Frederick ('Baron Corvo'), 72
Rossetti, Dante Gabriel, 49–50

'Saki', 12, 14, 50, 70, 140, 192
 'The Feast of Nemesis', 141
 'The Recessional', 142
 'The Romancers', 141
 'The Strategist', 142
 The Unbearable Bassington, 140–1
Santayana, George, 201
Saturday Review, 52

Scott, Sir Walter, 15–16, 48, 153, 190, 199
  The Bride of Lammermoor, 6
  The Heart of Midlothian, 15
  Rob Roy, 16
  St Ronan's Well, 16, 153
Seymour, Robert, 180
Shaw, Bernard, 118, 166
Shelley, Percy Bysshe, 159
Sherwood, Mary Martha, 137
Sidney, Sir Philip, 202
Sitwell, Edith, Osbert and Sacheverell, 221
Smith, Sydney, 24
Smith, Stevie, 61, 84
  Novel on Yellow Paper, 61
Smollett, Tobias, 128, 130, 180, 199
  Humphrey Clinker, 15, 128–31
  Peregrine Pickle, 15, 128
  Roderick Random, 128
Somerville, E. and Ross, Martin, 10, 11, 14
Southey, Robert, 158
Spectator, 114
Steele, Sir Richard, 63
Stein, Gertrude, 126
Sterne, Laurence, 3, 15, 61–70, 72, 75, 81, 83, 189
  A Sentimental Journey, 70, 72
  Tristram Shandy, 6, 61–70, 199
Strachey, Lytton, 221
Surtees, R.S., 10, 11, 14, 18, 180
  Jorrocks' Jaunts and Jollities, 180
  Mr Facey Romford's Hounds, 18
  Mr Sponge's Sporting Tour, 18
Swift, Jonathan, 5, 63, 68, 101–2, 125, 126, 128, 132, 192, 207
  Gulliver's Travels, 101–2, 125–6, 132
  'A Modest Proposal', 5
  A Tale of a Tub, 63

Taylor, Elizabeth, 213
Thackeray, W.M., 16, 30, 48, 74, 81, 92, 93, 95, 102, 110, 111, 136, 137, 186, 199–200, 214
  Barry Lyndon, 92–5
  Catherine, 92–3
  Christmas Books, 136
  The Newcomes, 95
  Novels by Eminent Hands, 48
  Rebecca and Rowena, 48–9, 136
  The Rose and the Ring, 136–8, 142
  Vanity Fair, 81, 110–13, 200
  The Yellowplush Papers, 227
Thirkell, Angela, 197
Tolkien, J.R.R., 195–6, 212
Travers, Ben, 12
Trevena, John, 71
Trollope, Anthony, 16, 17, 30, 74, 187, 188, 189, 190, 214
  Barchester Towers, 6, 17, 187–90
  The Bertrams, 16
  Framley Parsonage, 32
  The Last Chronicle of Barset, 17
  Miss Mackenzie, 16
  Orley Farm, 32
  Brown, Jones and Robinson, 30–2
  The Three Clerks, 32
  The Warden, 190
  The Way We Live Now, 32, 113
Twelfth Night, 165

Vulliamy, C.E., 38

Walpole, Horace, 130
Walpole, Hugh, 76
Ward, Mrs Humphrey, 24
Warner, Sylvia Townsend, 116, 209, 210, 211, 212, 213, 224
  The Flint Anchor, 209–10
  Kingdoms of Elfin, 212–13
  Lolly Willowes, 209
  Mr Fortune's Maggot, 209
  One Thing Leading to Another, 210–11
Waugh, Arthur, 191
Waugh, Evelyn, 3, 18, 25, 30, 116, 159, 190–5
  Black Mischief, 192, 194
  Brideshead Revisited, 6, 192–3
  'Cruise', 194
  Decline and Fall, 192
  A Handful of Dust, 191–2
  Helena, 194–5
  The Loved One, 192
  Men at Arms, 192, 194
  Put Out More Flags, 192

Scoop, 30, 191, 192, 194
Vile Bodies, 191
Work Suspended, 191, 193, 195
Webb, Mary, 71
Wells, H.G., 20, 26
   The History of Mr Polly, 26–7
   Kipps, 20
Whipple, Dorothy, 84
White, T.H., 136, 145
   The Elephant and the Kangaroo, 145–8
   The Sword in the Stone, 136
   They Winter Abroad, 120
Whyte-Melville, G.J., 14
Wilde, Oscar, 23, 24, 25, 50, 70, 201
   'The Decay of Lying', 24
   A House of Pomegranates, 50
   The Importance of Being Earnest, 70

Wilson, Angus, 3, 19, 33, 57–60, 135, 208, 213
   'A Little Companion', 208–9
   No Laughing Matter, 57–60
Wodehouse, P.G., 10, 12, 13–14, 18, 19, 70–1
   Leave it to Psmith, 14
   Right Ho, Jeeves, 13, 19
   Summer Lightning, 14
Woolf, Virginia, 1, 2, 57, 61, 209, 218
   Jacob's Room, 2
   The Waves, 57
Wordsworth, William, 158

Yates, Dornford, 12–13, 14, 70–1
Young, E.H., 209